COMPLICATING, CONSIDERING, AND CONNECTING MUSIC EDUCATION

COUNTERPOINTS: MUSIC AND EDUCATION

Estelle R. Jorgensen, *editor*

COMPLICATING, CONSIDERING, AND CONNECTING MUSIC EDUCATION

Lauren Kapalka Richerme

Indiana University Press

This book is a publication of

Indiana University Press
Office of Scholarly Publishing
Herman B Wells Library 350
1320 East 10th Street
Bloomington, Indiana 47405 USA

iupress.indiana.edu

© 2020 by Lauren Kapalka Richerme

All rights reserved

No part of this book may be reproduced or utilized in any form or by any means, electronic or mechanical, including photocopying and recording, or by any information storage and retrieval system, without permission in writing from the publisher. The paper used in this publication meets the minimum requirements of the American National Standard for Information Sciences—Permanence of Paper for Printed Library Materials, ANSI Z39.48-1992.

Manufactured in the United States of America

Cataloging information is available from the Library of Congress.
ISBN 978-0-253-04737-3 (hardback)
ISBN 978-0-253-04747-2 (paperback)
ISBN 978-0-253-04749-6 (ebook)

1 2 3 4 5   25 24 23 22 21 20

COMPLICATING, CONSIDERING, AND CONNECTING MUSIC EDUCATION

Lauren Kapalka Richerme

Indiana University Press

This book is a publication of

Indiana University Press
Office of Scholarly Publishing
Herman B Wells Library 350
1320 East 10th Street
Bloomington, Indiana 47405 USA

iupress.indiana.edu

© 2020 by Lauren Kapalka Richerme

All rights reserved

No part of this book may be reproduced or utilized in any form or by any means, electronic or mechanical, including photocopying and recording, or by any information storage and retrieval system, without permission in writing from the publisher. The paper used in this publication meets the minimum requirements of the American National Standard for Information Sciences—Permanence of Paper for Printed Library Materials, ANSI Z39.48-1992.

Manufactured in the United States of America

Cataloging information is available from the Library of Congress.
ISBN 978-0-253-04737-3 (hardback)
ISBN 978-0-253-04747-2 (paperback)
ISBN 978-0-253-04749-6 (ebook)

1 2 3 4 5   25 24 23 22 21 20

Contents

	Preface	*vii*
	Acknowledgments	*xv*
1	Rhizomatic Journeying	*1*
2	Who Are We?	*22*
3	Where Are We?	*43*
4	Considering Deleuzian Ethics	*67*
5	Reconsidering Considering	*84*
6	Musically Connecting With	*101*
7	When Is Music Education?	*127*
8	Rhizomatic Journeying	*150*
	Bibliography	*163*
	Index	*175*

Preface

William Ayers writes: "To be human is to be involved in a quest, a fundamental life project that is situated and undertaken as a refusal to accede to the given."[1] Similarly, I understand all philosophizing as a journey, one simultaneously personal and public. To focus on end points rather than paths minimizes the process of philosophizing, robbing travelers of the voyaging that, while at times arduous, often gives increased meaning to their temporary destinations. Undertaking such wandering demands a sense of adventure and a welcoming of the emotions that accompany sustained uncertainty.

While philosophizing may involve ephemeral resting points and momentary clarity, it inevitably reveals additional questions, confusion, and untraversed terrains. A nine-year-old boy whose philosophical musings went viral on the internet explains, "You never really know for sure if there is anything in the search. It's an endless quest without knowing what your quest is."[2] His statements illuminate that if one's philosophical journeying can be said to have a beginning, it is perhaps with a child's innate and at times relentless curiosity, wonderment, and creativity. Through their words and actions, teachers can extinguish or fan these dispositions, fostering or inhibiting students' traverses within and beyond the classroom.

Situated in my own ever-evolving narrative, the part of my philosophical wandering explored in this book began when an undergraduate mentor asked me: "What should be the relationship between music education and society?"[3] While the intervening years have not necessarily brought me any closer to an answer, the question has fostered what poststructuralist philosophers Gilles Deleuze and Félix Guattari might explain as an "*I do not know* that has become positive and creative."[4] Inspired by their work, I have stumbled on routes initially obfuscated by the weight of tradition and by my own previously unquestioned habits and values, at times finding joy in the vulnerability of being lost.[5]

The term "music education" is neither monolithic nor stagnant. It can refer to practices ranging from sight-singing with a professional choral conductor, to playing fiddle through observing and participating in a community group, to listening critically at a rap concert, to composing privately with help from an online forum. It can include the work of an elementary music specialist who sees hundreds of students a week, private teachers who prepare students for standardized performance exams, professional music ensembles that undertake community outreach, and music enthusiasts who create online videos teaching everything from accordion to Pro Tools.

While practices such as the master-apprentice model of instrument and voice instruction have persisted on multiple continents for centuries, relatively recent technological innovations have facilitated music education centered on multi-tracking, remixing, and creating mash-ups, endeavors unimaginable throughout the vast majority of human history.[6] Yet, even seemingly long-standing music education practices can include elements of variability. For example, contemporary students in traditional band, choral, and orchestral programs likely find themselves with increasing access to education in popular music-making as well as other genres outside of the Western cannon. In short, "music education" encompasses a collection of disparate, constantly changing practices.

Despite this diversity, current music education practices tend to have three potentially problematic qualities in common. First, music education practices often center on questions about content and pedagogy while neglecting teachers' and learners' unique attributes, including those related to their multiple environments. Leaders of groups ranging from music associations to teacher licensing committees divide individuals into categories such as "instrumental," "general music," "Gordon," and "music technology." Even when an "Orff teacher" serves a population of students very similar to that of a "Kodály educator" in a neighboring town, discussions about content and pedagogy often occur absent considerations of who and where one teaches.

Likewise, authors of policies such as national standards, International Baccalaureate exams, and competition requirements make little acknowledgment of differences between students or schools.[7] Yet, music educators frequently turn to such documents as their primary sources of guidance. When music educators neglect students' and communities' diverse needs and interests, they miss opportunities for musical and educative experiences particularly meaningful for a specific time and place. Even the very terms "educator," "students," and "community" have the potential to solidify people and practices, separating them from the continual change central to life beyond the classroom.

Second, contemporary music educators tend to treat music-making and education as amoral and apolitical processes. Extending the Enlightenment tradition of separating musical practices from functional ends,[8] music educators may conceive of their work as aiming toward transcendent conceptions of "good" music rather than as contingent on sociocultural practices that often propagate various systems of subjugation. By conceiving of the decision to emphasize Beethoven over Beyoncé in purely musical terms, they neglect any ethical or political implications of such action. Further, Julia Koza explains how music admission processes at the collegiate level favor white individuals while minimizing and excluding contributions from members of other races.[9] The same holds true for Pre-K–12 music instruction, which even when broadened to include practices such as guitar and ukulele, can promote racist divides by omitting genres such as rap and hip-hop.[10]

My point is not to assert that music educators should uncritically embrace all music-making; rather, these examples demonstrate how seemingly innocuous decisions can have potentially serious ethical implications. When misrecognized as apolitical and amoral, the ethical dilemmas hidden within all musical and educative practices go unexamined, and potentially more ethical alternatives remain unconsidered. In addition to neglecting possibilities for more ethical teaching and learning, such action denies students the opportunity to develop the dispositions and thought processes needed to make ethically conscious decisions throughout their lives. It may also reinforce a conception of ethics as pre-given and straightforward rather than complex and evolving in integration with one's own differing experiences.

Third, music makers often struggle to explain the purpose of their work in ways that are inclusive of divergent contemporary musical practices yet not superficial or relativistic. For example, the high school ensemble director who asserts that music promotes militaristic discipline may indirectly undermine the work of teachers who advocate for music education as an avenue for individual self-expression. Alternatively, authors of existing advocacy resources proffer that music education can promote everything from higher test scores, to better attendance, to creativity;[11] music education can be "good for" anything that reinforces teachers' personal values and convinces others of the importance of their existing work. While asserting narrow purposes for music education excludes various forms of musical engagement, a scattershot approach, particularly one based on unfounded rationale, can inhibit teachers and students from collectively expressing the significance of their endeavors. Music educators need not blindly adopt a single purpose or abandon an array of advocacy tactics useful within their respective contexts, but the absence of at least partial agreement about shared rationale may hinder support from administrators, politicians, and other stakeholders.

The uncritical acceptance of any and all purposes for music education is also problematic because it dissuades dialogue about values, potentially hiding troubling ulterior motives and limiting alternative possibilities. A teacher who cloaks the goal of personal glory through winning competitions in the guise of instilling a hard work ethic may miss how students lacking access to private lessons or those with different learning needs are excluded or degraded. Resistance to sustained thoughtful debate about possible purposes of music education leaves the field without examined arguments. Caught in a cycle of justifying what is, music educators and students miss opportunities to reimagine what could be.

Contextualized within my initial overarching question about possible relationships between society and music education, I wonder: How might twenty-first-century music educators respond to these three dilemmas? Consistent with my Western classical music background, my gut response to such an inquiry involves seeking solidified answers. Just as I aim to play the right note or to perform a stylistically correct interpretation, I wish nothing more than to proffer clear solutions. Yet, there exist no obvious answers to these quandaries, and positing ones would only deny and undermine their complexity as well as my own differing understandings. While one might perceive this acknowledgment of an absence of definitive solutions as an uncomfortable starting point, it can also enable the freedom of open possibilities. Often only when a hiker stops aiming for the summit can beauty and meaning be found in the meandering.

Resisting my own tendency to focus on destinations, I respond to the aforementioned problems by positing three processes in which music educators might engage: complicating, considering, and connecting. Although I address these processes independently, I conceive of them as occurring in ongoing integration, with each informing and transforming the possibilities for the others.[12] While I illuminate some rough sign posts and trail markers along the way, these processes ultimately serve as areas of exploration through which readers will need to forge their own unique paths. Each process rests on a single premise that I now explain in brief.

First, multifaceted people and places constitute the core of musical experiences. Take a moment and pick five adjectives that describe you. Are you intelligent, funny, kind, musical, and athletic? Maybe you are caring, interesting, introverted, demanding, and creative? Similarly, contemplate how you might describe any one of the students who you teach. Now consider what might be missing from your lists. For example, do any of your adjectives acknowledge your emotions or body? Alternatively, if asked to describe your teaching environment, would you think only about your classroom or would you consider your place within your school, local community, and multiple larger musical, educative, and human communities, ultimately at a global scale?

While the questions "Who are we?" and "Where are we?" may at first seem simplistic and unimportant, considerations of *what*, *how*, and *why* often presume certain human ontologies and students embedded within specific types of locations. Sandra Stauffer argues that foregrounding the questions *who* and *where* rather than *what*, *how*, and *why* may be "more fundamental for music education in the twenty-first century."[13] Building on her thinking, I posit that questions of content and pedagogy should grow from, rather than trace onto, considerations of self, others, and places.

Writing this book has caused me to rethink my cognitive-centric practices, but I continually struggle against such tendencies. Additionally, despite my own interest in people, places, and music-making beyond my past and present locations, this text remains North American–centered. I primarily draw on American music education authors and on examples formulated with reference to my experiences teaching and learning in American public schools.

The explorations undertaken here serve to challenge my own perceptions and practices as much as, if not more so than, those of readers. Following an introduction to poststructuralist thought in chapter 1, in chapters 2 and 3 I offer that music educators and students might complicate themselves and their multiple environments by engaging in three practices: embracing exclusions, emphasizing differing, and becoming. Each chapter ends by acknowledging the unique stories that teachers and students bring to their work and imagining how those narratives might inform and evolve through musically educative practices.

The second premise underlying this work, one associated with the process of considering, is that educative practices always have ethical implications. Students pick up on ethical dispositions hidden within teachers' everyday dialogue and actions. How does an educator engage with students who meet composition guidelines while resisting personal expressivity? To what extent does a teacher ignore, chide, or assist the weakest performers in a music ensemble? What people and content do educators exclude from musical spaces? When does an educator use artistic events to reinforce local norms, and when do educators work with students to challenge what music-making and society could be and become? Wayne Bowman summarizes: "Education is a fundamentally ethical undertaking and that, particularly to the extent it is concerned with matters like character, identity, cultivation, and change, music education is a fundamentally ethical enterprise."[14]

Given the limits of contemporary standardized education policies and practices detailed in chapter 1, music educators and students may find Gilles Deleuze's creative, potentiality-based ethics particularly meaningful. I begin chapter 4 with explanations of three key aspects of Deleuze's ethics: attending to context, welcoming complexity and instability, and favoring previously unimagined possibilities over the repetition of existing action. Despite the possible benefits of imaginative, event-based practices, Deleuze's assertions are potentially problematic because they can tend toward relativism and may undercut opportunities for political change. In response, I place Deleuze's work in a productive tension with Hannah Arendt's process-based ethics. Arendt's writings about imagining situations from multiple perspectives and making judgments serve as inspiration for my proposed process of considering more ethical music teaching and learning practices. In chapter 5, I further problematize and extrapolate on intersections of Deleuze's and Arendt's ethical writings, noting the need for dialogue and the importance of attending to one's own body, emotions, differing, and survival.

A third premise underlying this text is the idea that experiencing a sense of connection is part of what makes life meaningful. When I hear the word "connections," the tune "What You Own" from the musical *Rent* often begins playing in my head. In the song, two roommates articulate the tragedies, absurdities, and joys of American life in the 1990s. At one point, the singers reminisce about a recent evening during which they each felt "connection in an isolating age." While the twenty-first century provides increasing opportunities for interconnectivity between individuals throughout the world, it can also encourage disconnection as people become further compartmentalized. The prevalence of diverse technologies has made many humans less reliant on interactions with friends and neighbors, and individuals can use headphones and smartphones to avoid acknowledging the presence of those with whom they cross paths in public. Though not necessarily unique to any given time period, this sense of connection as a counter to isolation reveals why humans may value it.

In chapter 6, I argue that since humans often use music to foster various connections, connecting may serve as a unifying purpose for contemporary music education practices. Drawing on Deleuze's distinction between transcendence and immanence, I distinguish between "connecting to" stagnant entities and "connecting with" people and experiences that alter in and through the process. I offer that teachers and students might foster musical connections with their integrated cognition, bodies, emotions, and sociality as well as their local and global places. Feeling a sense of connection, however, does not mean that one has had an educative experience.

In chapter 7, I draw on Deleuze's emphasis on ongoing variability to posit that education occurs when one becomes aware of difference. Such awareness can foster a combination of arboreal growth that moves toward preset aims or hierarchies and rhizomatic growth that spreads creatively outward along diversifying trajectories. What the interplay between education and students' changing narratives might mean for the quality of educative experiences and the idea that teachers might differ *with* students are also explored. In chapter 8, I examine the integration of complicating, considering, and connecting as well as offer possible implications for practice, policy, and research.

With these processes in mind, I set out on this philosophical expedition. Yet, it is not only I who must do the traversing. Deleuze asserts that when engaging with a book, "The only question is 'Does it work, and how does it work?' How does it work for you?"[15] Since philosophy is never read, interpreted, or understood absent historically and socially constituted individuals residing in specific moments and places, it exists in ongoing integration with readers and the world. You, the reader, come to this uncertain voyage not only with your past experiences but with your present circumstances and anticipated goals and trajectories; your prior and potential future narratives will inform how you engage with this text.

Embarking on an adventure involves welcoming the risk of unknown experiences and accepting that you might become disoriented or even lost. It demands childlike wonderment and reflectivity that develops over time. While we might wander alongside friends and acquaintances, we ultimately author our own narrative accounts of the routes. As individuals momentarily joined in this journeying, our travels have already begun.

Notes

1. William Ayers, "Doing Philosophy: Maxine Greene and the Pedagogy of Possibility," in *A Light in Dark Times: Maxine Greene and the Unfinished Conversation*, ed. William C. Ayers and Janet L. Miller (New York: Teachers College Press, 1998), 7.
2. Robert Krulwich, "Socrates (In the Form of a 9-Year-Old) Shows Up in a Suburban Backyard in Washington," *National Public Radio*, March 27, 2013, http://www.npr.org/sections/krulwich/2013/03/27/175455214/socrates-in-the-form-of-a-9-year-old-shows-up-in-a-suburban-backyard-in-washingt.
3. Roger Rideout in discussion with the author, January 2004.
4. Gilles Deleuze and Félix Guattari, *What Is Philosophy?* Trans. Hugh Tomlinson and Graham Burchell (New York: Columbia University Press, 1994), 128.
5. For an extended philosophical investigation of the possibilities of being lost, see Lauren Kapalka Richerme, "Nomads with Maps: Musical Connections in a Glocalized World," *Action, Criticism, and Theory for Music Education* 12, no. 2 (2013): 41–59.
6. For a detailed description of how such practices might function in contemporary music teaching and learning scenarios, see, for example, Evan S. Tobias, "Toward Convergence: Adapting Music Education to Contemporary Society and Participatory Culture," *Music Educators Journal* 99, no. 4 (2013): 29–36.
7. In calling such documents "policies" I am taking Jones' definition of policy as referring to both "hard policies" that use carrots and sticks in order to mandate certain results and "soft policies," including curricula, course materials, and the work of music associations. Patrick M. Jones, "Hard and Soft Policies in Music Education: Building the Capacity of Teachers to Understand, Study, and Influence Them," *Arts Education Policy Review* 110, no. 4 (2009): 27–32.
8. For a detailed discussion of this separation, see Lydia Goehr, *The Imaginary Museum of Musical Works: An Essay in the Philosophy of Music* (New York: Oxford University Press, 2007).
9. Julia Koza, "Listening for Whiteness: Hearing Racial Politics in Undergraduate School Music," *Philosophy of Music Education Review* 16, no. 2 (2008): 145–155.
10. Adam Kruse, "Panel: Diversity & Inclusion in Music Education" (presentation, Big Ten Academic Alliance Music Education Conference, College Park, MD, October 5–7, 2016).
11. See, for example, "Broader Minded: Think beyond the Bubbles," *National Association for Music Education*, accessed January 5, 2016, http://www.nafme.org/wp-content/files/2014/05/Broader-Minded-Brochure.pdf.
12. In chapter 8, I use the physic phenomenon of quantum superposition to explain further the ongoing integration of complicating, considering, and connecting.
13. Sandra L. Stauffer, "Placing Curriculum in Music," in *Music Education for Changing Times: Guiding Visions for Practice*, ed. Thomas A. Regelski and J. Terry Gates (New York: Springer, 2009), 175.
14. Wayne Bowman, "Music as Ethical Encounter," *Bulletin of the Council for Research in Music Education* no. 151 (2000): 16.
15. Gilles Deleuze, *Negotiations: 1972–1990*, trans. Martin Joughin (New York: Columbia University Press, 1995), 8.

Acknowledgments

I WOULD LIKE TO offer my sincere gratitude to Estelle Jorgensen for empowering me to become a more thoughtful and critical thinker and writer. Most significantly, at a time when I was ready to abandon my narrative philosophical writing style, she offered the brilliant suggestion of reflectively owning my voice through a philosophical investigation of narrative. I am also thankful for the encouragement and support of my Indiana University colleagues and for the undergraduate and graduate students who unceasingly challenge and inspire me. In particular, Heather Beers, Jen Blackwell, Iantheia Calhoun, Dylan Fixmer, Sarah Robinson, Nick Roseth, Rose Sciaroni, and Stephen Shannon were gracious in providing me with extremely insightful comments and suggestions for improving this work. Additionally, I would like to extend my gratitude to Ann Clements, her class of Penn State graduate students, and the IU students taking E618 in the spring of 2017, all of whom read drafts of chapters and provided meaningful feedback.

This book would not have been possible without the unwavering love and support of my husband Phil. Our near daily intellectual conversations provoke, deepen, and liberate my philosophical thinking as well as motive me to become a better person. I am also forever grateful to Sandy Stauffer; through her caring mentorship, she inspired me to undertake this Deleuzian wandering.

Acknowledgments

I WOULD LIKE TO offer my sincere gratitude to Estelle Jorgensen for empowering me to become a more thoughtful and critical thinker and writer. Most significantly, at a time when I was ready to abandon my narrative philosophical writing style, she offered the brilliant suggestion of reflectively owning my voice through a philosophical investigation of narrative. I am also thankful for the encouragement and support of my Indiana University colleagues and for the undergraduate and graduate students who unceasingly challenge and inspire me. In particular, Heather Beers, Jen Blackwell, Iantheia Calhoun, Dylan Fixmer, Sarah Robinson, Nick Roseth, Rose Sciaroni, and Stephen Shannon were gracious in providing me with extremely insightful comments and suggestions for improving this work. Additionally, I would like to extend my gratitude to Ann Clements, her class of Penn State graduate students, and the IU students taking E618 in the spring of 2017, all of whom read drafts of chapters and provided meaningful feedback.

This book would not have been possible without the unwavering love and support of my husband Phil. Our near daily intellectual conversations provoke, deepen, and liberate my philosophical thinking as well as motive me to become a better person. I am also forever grateful to Sandy Stauffer; through her caring mentorship, she inspired me to undertake this Deleuzian wandering.

COMPLICATING, CONSIDERING, AND CONNECTING MUSIC EDUCATION

1 Rhizomatic Journeying

TRAVELING, WHETHER TO a nearby town or a different country, can raise consciousness about the often unquestioned habits guiding daily life. Waking up near a window situated alternatively to that in one's primary residence or confronting a breakfast contrasting usual morning routines may evoke awareness of the general dependability of everyday encounters. Likewise, observing how those in other places pace their speech and movements, interact with their families and neighbors, and use words and actions to indicate their values can illuminate that an individual's perceptions and practices are not universal but contingent on context and open to alteration.

Like traveling, engaging with philosophy has the potential to uncover taken-for-granted understandings about life. Philosophers encourage reflection on how seemingly natural music education practices hide assumptions about the nature of humans, music, teaching, and learning, as well as delimit "normal" relationships between music education and life beyond school walls.[1] When the rationale that underlies daily practices goes unquestioned, music educators may tend toward insularity and stagnation, perceiving their routines as inevitable.

Although traveling can at times invoke a desire for the safety and security of familiar habits, it can also empower voyagers to imagine and experiment with how they might alter their thinking and action upon their return home. Even journeying to another location within one's local community may lead to the adoption of an innovative way of arranging one's furniture or of practices such as walking more slowly or speaking with heightened energy. In the words of T. S. Eliot: "We shall not cease from exploration, and the end of all our exploring will be to arrive where we started and know the place for the first time."[2] The joy of traveling—whether physical, virtual, or imaginative—comes not from attempting to live apart from one's own home but from understanding and perhaps altering one's home through newfound insights.[3]

Similarly, engaging with philosophy provides opportunities not only to uncover assumptions and critique existing thinking and action, but to consider processes and questions that might guide one's future practices.[4] Like thoughtful travelers curious about and open to the possibilities of previously unimagined ways of being in the world, music educators can approach philosophical writings with a sense of adventure, balancing critical investigation with a desire to imagine teaching and learning as they might occur otherwise. Yet, just as individual wanderers must adapt new information to their specific home circumstances, music educators necessarily alter philosophical insights in light of their own experiences and situations.

Current Contexts

Although music educators are diverse individuals working in multifaceted contexts, a couple of overarching, potentially troubling, ideologies pervade aspects of almost all contemporary educative practices: standardization and career training. In the United States, while individual states began taking action toward educational accountability in the 1960s and 1970s,[5] the advent of No Child Left Behind in 2002 unified assessment collecting and reporting procedures. American policymakers continue to volley over the respective roles of federal and state governments in determining education policy, but standards and standardized assessments remain an unchallenged component of their discourse.[6] Stephanie Horsley explains that such practices are global phenomena, asserting that "streamlining education delivery in order to make it as economically efficient as possible" serves as one of many contemporary education leaders' primary goals.[7]

It is important to distinguish between standards and standardization.[8] While the setting of changeable aims for individuals and groups has facilitated educative practices for millennia,[9] the increasing emphasis on mass standardization occurred only recently. For example, despite the existence of locally developed music education standards in every state, American music educators went to great lengths to author the 2014 National Core Music Standards; these standards contain markedly more detail than the 1994 national music standards, and their authors wrote them with the now realized promise of accompanying voluntary national assessments.[10] These standards and assessments mimic the national music curricula in countries such as England, Singapore, and South Africa.[11] As Cathy Benedict noted in relation to the 1994 standards, the writers of these and other twenty-first-century policies suggest a desire to stabilize music education practices with the confining structures and top-down control pervasive in other subjects.[12]

Standardized educational practices are problematic for two reasons. First, they limit teachers' and students' opportunities to embrace divergent, continually changing music-making occurring beyond school walls. In addition to variable practices within local musical communities, humans currently have access to more disparate information than at any other time in history. The internet enables curious students not only to find out about and listen to music from places across the globe, but also to view instructional videos for everything from composing with DJ software to Hindustani vocal technique to bassoon-reed making. These interconnections facilitate the creation of evolving musical hybrids that defy the boundaries of genres, styles, and Western classical music terminology.

In contrast with such ongoing variation, standardized goals and assessments can encourage teachers and students to move toward a more simplified and universal view of their discipline. In the process, they deny students access to the skills and dispositions needed to interface with significant aspects of twenty-first-century music-making. For example, a student interested in making a composition that combines qualities of gamelan performances and Scandinavian rock music may not find such action compatible with the current eighth grade "creating" Model Cornerstone Assessment, which requires composing a song with a clear beginning, middle, and end, and evaluating based on "craftsmanship" and "expressivity."[13] While the authors of these and other standards and assessments documents note their adaptable nature, because standards and assessments reference certain types of music-making while omitting others, they have the potential to dissuade teachers and students from engaging with musical practices that do not fit easily within their discourse.

Yet, in the absence of standards, teachers may base their instruction solely on their own narrow interests or on limited curricula. Indeed, authors of the 2014 American National Core Music Standards attend to a wider variety of practices than many music educators currently address on a regular basis. The problem is not that standards and assessments prohibit any variety, but that the uncritical universal adoption of them (standardization) limits additional divergent musical ventures potentially more meaningful for specific students at a given time and place. Estelle Jorgensen summarizes, "When standards foster convergent thinking and are normative and static propositions that may be irrelevant for a particular instructional situation, they are repressive to teacher and student alike."[14]

Second, standardization becomes detrimental when it encourages compartmentalization. Standards and standardized assessments create boundaries between ideas and practices. For example, the American National Core Music Standards divide the processes of "creating," "performing," "responding," and "connecting," as well as reinforce distinctions between "ensemble performing," "technology," and "composition/theory." Standards and standardized assessments also produce and reinforce borders between artistic disciplines, between the arts and other subjects, and between formal education and practices beyond the classroom or studio. Such divides run counter to the interconnected nature of twenty-first-century life.

Many contemporary careers demand interdisciplinary skill sets, and most adults will hold a variety of changing jobs over the course of their lifetimes. Likewise, people need not limit their nonwork activities to a single subject or disciplinary subset. One can imagine individuals who spend evenings recording improvised instrumental riffs that they then remix and later apply to homemade videos. Subsequently, they may share these films with close friends, at a local art gallery or community center, or through a website frequented by enthusiasts of similar creations. Such actions illuminate the limits of strict divides between music performing, technology, and composition; between music, film, and other disciplines; and between a person's home, local, and global musical communities. Yet, the standardized silos within music education and between music and other disciplines resist the skills and dispositions needed for such forms of lifelong musical engagement.

A second theme permeating current education discourse and practice is the assertion that education serves primarily as a means of job training. The rhetoric of international competitiveness has influenced American education policy since at least the launch of Sputnik in 1957.[15] Yet, contemporary policymakers increasingly conceive of education as primarily a means of producing efficient workers who will further political-economic agendas in a global capitalist marketplace. Randall Allsup argues that for such individuals, schools "are markets like any other" and should be judged effective by outcomes such as "enlarging a province or state's employment rolls or increasing a nation's gross domestic product."[16] Horsley notes the global nature of such thinking, explaining one of the worldwide goals of many current education practices as "creating employable citizens within a largely globalized economic structure in order to support national or regional economies."[17]

While a career-centric rationale for education is perhaps particularly detrimental for music educators, few of whose students will likely pursue music careers, it is also problematic for educators of all subjects and for societies in general. Like standardization, a job training rationale for education can have the troubling effects of limiting engagement with assorted, constantly changing ideas and practices and compartmentalizing understandings and actions. Additionally, the increasing interconnectivity of twenty-first-century life means that personal and professional decisions can have far-reaching ethical implications. For instance, while for much of human history choices about what food to consume or what clothing to wear primarily affected those within one's local geographic area, they now often have a powerful influence on humans in disparate parts of the globe. Likewise, issues such as global warming, unequal resource distribution, and women's rights exist at the confluence of local and global value systems, policy documents, and actions.

Contemporary ethical decision-making necessitates acknowledging complex, evolving relationships and debating problems that defy singular solutions. Leading by example, a teacher narrowly focused on the skills needed for employment reinforces the covert message that students should follow instructions rather than think creatively about ethical dilemmas. Such action neglects to prepare students for both civic life in their own regions and their roles as thoughtful global citizens.

In exposing the problems of a primarily economic rationale for education, I am not asserting that educators should refrain from teaching skills and understandings needed for future employment. Yet, as authors such as Nel Noddings have argued, such learnings might occur alongside and in integration with insights and experiences not directly tied to job training.[18] The problem of contemporary education policy and practice is not the acknowledgment of the need to consider students' potential careers, but the absence of any other significant aims for education, including ethical ones.[19]

This problematization of educational standardization and career-centrism hints at what such practices neglect, including complexity, ethics, and relationships with and within changing local and global musical communities. My interest in these often excluded qualities and considerations is not unique. Benedict critiques confining music education methodologies and asserts the possibilities of embracing diverse, context-specific aims, and Patrick Schmidt encourages music educators to welcome complexity, including seeking out the musical meanings that they tend to omit.[20] Similarly, Jorgensen welcomes divergent viewpoints by challenging the profession to move beyond an either/or mentality to a dialectics of "this is with that,"[21] while Allsup posits the need for an open philosophy that embraces the "muddle."[22] Although I attend to contrasting details and points of interest, these thinkers and I pause at similar vistas, and my travels rely on their critiques of existing routes. Most significantly, my philosophical journeying parallels and at times joins trails Elizabeth Gould blazed using the ideas of authors often labeled "poststructuralist." Like Gould, I find that poststructuralist writers inspire intriguing, creative alternatives to well-worn music education paths.

In light of the limitations of standardization and a career-centric rationale for education, what makes poststructuralist philosophy "better" than other writings at facilitating reimaginings of music education practices? Asking this question negates the fluidity, diversity, and context-based functionality central to most poststructuralists' work. In contrast with the longstanding Western philosophical practice of aiming to convince readers about the correctness of one's arguments, poststructuralist authors Gilles Deleuze and Félix Guattari explain: "Philosophy does not consist in knowing and is not inspired by truth. Rather, it is categories like Interesting, Remarkable, or Important that determine success or failure."[23] Deleuze and Guattari conceive of readers not as judges in need of persuasion but as explorers in search of adventure; their philosophy can only be temporarily "better" or "useful" if readers find that it inspires their journeying. Since poststructuralist philosophy remains relatively unexplored in music education,[24] an overview of its authors' practices provides context for the remainder of this text.

When Is Poststructuralism?

Closely related to postmodernism and a subset of continental philosophy, the poststructuralist movement began in 1960s France. Poststructuralist writers sought to counter structuralism, whose adherents treated difference as superficial, arguing that overarching systems and structures underlie all aspects of human culture.[25] The term "poststructuralism" encompasses the writings of a variety of diverse authors, including Deleuze and Guattari, Jacques Derrida, Michel Foucault, Julia Kristeva, and Jean-François Lyotard. Although these authors did not define their writings as "poststructuralist," American academics subsequently designated them as such.[26] Resisting confinement within a single category or label aligns with key aspects of poststructuralists' philosophical practices.

While poststructuralist authors generally acknowledge the existence of forms of organization, they challenge structuralist writers' treatment of systems as universal and foundational. James Williams, author of the book *Understanding Poststructuralism*, states: "Wherever sameness and identity are taken as foundations, poststructuralism uncovers concealed differences."[27] Given this emphasis on difference and differing, I titled this section "When Is Poststructuralism?" rather than "What Is Poststructuralism?" To ask "What is poststructuralism?" leads to singular answers, endowing the movement and its thinkers with stagnant identities. Conversely, asking "When is poststructuralism?" highlights the temporal nature of poststructuralist endeavors. Poststructuralism is not a set of solidified arguments or conclusions but rather a "practice," a way of becoming in and with the world rather than abstracted from it.[28]

While each poststructuralist writer enacts unique practices, Williams explains general similarities in their undertakings. These include poststructuralists' highlighting of the limits of knowledge and knowing.[29] For example, imagine reading a composer's explanation of a specific musical piece. While teachers and students might typically focus on what the composer said, poststructuralists generally emphasize omissions. What does the composer neglect from their description of "love"? What are the communicative limits of words, including love? Yet, poststructuralist authors do not usually highlight omissions in order to balance or oppose the known; rather, they embrace limits as productive and central to experience. A poststructuralist composer might, for instance, experiment with how texts or harmonies generally considered unrelated to "love" could foster differing understandings of and experiences with love. Limits are not secondary but positive in their own right.[30]

Furthermore, poststructuralists tend to conceive of limits as existing in constant flux. Williams explains: "Poststructuralism is not against this and for that—once and for all.... It is for the resulting positive disruption of settled oppositions."[31] Poststructuralist writers resist stagnation and solidified directives, even in relation to limits, instead favoring uncertainty and ongoing differing. The teacher and students who explore that which a composer excluded would never reach a definitive resolution; their understandings and engagement would differ each time they returned to the question. Similarly, poststructuralists—often ambiguous and creative in their writing—generally conceive of their work as challenging single interpretations and universally communicable meanings.[32] They instead empower readers to engage with their writings in ways unique to each individual's circumstances.

This emphasis on changing, divergent interpretations extends beyond reading to everyday thinking and action. Through their experimental and provocative authorship, poststructuralist authors typically aim to show "how the limits of knowledge can be crossed and turned into disruptive relations."[33] Working within this turmoil, these writers tend to encourage readers to strive for a "better" world without fixing their images of what that world should be.[34] While poststructuralists do not pursue chaos for its own sake, they articulate the problems of static ends that inhibit creative possible futures.

Utilizing poststructuralist practices in music education, Deborah Bradley draws on Lyotard's writings to critique Wisconsin's preservice music teacher assessment guidelines.[35] She explains how this policy discourse restrains possibilities by excluding certain ways of being musical. Alternatively, June Boyce-Tillman uses Derrida's work to provide philosophical grounding for a gathering titled Space for Peace, which hosts participants ranging from community choirs to a Muslim imam to a Bahá'í singer.[36] Derrida's attention to the process of exclusion can inspire innovative musically educative experiences emphasizing difference and unpredictable variability.

In addition to illustrating possible practical applications of poststructuralist thought, Bradley's and Boyce-Tillman's engagement with individual poststructuralist authors, as opposed to poststructuralism more broadly, demonstrates the accepted scholarly approach to such ideas. Despite some overarching similarities across poststructuralist authors' writings, there exist marked differences in their assertions. For example, although Derrida, Foucault, and Deleuze all investigate issues related to the nature of being (ontology), they do so through contrasting practices. Todd May explains that Derrida's investigations into the limits of language led him to reject not specific human ontologies but "the terms used to fix any ontology."[37] If language does not enable clear communication, then definitions of human nature necessarily remain incomplete, and therefore the philosophical project of ontology is inherently flawed.

Alternatively, Foucault critiques inquiries into humans' nature by reframing apparent ontological matters as historical ones. By revealing the social construction of what people consider "normal," and thus "human," including with regard to mental illness and sexual practices, Foucault argues that ontological investigations propagate politically motivated boundaries under the guise of universal truths.[38] Conversely, as I explore further throughout this text, Deleuze conceives of imaginative, boundary-defying ontological investigations as central to considering how one might live.³⁹ In short, while Derrida, Foucault, and Deleuze all reject ontological investigations seeking stable "truths," their varying engagements result in divergent philosophical projects.

Given the distinct nature of each poststructuralist author's practices, attempting to combine their ideas into a unified philosophy would result in either assertions too broad to be useful or specific arguments that would align with some writers while contradicting others. For this reason, a text drawing on poststructuralist philosophy must necessarily favor the work of some authors while minimizing that of others. While I constructed this book with an awareness of and occasional references to a varied array of poststructuralist writings, I focus on the thinking of coauthors Gilles Deleuze and Félix Guattari.

Trained in philosophy at the Sorbonne (University of Paris), Gilles Deleuze (1925–1995) taught at various schools in France. He eventually found a permanent position at The University of Paris VIII in Vincennes, which he held from 1969 until his retirement in 1987. Drawing inspiration from the works of Lucretius, Spinoza, Hume, Nietzsche, and Bergson while defining himself as "an enemy" of Kant,⁴⁰ Deleuze wrote both alone and with Félix Guattari (1930–1992), a practicing psychoanalyst who engaged in political activism. Guattari trained with the French psychoanalyst and philosopher Jacques Lacan and spent most of his life working at an experimental psychiatric clinic.

Deleuze and Guattari wrote together following the May 1968 protests in France, during which students and, later, workers went on strike against university and government authorities. Denise Green explains the impact that the May 1968 events had on Deleuze's work, asserting: "Far from writing being the expression of a unique vision or belief, philosophers such as Deleuze thought it should be an open and almost involuntary response to the events of one's time."⁴¹ For Deleuze and Guattari, philosophy served not just as an intellectual exercise but as a creative interaction with life.⁴²

In music education, Elizabeth Gould draws extensively on the work of Deleuze and Guattari, using it to probe issues related to feminism, heteronormativity, social justice, and creativity.⁴³ Alternatively, Deleuze's work inspired Michael Szekely to conceptualize the practice of "becoming-musician," arguing for an envisioning of music education as a process rather than an entity.⁴⁴ David Lines has challenged the confines within and beyond the music education profession, including those related to "music piece," "skilled music performer," and economic rationalism.⁴⁵ In response, Lines poses Deleuzian ideas related to mutation, events, affects, and uncertainties.⁴⁶

Despite this attention, Estelle Jorgensen and Iris Yob assert that aspects of Deleuze and Guattari's philosophy remain ripe for further exploration. Referencing Deleuze and Guattari's writings about becoming, desiring, nonconformity, difference, dynamism, resistance, and eccentricity, they state: "These are truly big ideas that have yet to penetrate education to any depth, and there has probably never been a more compelling time to do so when every impulse in educational organization and policy making is toward setting standards for all to reach at each step along the way, massification of texts and curricula, and obliteration of the individual teacher and specific learner from the equation."[47] In the coming chapters, I take up Jorgensen and Yob's challenge.

The current standardized, career-centric educational climate fosters new dilemmas that existing music education Deleuzian writings could inform. It also provides opportunities for investigating musical issues largely unexplored through a Deleuzian lens, including those related to human ontology, ethics, and educative experiences.

Enter the Rhizome

In addition to offering imaginative practices for engaging with lived experiences, Deleuze and Guattari create alternative ways of doing philosophy. In their coauthored book *What Is Philosophy?* they explain their practice of philosophizing, writing, "Philosophy is the art of forming, inventing, and fabricating concepts."[48] Deleuze and Guattari elaborate that concepts are connective and lack hierarchies or other structural models.[49] Rather than stagnant, logically ordered ideas, Deleuze and Guattari conceive of concepts as changing entities that form disparate relationships and alter over the course of their writing.

Deleuzian scholar John Rajchman notes the rhizomatic nature of their processes, stating: "[Deleuze's philosophy] proceeds by continuous variation of concepts and problems, constantly going back to an earlier point to insert it in a new sequence, and spreads like a rhizome rather than branching out from roots or building up from foundations."[50] If you have never encountered the term "rhizome," then I encourage you to pick up the closest internet-enabled device and search for images of rhizomes.

Botanical rhizomes, such as ginger, seek neither a particular shape nor territory of residence. Unlike plants that have roots anchoring them into a given location and leaves and buds that grow only at specific points, rhizomes develop freely, shooting off in new directions and burgeoning into new places.[51] Horizontal growth frees different sections of a botanical rhizome to expand variably, avoiding preset hierarchies as they form their own paths and interact with their surroundings.

These qualities of organic rhizomes inform Deleuze and Guattari's concept of the rhizome. They write that the rhizome "has neither beginning nor end, but always a middle (*milieu*) from which it grows and which it overspills."[52] Rhizomatic practices neither occur in a set order nor move toward preplanned goals. Instead, rhizomatic thinking and action, including Deleuze and Guattari's philosophizing, meanders freely. Those undertaking it search not for completeness, but for diversity and potential ruptures, each of which holds value in its own right. Moving rhizomatically involves relishing the uncertainty of a middle that overflows the boundaries confining and dividing everyday endeavors.

Viewing a plethora of rhizomes on an electronic device within a matter of seconds is itself a rhizomatic practice. Curious searchers may end up wandering to unanticipated web pages, ranging from how to grow and cook rhizomes to animals that eat rhizomes. The act of clicking through diverse, nonsequenced links mirrors the rhizome's horizontal motion and divergent connections. While rhizomatic practices can occur absent technology, the variegated, continually changing information and ideas available through the internet enable more complicated understandings than, for instance, the limited images and explanations found in a printed encyclopedia.

Mary Reichling explains that the methods of a music education philosophical inquiry should match its content.[53] Deleuze and Guattari posit a similar idea, writing, "There is no difference between what a book talks about and how it is made."[54] Yet, Reichling's use of the word "methods" is problematic in terms of Deleuze and Guattari's ideas because it denotes a systematic procedure. Writers using philosophical "methods" take an ordered approach to the content under their investigation and aim for clear conclusions.

By using what Rajchman terms "nonmethodological rigor"[55] in order to disturb rather than to settle,[56] Deleuze and Guattari's writings remain at odds with philosophical "methods" mandating clarity and resolve. Claire Colebrook summarizes: "There is a problem with talking about 'method' in Deleuze, simply because his whole approach to life and thinking set itself against any idea that we should approach problems with ready-made schemas, questions or systems. Philosophy, especially, ought to be creative and responsive, forming its questions through what it encounters."[57] Like botanical rhizomes that grow in interaction with the obstacles and fertile possibilities in their immediate vicinities, Deleuze's philosophizing derives from the challenges and imaginings that the world's changing circumstances enable.

Deleuze and Guattari's distrust of "method" extends beyond the process of philosophizing;[58] their concept of the rhizome, in connection and evolution with other ideas, provides a means of problematizing the forms of organization that permeate daily life. For example, early on in my engagement with Deleuze's work, I struggled with the question of how to create figures consistent with his philosophy. Putting terms into common geometric shapes, such as squares and circles, reinforced rather than challenged existing hierarchies and structures. This does not mean that familiar geometries serve no purpose, but engaging with Deleuze's writings caused me to consider how they propagate certain ways of perceiving and interacting with the world while omitting others.

While flying in an airplane, I looked out the window in hopes of finding inspiration for alternative arrangements. At first, I could see only the elements that I had already rejected. I noticed crops growing in circles, square plots of land, and perpendicular roads. Eventually an untamed group of trees caught my eye. Their shape reminded me of a botanical rhizome. I suddenly began to see rhizomes everywhere: in the flows of river tributaries carving into fields, in the way housing developments connected with each other, and in the patterns of growth within circular and square fields.

I encourage you to take a moment and look for examples of rhizomes in your immediate location. Can you notice rhizomatic designs on nearby furniture, rhizomatic arrangements of items on a shelf, or rhizomatic patterns beneath your feet? How is looking for rhizomes different from the way that you normally interpret your surroundings? In what ways do your emotions change during this exercise? When I started to notice the rhizomes outside of my airplane window, I have to admit that I had a moment of panic. I am comfortable in a world of squares, organization, and repeated patterns. Even now, turning my focus toward the unbounded confusion of diverse rhizomatic arrays cause me to feel uncertain and vulnerable. Yet, like the traveler who returns home with newfound insights, engaging with concepts such as the rhizome can reveal the limits of one's current predilections and habits. While I may choose to focus on the squares and circles that surround me, I can no longer conceive of such action as my only option.

Education discourse and practice foregrounding standardization and future employment rely on the clear conclusions and systematic approaches indicative of philosophical methods and a methodological approach to life. They demand preplanned, logically sequenced instruction designed to meet delimited goals as orderly and efficiently as possible. While philosophers can and do use philosophical methods to critique and reimagine such thinking and action, doing so in part reinforces the reliance on the forms of organization that they seek to counter. Deleuze and Guattari's practice of philosophizing challenges the necessity of singular, hierarchical, and clarity-based approaches that underlie contemporary education discourse and practice, freeing possibilities not only for philosophy but for all aspects of living.

For those able and willing to pore over single sentences and simmer in confusion as abstract concepts change over hundreds of densely packed pages, Deleuze and Guattari's work can offer philosophical insights unavailable through any secondary interpretation. In order to facilitate readers' experiences with Deleuze and Guattari's radical writing, I have retained much of their terminology and quote regularly from them. I also encourage interested readers to use Deleuze and Guattari's writings as companions to this text. However, even within the music education philosophy community, few have undertaken sustained engagement with their work. For example, in her prepared response to

Elizabeth Gould's Deleuzian paper at the 2017 International Society for the Philosophy of Music Education Symposium, senior scholar Hanne Fossum posited that the field needs philosophers to explain poststructuralist ideas more clearly before utilizing them.

Given the potential for poststructuralist practices to confront and offer alternatives to timely music education dilemmas, the purpose of this book is twofold: to explain aspects of poststructuralist philosophy in a way that is accessible for readers and to draw on these ideas in order to posit my own philosophy of music education. Coherent explanations of Deleuze and Guattari's concepts are antithetical to their rhizomatic philosophizing and in part reinforce the hierarchical, cognitive-centric systems that I critique. While I acknowledge that my structured writing limits the transformative potential of poststructuralist writings, in agreement with Fossum, I have chosen to craft clarified versions of these unique ideas in the hope that they might have a broad impact on music education.

Limits of Poststructuralism: Narratives Proceed from the Middle

As the staggering amount of misleading, agenda-driven, and blatantly false information on the internet reveals, rhizomatic processes are not without problems. When individuals cannot distinguish between empirical facts and myths about everything from election fraud to the percentage of crimes committed by certain ethnic groups, the lack of clear hierarchies becomes detrimental to societal well-being. Far from denying the existence of material circumstances, Deleuze asserts that all philosophizing functions in integration with them. However, the abstract, disembodied nature of the rhizome and other Deleuzian concepts leaves them particularly vulnerable to self-serving, disingenuous uses. Integrating Deleuze's philosophizing with the work of authors addressing humans' narrative construction of reality may mitigate these potential drawbacks.

Noting the embodied-experiential nature of knowledge formation, narrative researchers assert that humans' stories play a crucial role in their perceptions and actions.[59] Drawing on the work of philosophers including Dewey and Foucault, Margaret Barrett and Sandra Stauffer explain stories as "a means of sense making, a way in and through which we represent, interrogate, and interpret experience and come to know ourselves and others."[60] For example, while one student may deem a band concert significant, causing them to reauthor their current self-story in order to emphasize membership in that group, another student may not endow the event with such import. Individuals' changing understandings and valuations of their everyday endeavors and future trajectories develop and alter through the telling and retelling of stories.

While narratives, like philosophical methods, can reinforce existing ordered knowledge and practices, they can also can function rhizomatically, challenging clarity, straightforward answers, and stagnant systems. When individual narratives serve as what Barrett and Stauffer describe as "a means by which we might trouble certainty, and raise questions concerning the 'taken-for-granted,'"[61] they provide counters to grand narratives that subsume differences and solidify existing hierarchies. As explained further in the coming chapters, such action involves attending not only to one's own narratives but to a multitude of divergent narratives, including those from individuals marginalized within contemporary societies. While these narratives cannot stop the spread of misinformation that undermines thoughtful citizenship, they may provide a counter to it.

Although Deleuze does not directly address humans' narrative construction of reality, such understandings generally align with his overall philosophical project as well as with poststructuralist philosophy more broadly. Jean Clandinin and Jerry Rosiek call poststructuralism "the natural home to narrative inquiry," adding, "Post-structuralism focuses attention on the linguistic and narrative structure of knowledge."[62] They argue that differences between narrative inquiry and poststructuralism "are a matter of emphasis," explaining that narrative inquirers sometimes work within problematic social discourses longer than poststructuralist authors.[63]

More specifically, Deleuze's literary style of writing and the variable nature of his individual concepts suggest alignment with narrative philosophizing. Noting how his and Guattari's practices break from previous philosophical inquiries, Deleuze states: "For ages people have used [concepts] to determine what something is (its essence). We, though, are interested in the circumstances in which things happen: in what situations, where and when does a particular thing happen, how does it happen, and so on? A concept, as we see it, should express an event rather than an essence."[64] By focusing on individual occurrences and the processes that enable them, Deleuze implies that philosophical creations can have narrative qualities. His concepts are not transcendent ideas but narrative entities with their own histories and evolving futures.

In addition to integrating narrative writings with poststructuralist philosophy, I use narrative as a philosophical tactic.[65] The purpose of such action is twofold: to acknowledge in part the roles narratives play in my own and readers' philosophizing and to make Deleuze's abstract concepts more tangible. If all humans are narrative beings, then when individuals read, write, and think about philosophy, they do so not from minds divorced from their bodies and past and present experiences. Maxine Greene explains: "I could not separate my feeling, imagining, wondering consciousness from the cognitive work assigned for me to do. Nor could I bracket out my biography and my experiences of embeddedness in an untidy, intersubjective world."[66] As the airplane story in the previous section demonstrates, my own experiences influence my understandings of and engagements with poststructuralist philosophy. Since philosophers can never completely separate their own narratives from their philosophizing, sharing those narratives provides readers a deeper and more honest picture of a philosopher's perspectives, confronting directly the longstanding Western philosophical assumption that cognition can occur disconnected from embodied experiences.[67]

If a philosopher's narratives inform their writing, then it follows that a reader's narratives will affect how they interpret those ideas. In *Poststructuralism: A Very Short Introduction*, Catherine Belsey points to Roland Barthes' writings about the "death of the author" and the "birth of the reader" as one of the defining moments that enabled the poststructuralist movement.[68] Barthes asserts the potential problems of relying on aspects of an author's identity to determine a text's meaning. Belsey summarizes: "Barthes wants us to read the text itself, not something else that we imagine would provide a clue to it, or a guarantee of the correctness of our interpretation."[69] For example, while knowing specifics about the sad circumstances Edgar Allen Poe endured throughout his life may provide insight into his writings, such understandings can never reveal singular "true" or "correct" interpretations of his works. Instead, Barthes argued that a text's layers of meaning ultimately derive from the reader's impressions, which evolve with each rereading. These changing interpretations, which have no "formal guarantees" elsewhere, retain primary importance.[70]

Centering a reader's engagement with a text involves encouraging reflection on how their narratives inform their evolving understandings. By enabling readers to look for moments of alignment and disconnection between authors' stories and their own, philosophers who integrate their personal narratives into their writings foster attention to readers' narratives. Positing the value of utilizing narratives within philosophical writings, Patricia O'Toole explains: "When talking in theoretical terms, it's easy to assume a common practice; narratives provide material examples from which to argue or to imagine differences."[71] When readers' experiences contrast those articulated by a philosopher, while total agreement may remain elusive, stories provide points of entry and increased opportunities for empathy.

Additionally, given the abstract and complicated nature of Deleuze's concepts combined with the relative scarcity of Deleuzian-inspired philosophical writings in music education, narrative examples may empower readers to make more meaningful connections with everyday teaching and learning scenarios. O'Toole asserts that storytelling offers readers "the opportunity to adapt 'with' as opposed to adapt 'to' structures of knowledge."[72] Rather than omitting the uniqueness of their own circumstances and experiences, music educators and students adapting "with" become cophilosophers who conceive of their imaginative wanderings in dialogue with their current practices. Although not addressing narrative specifically, Deleuze makes similar assertions about the need for readers' active engagement. May summarizes: "Deleuze offers a radically different way to approach living. . . . As long as we turn to his work not to settle old questions or old scores but instead to become unsettled. In short, as long as we are willing to do philosophy."[73] Reading a writer's own narratives about being and becoming philosophical may facilitate one's experimentations with such actions.

When Is Philosophy?

Despite these possible benefits, using narrative as a philosophical tactic has notable drawbacks. The limited nature of any one philosopher's experiences means that the narratives they tell favor certain music teaching and learning scenarios while excluding others. Also, given that philosophers often form their ideas while working at the collegiate level, they may lack personal narratives about the innovative ways that their newfound thinking played out in contemporary Pre-K–12 music education. More troublingly, integrating narrative with theoretical writings can encourage readers to valorize and replicate those narratives, potentially reinforcing preset ways of thinking, being, and becoming, rather than to adapt the underlying philosophical ideas in ways meaningful for their unique teaching circumstances.

Philosophers can never eliminate such possibilities, but they can construct their narratives in ways that encourage readers to understand them as what Mikhail Bakhtin calls "novels" rather than "epics." Epics contain the language of tradition and display a "profound piety" toward an unchanging subject in a world possessing completed values and meanings.[74] Conversely, authors of novels treat characters as evolving, exposing their negative and positive features in order to demonstrate how they learn from life.[75]

While epics can certainly illuminate important insights about humanity, novel characters emphasize humans' imperfect and unfinished nature. For instance, in contrast with "epic" characters such as Prometheus, the seemingly flawless Greek god who brought humans fire stolen from Mount Olympus, Harry Potter exemplifies the qualities of a "novel" character. Harry gets caught breaking rules, makes poor judgments about other characters' motives, and does not always play on the winning Quidditch team. The physical scar on his forehead serves as a reminder of his own vulnerability. Yet, the Harry Potter novels have spurred more fan fiction than any other stories to date, suggesting that imperfect, changeable characters have the potential to inspire innovative, divergent practices. By drawing inspiration from novels rather than epics, music education philosophers can aim to construct narratives that resist coming across as prescriptive and lofty, encouraging imaginative adaptations rather than unthoughtful copies.

Since those fully embracing Deleuze and Guattari's work would unceasingly challenge any stagnated structure, they would ultimately reimagine all existing narratives, including every current form of music education. However, this does not mean that Deleuze and Guattari preclude using poststructural ideas to foster incremental changes. Despite the radical nature of their overall project, Deleuze and Guattari frequently reference the possibilities of small reimaginings. For example, while they note that a tree might become a rhizome,[76] they also envision rhizomes forming in the crooks of a tree's branches.[77] Adrian Parr summarizes that for Deleuze, "Philosophical thinking works to create a future that is different, yet informed by the past and present."[78] As such, ongoing minor deviations from the past and present align with their project. For me, these modest deviations, what John Kratus might call "small acts of subversion,"[79] remain one of the most underdeveloped applications of poststructuralist thought.

Since the novel-like narratives in this book grow from my own inevitably limited experiences, they serve as but initial steps along my continuing Deleuzian-inspired venture. Although compatible with Deleuze and Guattari's stated philosophy, I acknowledge that the straightforward nature of my narratives resists their style of philosophizing. Yet, I am skeptical of positing grandiose epic-like imaginings, particularly given that such action would not account for the needs of specific people and places. While readers may find less drastic inspiration in Harry Potter's values and motivations than in Prometheus's, because they likely identify with Harry's fallibility, they may be more inclined to learn from him. Likewise, I have chosen my novel-like narratives in the hope that their relatable nature will inspire readers' own unique imaginings, including markedly more revolutionary ones.

If humans understand themselves, others, and their environments through the evolving stories they think, feel, and tell, then their own changing narratives influence not only how they engage with philosophical writings but how such endeavors may in turn alter those narratives. Deleuze proposes an "intensive" way of reading in which the book meets the outside, one flow in contact with others.[80] Reading should consist of "a series of experiments for each reader in the midst of events that have nothing to do with books."[81] While a person might pick up a philosophical tome and deem that the writing *is* philosophy, if their narrative remains unchanged by their reading, then they have not *experienced* philosophy. Just as various travelers journeying to the same location likely return home with divergent insights, individual readers necessarily determine the meaning and value of poststructuralist writings in relation with their applicability for their own unique situations.

Focusing on the question "When is philosophy?" emphasizes readers' changing philosophical encounters, including how they come to live philosophically. The author is dead; this is now your journey. You will determine how you move through it, where you arrive at the end of it, and in what ways your narrative changes over the course of it. How might these explorations continue to affect your practices and stories in the future? Absent a clear starting point and planned trajectory, perhaps—like the rhizome—you proceed from the middle.

Notes

1. Wayne Bowman, *Philosophical Perspectives on Music* (New York: Oxford University Press, 1998); Hildegard Froehlich and Carol Frierson-Campbell, *Inquiry in Music Education* (New York: Taylor and Francis, 2012); Roger Phelps, Lawrence Ferrara, and Thomas Goolsby, *A Guide to Research in Music Education,* 4th ed. (Metuchen, NJ: Scarecrow Press, 1993).

2. T. S. Eliot, *Four Quartets* (Orlando, FL: Harcourt, Inc., 1943), 59.

3. While one may read this emphasis on traveling as colonialist, I have attempted to avoid this interpretation by clarifying that journeying need not involve exotic places or even physical movement. Yet, one cannot escape the reality that some people have greater access to more types of traveling than others. Likewise, some individuals are privileged enough to have the time and resources to read philosophy while circumstances deny or minimize others' opportunities for such engagement. Indeed, being a teacher carries a certain amount of privilege. In chapters 4 and 5, I return to these concerns, addressing the role ethics might play in teaching and learning.

4. See, for example, Kenneth Aigen, "Philosophical Inquiry," in *Music Therapy Research: Quantitative and Qualitative Perspectives,* ed. Barbara Wheeler (Phoenixville, PA: Barcelona Publishers, 1995), 447–484; and David J. Elliott, *Music Matters: A New Philosophy of Music Education* (New York: Oxford University Press, 1995).

5. Jal Mehta, *The Allure of Order: High Hopes, Dashed Expectations, and the Troubled Quest to Remake American Schooling* (New York: Oxford University Press, 2013), 64–83.

6. Alyson Klein, "ESEA Reauthorization: The Every Student Succeeds Act Explained," *EdWeek,* November 30, 2015, http://blogs.edweek.org/edweek/campaign-k-12/2015/11/esea_reauthorization_the_every.html?r=501001509; US Department of Education, "ESEA Flexibility Policy Document," December 18, 2015, http://www2.ed.gov/policy/elsec/guid/esea-flexibility/index.html.

7. Stephanie Horsley, "Globally Convergent Accountability Policies and the Cultural Status of State Funded School Music Programs: A State-Level Comparison," in *Biennial International Seminar of the Commission on Music Policy: Culture, Education, and Media,* ed. Peter Gouzouasis (Vancouver: University of British Columbia, 2014), 74.

8. Lauren Kapalka Richerme, "Uncommon Commonalities: Cosmopolitan Ethics as a Framework for Music Education Policy Analysis," *Arts Education Policy Review* 117, no. 2 (2016): 87–95.

9. See, for example, Nan Cooke Carpenter, "Music in the Medieval Universities," *Journal of Research in Music Education* 3, no. 2 (1955): 136–144; and Rebecca Newberger Goldstein, *Plato at the Googleplex: Why Philosophy Won't Go Away* (New York: Pantheon Books, 2014).

10. State Education Agency Directors of Arts Education, "National Core Arts Standards," 2014, http://nationalartsstandards.org/.

11. See, for example, The College Board, "International Arts Education Standards: A Survey of the Arts Education Standards and Practices of Fifteen Countries and Regions," 2013, https://www.nationalartsstandards.org/sites/default/files/College%20Board%20Research%20-%20International%20Standards_0.pdf; Department of Education, "National Curriculum in

England: Music Programmes of Study," 2013, https://www.gov.uk/government/publications/national-curriculum-in-england-music-programmes-of-study; and Antoinette Hoek, "South African Unit Standards for a General Music Appraisal Programme at NQF Levels 2-4, with Special Reference to Ensemble Specialisation for Available Instruments," 2001, https://pdfs.semanticscholar.org/3709/f6d49ef6d469457a20e6b9ff936da1ce1895.pdf?_ga=2.162131961.454580314.1567603790-1463185626.1567603790.

12. Cathy L. Benedict, "Naming Our Reality: Negotiating and Creating Meaning in the Margin," *Philosophy of Music Education Review* 15, no.1 (2007): 23–36.

13. National Association for Music Education, "Music Model Cornerstone Assessment: Artistic Process: Creating 8th Grade General Music," 2017, https://nafme.org/wp-content/files/2014/11/Grade_8_GenMus_Creating_MCA.pdf. See an extended discussion of these ideas in Lauren Kapalka Richerme, "Measuring Music Education: A Philosophical Investigation of the Model Cornerstone Assessments," *Journal of Research in Music Education* 63, no. 3 (2016): 274–293.

14. Estelle Jorgensen, *Transforming Music Education* (Bloomington: Indiana University Press, 2003), 17.

15. See, for example, John Rudolph, *Scientists in the Classroom* (New York: Palgrave, 2002).

16. Randall E. Allsup, "The Eclipse of Higher Education or Problems Preparing Artists in a Mercantile World," *Music Education Research* 17, no. 3 (2015): 253.

17. Horsley, "Globally Convergent Accountability Policies," 74.

18. Nel Noddings, *Happiness and Education* (New York: Cambridge University Press, 2004).

19. Richerme, "Uncommon Commonalities."

20. See, for example, Benedict, "Naming Our Reality"; Cathy Benedict, "Processes of Alienation: Marx, Orff and Kodaly," *British Journal of Music Education* 26, no. 2 (2009): 213–224; Patrick Schmidt, "Ethics or Choosing Complexity in Music Relations," *Action Criticism and Theory for Music Education* 11, no. 1 (2012): 149–168; Patrick Schmidt, "What We Hear Is Meaning Too: Deconstruction, Dialogue and Music," *Philosophy of Music Education Review* 20, no. 1 (2012): 3–24.

21. Estelle Jorgensen, *In Search of Music Education* (Urbana: University of Illinois Press, 1997), 56.

22. Randall E. Allsup, *Remixing the Classroom: Toward an Open Philosophy of Music Education* (Bloomington: Indiana University Press, 2016), 22.

23. Gilles Deleuze and Félix Guattari, *What Is Philosophy?* Trans. Hugh Tomlinson and Graham Burchell (New York: Columbia University Press, 1994), 82.

24. For example, writing about music education researchers who have utilized poststructuralist authors, including Deleuze and Guattari, David J. Elliott and Marissa Silverman note that despite deepening music education philosophy, "The practical relevance of this work is less evident in everyday teaching and learning." David J. Elliott and Marissa Silverman, *Music Matters: A Philosophy of Music Education,* 2nd ed. (New York: Oxford University Press, 2015), 122.

25. Catherine Belsey, *Poststructuralism: A Very Short Introduction* (Oxford, UK: Oxford University Press, 2002), 42–44.

26. Mark Poster, *Critical Theory and Poststructuralism: In Search of a Context* (Ithaca, NY: Cornell University Press, 1988), 6.

27. James Williams, *Understanding Poststructuralism* (Chesham, UK: Acumen, 2005), 145.
28. Ibid., 6.
29. Ibid., 1.
30. Ibid., 2.
31. Ibid., 4.
32. Ibid., 14.
33. Ibid., 22.
34. Ibid., 21.
35. Deborah Bradley, "In the Space between the Rock and the Hard Place: State Teacher Certification Guidelines and Music Education for Social Justice," *Journal of Aesthetic Education* 45, no. 4 (2011): 79–96.
36. June Boyce-Tillman, "Music and the Dignity of Difference," *Philosophy of Music Education Review* 20, no. 1 (2012): 25–44.
37. Todd May, *Gilles Deleuze: An Introduction* (Cambridge, UK: Cambridge University Press, 2005), 14.
38. Ibid.
39. Ibid., 15.
40. Brian Massumi, "Translators Forward: Pleasures of Philosophy," in *A Thousand Plateaus: Capitalism and Schizophrenia,* trans. Brian Massumi (Minneapolis: University of Minnesota Press, 1987), ix–xv.
41. Denise Green, *Metonymy in Contemporary Art: A New Paradigm* (Minneapolis: University of Minnesota Press, 2005), 61.
42. May, *Gilles Deleuze,* 19.
43. Elizabeth Gould, "Nomadic Turns: Epistemology, Experience, and Women University Band Directors," *Philosophy of Music Education Review* 13, no. 2 (2005): 147–164; Elizabeth Gould, "Dancing Composition: Pedagogy and Philosophy as Experience," *International Journal of Music Education* 24, no. 3 (2006): 197–207; Elizabeth Gould, "Social Justice in Music Education: The Problematic of Democracy," *Music Education Research* 9, no. 2 (2007): 229–240; Elizabeth Gould, "Thinking (as) Difference: Lesbian Imagination and Music," *Women and Music: A Journal of Gender and Culture* 11, no. 1 (2007): 17–28; Elizabeth Gould, "Devouring the Other: Democracy in Music Education," *Action, Criticism, and Theory for Music Education* 7, no. 1 (2008): 29–44; Elizabeth Gould, "Women Working in Music Education: The War Machine," *Philosophy of Music Education Review* 17, no. 2 (2009): 126–143; Elizabeth Gould, "Feminist Imperative(s) in Music and Education: Philosophy, Theory, or What Matters Most," *Educational Philosophy and Theory* 43, no. 2 (2011): 130–147; Elizabeth Gould, "Uprooting Music Education Pedagogies and Curricula: Becoming Musician and the Deleuzian Refrain," *Discourse: Studies in the Cultural Politics of Education* 33, no. 1 (2012): 75–86.
44. Michael Szekely, "Musical Education: From Identity to Becoming," in *The Oxford Handbook of Philosophy in Music Education,* ed. Wayne Bowman and Ana Lucía Frega (New York: Oxford University Press, 2012), 163–179.
45. David Lines, "Deleuze and Music Education: Machines for Change," in *Cartographies of Becoming in Music Education: A Deleuze-Guattari Perspective,* ed. Diana Masny (Rotterdam: Sense Publishers, 2013), 23–33; David Lines, "Deleuze, Education and the Creative Economy," in *Nomadic Education: Variations on a Theme by Deleuze and Guattari,* ed. Inna Semetsky (Rotterdam: Sense Publishers, 2008), 138–139.
46. Ibid.

47. Estelle R. Jorgensen and Iris M. Yob, "Deconstructing Deleuze and Guattari's *A Thousand Plateaus* for Music Education," *Journal of Aesthetic Education* 47, no. 3 (2013): 51–52.
48. Deleuze and Guattari, *What Is Philosophy?*, 2.
49. Ibid., 91.
50. John Rajchman, *The Deleuze Connections* (Cambridge, MA: The MIT Press, 2000), 24.
51. May, *Gilles Deleuze*, 133.
52. Gilles Deleuze and Félix Guattari, *A Thousand Plateaus: Capitalism and Schizophrenia*, trans. Brian Massumi (Minneapolis: University of Minnesota Press, 1980), 21 (italics in the original).
53. Mary Reichling, "On the Question of Method in Philosophical Research," *Philosophy of Music Education Review* 4, no. 2 (1996): 117–127.
54. Deleuze and Guattari, *A Thousand Plateaus*, 4.
55. Rajchman, *The Deleuze Connections*, 24.
56. May, *Gilles Deleuze*, 19.
57. Claire Colebrook, *Gilles Deleuze* (New York: Routledge, 2002), 46.
58. Colebrook explains, "If Deleuze has a method it is that we should never have *a* method, but should allow ourselves to *become* in relation to what we are seeking to understand." Ibid (italics in the original).
59. See, for example, Jerome Bruner, "The Narrative Construction of Reality," *Critical Inquiry* 18, no. 1 (1991): 1–21; Jerome Bruner, "Life as Narrative," *Social Research* 71, no. 3 (2004): 691–710; and Walter R. Fisher, *Human Communication as Narration: Toward a Philosophy of Reason, Value, and Action* (Columbia: University of South Carolina Press, 1987).
60. Margaret S. Barrett and Sandra L. Stauffer, "Resonant Work: Toward an Ethic of Narrative Research," in *Narrative Soundings: An Anthology of Narrative Inquiry in Music Education*, ed. Margaret S. Barrett and Sandra L. Stauffer (New York: Springer Science+Business Media, 2012), 1.
61. Ibid.
62. D. Jean Clandinin and Jerry Rosiek, "Mapping a Landscape of Narrative Inquiry: Borderland Spaces and Tensions," in *Handbook of Narrative Inquiry: Mapping a Methodology*, ed. D. Jean Clandinin (Thousand Oaks, CA: Sage, 2007), 52. I am grateful to Sandy Stauffer for directing me to this source and to the Bakhtin's work.
63. Ibid.
64. Gilles Deleuze, *Negotiations: 1972–1990*, trans. Martin Joughin (New York: Columbia University Press, 1995), 15.
65. Such action is consistent with writings including: Boyce-Tillman, "Music and the Dignity of Difference;" Deborah Bradley, "Oh, That Magic Feeling! Multicultural Human Subjectivity, Community, and Fascism's Footprints," *Philosophy of Music Education Review* 17, no. 1 (2009): 56-74; Elizabeth Gould, "Legible Bodies in Music Education: Becoming Matter," *Action, Criticism, and Theory in Music Education* 6, no. 4 (2007): 201–223; and Julia E. Koza, "My Body Had a Mind of Its Own: On Teaching, the Illusion of Control, and the Terrifying Limits of Governmentality (Part I)," *Philosophy of Music Education Review* 17, no. 2 (2009): 98–125.
66. Maxine Greene, *Releasing the Imagination: Essays on Education, the Arts, and Social Change* (San Francisco: Jossey-Bass), 113.
67. See, for example, George Lakoff and Mark Johnson, *Philosophy in the Flesh: The Embodied Mind and Its Challenge to Western Thought* (New York: Basic, 1999). I further address the inseparability of humans' minds and bodies in chapter 2.

68. Belsey, *Poststructuralism*, 20–21.
69. Ibid.
70. Ibid., 22.
71. Patricia O'Toole, "Threatening Behaviors: Transgressive Acts in Music Education," *Philosophy of Music Education Review* 10, no. 1 (2002): 5.
72. Ibid.
73. May, *Gilles Deleuze*, 25.
74. Mikhail Bakhtin, *The Dialogic Imagination*, ed. Michael Holquist, trans. Caryl Emerson and Michael Holquist (Austin: University of Texas Press, 1981), 16.
75. Ibid., 10.
76. Deleuze and Guattari, *A Thousand Plateaus*, 17.
77. Ibid., 15.
78. Adrian Parr, *Deleuze and Memorial Culture* (Edinburgh: Edinburgh University Press, 2008).
79. John Kratus, "The Role of Subversion in Changing Music Education," in *Music Education: Navigating the Future*, ed. Clint Randles (New York: Routledge, 2015).
80. Deleuze, *Negotiations*, 8.
81. Ibid., 9.

2 Who Are We?

Asking what it means to be human is at once a fundamental philosophical quandary and a question so often taken for granted that it can seem absurd to ponder. Although evidence suggesting that any other creature contemplates the nature of its own existence has yet to materialize, humans have spent millennia perplexed by and arguing about their ontology. Despite these ongoing debates, one might assert that such inquiries have little impact on or meaning for daily life. We know what it means to be human because we are human. Why deliberate the matter further?[1]

Engagement with the question "Who are we?" can surface obliquely in two types of commonplace encounters. The first occurs when someone expresses a thought, feeling, or experience that a person previously believed uniquely their own. An example of this includes reading a novel in which a description of love, friendship, or loss resonates with one's own private encounters. Similarly, I recall my ninth-grade color guard instructor describing and celebrating the emotions and chills that can arise in integration with artistic performances. While I had long recognized such experiences as the driving reason why I participated in music and dance activities, I do not recall any teacher before her acknowledging their existence. Learning that I could in part communicate these emotional aspects with others enabled me to find moments of solace in the fatigue and loneliness that can at times accompany artistic engagements.

This simple narrative illustrates that how teachers and students think about and engage with their own and others' humanity can have a notable impact on musically educative experiences. The same goes for humans' bodies and socialization; music teaching and learning that emphasizes the embodied aspects of producing sound or focuses on an ensemble's social dynamics contrasts endeavors primarily based on cognition. Yet, as exemplified by the vast majority of standards and standardized assessments permeating general Pre-K–12 education policy and practice, contemporary educational leaders tend to favor cognition while omitting attention to humans' other qualities. Such action can further a detrimental conception of students as mere brains developing to serve regional and global economies.

Likewise, although the notion that making music involves individuals' bodies, emotions, and sociality may seem obvious, music education discourse tends to highlight cognition alone. For example, the authors of the 1994 American

National Music Standards make no mention of the words "emotion" or "body" and only obliquely reference students' sociality through "performing in groups" and "understanding music in relation to . . . culture."[2] While the authors of the 2014 American National Core Music Standards attend to the social nature of musical endeavors, they do not address students' bodies and only note music's "emotional impact" in two substandards.[3] Moreover, one need only read the article titles in leading music education research journals to see the emphasis placed on music cognition separate from the other three facets, a trend that has persisted for decades.[4] Although authors such as June Boyce-Tillman, Wayne Bowman, David Elliott and Marissa Silverman, Harold Fiske, J. Scott Goble, Randall Pabich, and Iris Yob have posited the integrated nature of humans' multiple aspects of being,[5] even many contemporary critiques of music education continue to reproduce a human ontology based almost exclusively on cognition.[6]

A second event that may cause people to question the nature of being human occurs when people interact with those who they deem "other" or "different." Confrontations with variations in physical appearance, social customs, and exhibitions of thinking and feeling can illuminate different ways of being and becoming human. When such awareness leads to strict distinctions, including exclusions based on ability, class, gender, race, or other qualities, teachers and students miss chances to enrich their own lives by learning from and through human diversity. More problematically, as demonstrated by the current deplorable transcontinental rhetoric regarding immigrants and refugees, divides between certain groups of humans can facilitate the mistreatment of those deemed as deviant from "us."

In asking "Who are we?" I use the term "we" to mean all humans. Troubling solidified distinctions between "us" and "others" challenges physical and metaphorical walls separating those engaging in various forms and styles of music-making and between so-called "musicians" and "nonmusicians." Yet, my call for a more universal understanding of "we" has the tendency to imply an American, white, middle-class worldview. "We" becomes problematic when it minimizes differences and omits injustices.

Working within these various tensions, my project involves complicating what it means to be human. This includes honoring differences while challenging stagnant, hierarchical divisions between certain humans. Ongoing complications counter and enable alternatives to an educational milieu favoring standardized, cognitive-centric understandings that deny students opportunities for divergent explorations of shared aspects of their complex humanity.

Embracing Exclusions: Embodiment, Emotion, and Sociality

The contemporary neglect of teachers' and students' bodies, emotions, and sociality necessitates attention not only to their role in music-making but to their integrated nature, including with cognition.[7] Paralleling Deleuze's own philosophical practices, I augment philosophical writings with those of researchers in other fields, including cognitive linguistics, neuroscience, and sociology. Such action enables further understandings regarding the intricacy and inseparability of humans' various qualities. Most of the authors on whom I draw are structuralists, meaning that they assert the existence of overarching systems that underlie human action, thinking, and feeling. While these foundations remain at odds with Deleuze's poststructuralist assertions, by utilizing the Deleuzian concepts of multiplicities and the nomad in subsequent sections of this chapter, I reimagine these authors' work in ways consistent with Deleuze's overall project.

Given the difficulty of discussing cognition, embodiment, emotion, and sociality simultaneously, authors generally address no more than two or three at a time. While these four human qualities function in ongoing integration, because of the limits of language I begin with an exploration of two qualities, cognition and embodiment, and subsequently add emotion and then sociality. In order to further undermine the tendency to ascribe a certain hierarchy to these inseparable qualities, I randomly varied the order in which I name them.

Embodied and Cognitive

As a first-year teacher at a predominantly white, blue-collar high school in western Massachusetts, I made the poor decision of programming Norman Dello Joio's *Scenes from "The Louvre"* for our December band concert.[8] Despite my efforts, students took little interest in the piece and struggled with its technical and artistic demands. As I frantically tried to prepare the band, I thought primarily about music cognition: Did they know the rhythms? Could they respond to the articulation markings? Would they match phrasing across the ensemble? Besides occasionally asserting, "Sit with good posture" or "Use better breath support," my instruction largely ignored students' bodies, perceiving them as mere extensions of their minds. If their minds could comprehend the conventions of Western classical music, I thought, their cognition would control their bodies. Yet, both recent scientific research and my own meaningful musical experiences reveal the falsity of such a mind-body dichotomy.

Cognitive linguists George Lakoff and Mark Johnson assert that all thinking, from basic to abstract, from individual reason to socially constructed "truths," derives from and relies on the inseparability of mind and body. In addition to this mind-body integration, Lakoff and Johnson explain the body's pivotal role in constructing humans' conceptions of reality.[9] They write, "Human concepts are not just reflections of an external reality, but ... crucially shaped by our bodies and brains, especially by our sensorimotor system."[10] Going further, Lakoff and Johnson describe that humans come to understand abstract concepts through their embodied worldly experiences.[11] For instance, humans use spatial metaphors to distinguish between categories, often envisioning them as containers with an interior and exterior.[12] Banana belongs "in" the category of fruit while asparagus belongs "out of" that category.

Bowman draws on these metaphors to explain how ideas such as being "in" a key or "out of" a key relate to embodied experiences.[13] If the high school students understood that they played sections of *Scenes from "The Louvre"* "in" tune or "out of" tune and "in" time or "out of" time, they did so not through minds disconnected from their bodies, but as a result of an inseparable body-mind. Bowman elaborates, "Each of these fundamentally musical phenomena—timbre, gesture, groove, movement, growth, and attenuation—are bodily mediated, corporeal acquisitions."[14] I could have related the contrasting tempos and articulations within Dello Joio's piece to ways of walking or dancing, or compared his subtle musical gestures to differences in facial expression or speech inflection. Yet, as I prepared the band for our December concert, I ordered students' bodies into proper playing positions and encouraged them to hold notes longer or to play passages faster, but I rarely asked them to reflect on their bodies or to use their bodies to assist them in gaining musical understandings.

One might argue that instructional methods such as Dalcroze, Kodály, and Orff encourage educators to acknowledge the integration of body and mind during musical endeavors. In the Dalcroze method, teachers assist learners in developing a group of aural and kinesthetic images that they can both translate into symbols and perform,[15] and educators utilizing Kodály create a kinesthetic connection between the Curwen hand signs[16] and solfége syllables.[17] Alternatively, those engaged in Orff pedagogy emphasize the basic elements inherent in music, dance, and speech, aiming for a unity of word, music, and movement.[18] In agreement with Bowman and Kimberly Powell, I posit that while Dalcroze, Kodály, and Orff foster body-mind awareness during musical engagement, these methods de-emphasize the body as students grow older. As such, they do not facilitate lifelong attention to the mind-body's role in all musical experiences.[19]

While teachers might reimagine aspects of Western classical music-making through embodied perspectives, they can also facilitate such understandings via engagement with other musical traditions and innovations. For instance, Ghanaian drumming teacher David Locke explains that such music-making demands "group-oriented, body-mind intelligence rather than a self-oriented, visual-analytical approach."[20] He continues: "New students should experience physical sensations as directly as possible, with minimal filtering through familiar concepts of music theory."[21] Engaging with musical traditions and innovations that provide the body a pronounced role counterbalance the cognitive-centric aspects of Western classical music-making. In short, the ways in which the body and mind interconnect depends in part on the type of musical practice and form of instruction. Musical experiences never occur absent of their integration. However, as my opening color guard narrative demonstrates, artistic endeavors involve more than just a body-mind.

Emotional, Embodied, Cognitive

Imagine yourself feeling sad, afraid, or happy. Do you feel changes in your mind-body?[22] Neuroscientists such as Antonio Damasio and Paul Ekman detail the relationship between physiology and emotion, often defining the existence of emotions in terms of bodily responses.[23] For instance, Damasio explains that emotional responses cause changes in body, body landscape, and the brain landscape,[24] and Ekman argues that all emotions possess a "distinctive physiology."[25]

Lars-Olov Lundqvist, Fredrick Carlsson, Per Hilmersson, and Patrik Juslin have studied these relationships during musical endeavors.[26] Upon measuring the muscle activity of people listening to popular music, they found that "happy music" induced markedly different physiological changes, such as greater skin conductance and lower finger temperature, than "sad music."[27] Summarizing similar findings from a variety of sources, Elliott and Silverman argue, "Music is a socially embedded, corporeal phenomenon such that . . . musical emotions do not arise from 'music cognition' alone."[28]

Despite the paramount role emotions play in my own musical engagement, they went almost totally unacknowledged in my classroom. While teaching *Scenes from "The Louvre,"* I did on rare occasions ask students to portray certain emotions, imploring them to feel the longing sadness in the introduction of the second movement and the happiness, joy, and excitement that ensued with the entrance of the main theme. Yet, I talked about emotions as if one's mind could conjure them on cue and apart from embodied reactions; I neither wondered whether students had visceral reactions linked to their changing emotions nor contemplated how students' emotions interplayed with their cognition during musical experiences.

Damasio explicitly challenges the divide between cognition and emotion, asserting that emotion does not exist apart from reasoning.[29] Likewise, enumerating recent changes in scientists' conceptions of reason, Lakoff and Johnson summarize, "Reason is not dispassionate, but emotionally engaged."[30] Given the body-mind integration detailed above, it follows that cognition, embodiment, and emotions unceasingly intermix, each informing and affecting the others.

Contemporary music philosophers such as Peter Kivy and Jenefer Robinson write specifically about listening and emotion, positing that emotional responses occur in union with various cognitive understandings.[31] Robinson notes that when listening to music, "I may be moved by the beauty and craftsmanship of the music, as well as temporarily bewildered, then pleasantly surprised and delighted by the clever harmonic, melodic, and rhythmic development."[32] An elongated rock guitar solo, extended tabla improvisation, classical cadenza, or prolonged silence before the closing gong of a gamelan piece all serve to create suspense. Regardless of their knowledge of specific terminology, those familiar with the conventions of each genre often feel certain emotions as their cognitive anticipations of musical resolutions become disrupted. Conversely, while engaging with *Scenes from "The Louvre,"* I became frustrated when students' musical knowledge did not enable them to experience those same cognitive expectations and accompanying emotions. In assuming that the group and I could and should have equivalent emotional experiences, I neglected how the interplay of a student's emotions, body, and cognition might differ from my own and from those of their peers.

Although music philosophers such as Kivy write almost exclusively about the relationship between formal musical structure and emotion,[33] other cognitive-embodied understandings can also influence emotional responses to music. James Averill's research provides a foundation for considering how thoughts about nonmusical elements occur inseparable from one's emotions during musical endeavors.[34] He argues that humans' appraisals of objects, people, and situations work in union with their embodied-emotions, explaining that interpretations of events rather than the events themselves determine the emotions someone will feel.[35] While playing *Scenes from "The Louvre,"* students' cognitive evaluations of me and of their fellow students may have interfaced with their embodied-emotions as much, if not more so, than thoughts related to the music itself. Additionally, Robinson posits that the emotions of a singer, apart from the structure of the music, can move listeners.[36] Audience members react differently to a singer's personal sadness permeating a traditionally "happy" tune than to a joyful rendition of the same song.

Given that humans have physiological responses when experiencing emotions, it seems logical that one can interpret, at least in part, another's emotional state by observing their body. For example, a teacher observing a reluctant student improvising a solo might notice the redness in their cheeks, the nervous shaking of their hands and arms, or the excitement in their open eyes. Through these observations the teacher and other students can partly deduce the performer's emotions. Researchers have supported such perceptions, documenting the ability of people to identify others' emotions through their facial expressions and demonstrating that even stagnant bodies devoid of facial features can articulate certain emotions.[37]

Neuroscientists such as Istvan Molnar-Szakacs and Katie Overy relate such ideas to music, positing that mirror neurons allow for the embodied communication of emotion during music-making.[38] They state, "According to the simulation mechanism implemented by the human mirror neuron system, a similar or equivalent motor network is engaged by someone listening to singing/drumming as the motor network engaged by the actual singer/drummer; from the large-scale movements of different notes to the tiny, subtle movements of different timbres."[39] In other words, when people hear music produced by another human, their brains react in part as if they themselves had produced the sounds. Listening to a singer-songwriter perform a sorrowful composition causes reactions in one's mirror neurons corresponding to the physical actions that would allow them to sing sadly. Likewise, imagine pairs of students who take turns improvising or reinterpreting music with the aim of portraying certain emotions while simultaneously attending to the accompanying physiological changes that they experience. Teachers and students could extend these empathetic exercises by utilizing different styles of music, including those they might initially deem "foreign," and involving others in their school, local community, and beyond.

Social, Emotional, Embodied, Cognitive

So if all humans are inseparably cognitive, embodied, and emotional beings, what accounts for the immense diversity of human practices and values that exist within and between contemporary societies? Why would I, a classically trained oboist, react one way in a master class while a Japanese oboist, Navajo flutist, or Norwegian rock guitarist likely act and respond differently? While social interactions do not necessarily account for all forms of human variation, humans' social nature allows for and encourages physically or virtually connected human beings to think, act, and show emotion in similar ways.

Scholars such as Pierre Bourdieu and Christopher Small posit various theories about the interaction between cognition and sociality during artistic experiences.[40] Bourdieu explains that humans socially construct the value of artworks, writing, "The work of art is an object which exists as such only by virtue of the (collective) belief which knows and acknowledges it as a work of art."[41] This shared value occurs through and further reinforces artistic fields in which those in power determine art's worth.[42] Similarly, Bourdieu explains how listeners' past and present social experiences affect their musical understandings. He asserts that although they do not overtly recognize the process, listeners constantly "decipher" artworks through their familiar cultural codes.[43] Rather than focusing on works of art, Small emphasizes the social-cognitive interactions occurring during musical endeavors, stating, "Since how we learn which relationships are of value and which are not is a matter of our experience, it is to be expected that although each person has their own ideas of relationships, those held by members of the same social group, whose experiences are broadly similar, will also tend to be broadly similar and in that way serve to reinforce one another."[44]

The value I placed on playing *Scenes from "The Louvre"* developed through many layers of social relationships: my public-school band director, my private oboe teacher, my community youth orchestra, conductors and fellow competitors at school-sponsored music festivals. These and other experiences with classical music fostered my valuation of Dello Joio's music by providing me with the knowledge needed to understand his conventions. When the high school students expressed disinterest in or a dislike of *Scenes from "The Louvre,"* I attributed their opinions to a lack of cognitive understanding, failing to recognize the inseparability of their thinking and sociality. While my socialization led me to explain logically the piece's value to band members, citing Dello Joio's interesting use of harmonies and varying timbres, my words confronted minds socialized since birth to understand and prize cultural codes that conflicted with those I asserted.

Researchers have also found that members of specific cultural groups tend to react with similar emotions when experiencing certain events.[45] Damasio states, "The classes of stimuli that cause happiness or fear or sadness tend to do so fairly consistently in the same individual and in individuals who share the same social and cultural background."[46] The same tendency applies to musical practices,[47] as illustrated by the contrasting discourse surrounding the emotional aspects of music-making used by members of different cultures. For example, Kathleen Higgins notes that artists from India aim for audience members to experience one of the eight basic *rasas*, "the essential flavors of emotion," including erotic, comic, pathetic, furious, heroic, terrible, odious, and marvelous.[48] This list clearly contrasts the more limited emotions labeled by Western music philosophers such as Kivy.[49] Even within a given culture, socialized norms related to certain musical genres and locations can lead to contrasting shared physical manifestations of emotions. The emotional restraint typical within Western concert halls contrasts the clapping following improvisations at a jazz club or the exuberant singing and shouting at a rock concert.

Through their critiques, authors such as Patricia O'Toole and Elizabeth Gould have problematized the place of socialized bodies in traditional Western art music experiences.[50] O'Toole notes the social-embodied aspects of a choral rehearsal, explaining that the positioning of members' bodies creates docility and discourages contact between choir members who view each other only peripherally.[51] Gould instead focuses on the inseparability of sociality and embodiment throughout collegiate music students' experiences, writing, "Virtually all students entering university music programs . . . willingly give up control of their bodies to their omniscient music teachers and conductors."[52] These individuals can dictate everything from when and where students sit, stand, and use the restroom to the timing and style of breathing to arm and finger position. Likewise, in my band classroom, the integration of my socialization and embodiment left unquestioned both my imposing stance at the front of the room and students' attentive perching on chairs arranged in semicircles. Had I recognized this positioning as changeable rather than assuming it as "natural," I might have experimented with alternatives—perhaps integrating myself as but one member of a single circle or forming instrument pods with changing leaders—and encouraged students to do likewise.

In short, musical experiences necessitate humans' bodies, emotions, sociality, and cognition. While music makers may not always acknowledge or attend to the integration of these four qualities, they nonetheless function as inseparable components rather than distinct entities. My explanation thus far, however, is problematic because it treats these four qualities as relatively stagnant. The ways in which my own and each student's intermixing emotions, sociality, cognition, and body differed over the course of a single rehearsal, throughout our preparation for the December concert and beyond necessitate attention.

Emphasizing Differing: Multiplicities

Gilles Deleuze and Félix Guattari's concept of "multiplicities" offers further understandings of how humans' inseparable qualities connect and integrate. They explain multiplicities as "heterogeneous terms in symbiosis."[53] Like the brightly colored objects within a kaleidoscope, groups of distinct yet interconnected qualities, ideas, or materials constitute a multiplicity. Just as the joy of a kaleidoscope comes from the countless temporary arrangements of the pieces that momentarily settle at its base, multiplicities emphasize the endless potential configurations of a given set. Yet, in the case of both multiplicities and kaleidoscopes, these ephemeral orderings give way to ongoing intermixing.

In fabricating the concept of multiplicities, Deleuze and Guattari aimed to challenge the dichotomy between parts and whole. They write, "It was created precisely in order to escape the abstract opposition between the multiple and the one, to escape dialectics, to succeed in conceding the multiple in the pure state, to cease treating it as a numerical fragment of a lost Unity or Totality or as the organic element of a Unity or Totality yet to come."[54] Conceiving of humans as multiplicities enables our various integrated qualities to hold value apart from a unified "being." This means, for instance, that one can talk about emotion and its interrelations without subordinating it to a cognitive-centric vision of a whole human. Since multiplicities resist a stagnant hierarchy between their facets, utilizing the concept demands providing each human quality attention in its own right, resisting the treatment of any one as perennially superior to the other three.

Deleuze and Guattari further distinguish between what they term "discrete multiplicities" and "continuous multiplicities."[55] This contrast mirrors their distinction between two types of difference. Deleuze and Guattari differentiate discrete or numeric difference from continual or qualitative difference, writing, "Either the variables are treated in such a way as to extract from them constants and constant relations or in such a way as to place them in continuous variation."[56] In other words, there exist both difference between discrete identities and difference as a continual process.

Statements such as "The apple is *different from* the asparagus," "The city is *different from* the countryside," and "Listening is *different from* composing" exemplify discrete differences. The apple, city, and practice of listening have a different identity than the object, place, or practice named in the latter half of each sentence. A discrete multiplicity accentuates differences between the qualities, ideas, or materials it contains. While the elements within a discrete multiplicity remain conjoined, they each hold independent value.

Conversely, statements including "The shadow *differs* as the sun moves across the sky," "The seashore *differs* as the tide goes out," and "The Ewe drumming song 'Gahu' *differs* as it passes via aural tradition from one generation to the next" imply continual or qualitative difference. The shadow, seashore, and song differ not from other identities but *from themselves* over time. Continuous multiplicities emphasize their own ongoing differing and interconnections. Changing relations among integrating elements take precedence over distinctions between elements.

Conceiving of humans as embodied, social, cognitive, emotional multiplicities relies on aspects of both discrete and continuous multiplicities. While never completely separable, the four human qualities are discrete in that, at a specific time, individuals can attend to one quality more than the others. Although at no point do any of the four qualities cease to exist or integrate, a student can move from a more cognition-centric musical experience to a more emotional one, and so on. These changes in intensity suggest that human qualities also in part constitute a continuous multiplicity. Transitioning from a more emotional musical moment to a more embodied-social one emphasizes motion among qualities, rather than distinctions between them. While the objects in a kaleidoscope function solely as a discrete multiplicity, changing formation but always retaining their individual shapes and colors, human sociality, emotion, cognition, and embodiment vary in intensity over time.

Humans' integrated qualities also function as a continuous multiplicity when they affect each other through their meetings. A student performing *Scenes from "The Louvre"* might experience their socialized cognition assign varying values to their music-making. Meanwhile, their immediate social environment, a room of peers and a teacher—each of with whom they possess a certain relationship—interfaces with specific, continually changing emotions. Concurrently, their cognition might aim to control their emotions and bodily actions in socially acceptable ways, while their body-mind might recall past social experiences, reacting to everything from the musical notation to auditory changes to physical distractions. Although any prose account of the interplay between these four qualities reads like a linear story, the integrated concepts of discrete and continuous multiplicities enable understandings of and experimentations with how they function simultaneously and inseparably, each differing individually while concurrently affecting the others.

Applying such thinking to my instruction, I might have asked students to portray a different emotion each time they performed a specific passage, suggesting that they pay attention to their inseparable bodies and sociality while doing so. Alternatively, the students and I might have altered our bodies and social interactions while attempting to communicate a unified musical emotion. We could also have reflected on how such experiences differed, both over time and from our "typical" musical engagements. To what extent did our existing ideas of "band" confine this differing and with what alternatives might we experiment?

Mere attention to such differing, however, does not necessarily change teachers' and students' dispositions and ways of engaging with each other and the world. Embracing new possibilities for humanity's complicated nature, including troubling divides separating individuals from aspects of themselves and from others, demands more than awareness. Having explored the question "Who are we?" I now consider "Who might we become?"

Becoming-a-Body-without-Organs

In their later writings, Deleuze and Guattari use the term "becoming" to explain particular kinds of differing.[57] Stated differently, "becoming" is not a practice in and of itself. In clarifying what one might become, they write, "There is no becoming-majoritarian; majority is never becoming. All becoming is minoritarian."[58] Through the terms "majoritarian" and "minoritarian" Deleuze and Guattari do not refer to numerical distinctions but to norms and power relations.[59] For example, even in populations where women outnumber men, because the idea of "man" still typically serves as the dominant model of humanity, one can become-woman but not man.[60]

This does not mean that a man becoming-woman somehow physically transforms into a woman or that he tries to imitate the actions of a stereotypical "woman." Deleuze and Guattari explain: "The act of becoming is a capturing, a possession, a plus-value, but never a reproduction or an imitation."[61] Becoming-woman involves the extension and innovation of self rather than the replication of an "other." Explaining Deleuze and Guattari's writings about becoming-animal, Claire Colebrook writes: "Becoming-animal is not, then, attaining the state of what the animal *means* (the supposed strength or innocence of animals); nor is it becoming what the animal *is*. It is not behaving like an animal. Becoming-animal is a feel for the animal's movements, perceptions and becomings: imagine seeing the world as if one were a dog, a beetle or a mole."[62] A man becoming-woman would therefore extend his own self possibilities by sensing the world as if he were a woman.[63]

Deleuze and Guattari's concept of the "body without organs" or "BwO" offers possibilities for minoritarian becomings related to humans' multiple qualities. Like most of Deleuze and Guattari's concepts, the body without organs defies easy explanation. Deleuze and Guattari describe the BwO as "the unformed, unorganized, nonstratified, or destratified body and all its flows" and as "connection of desires, conjunction of flows, continuum and intensities."[64] The body without organs involves neither bodies nor organs; rather, it is the difference and differing—the ongoing changes of intensity and meetings of particles—that constitute existence. In Michael Peters' words, the BwO "is the play of forces, both mutable and endlessly transformable."[65] Movement, motion, and direction rather than fixed states or positions compose the body without organs.[66]

Do you find the concept of a body without organs confusing? The experience of uncertainty is consistent with Deleuze and Guattari's intentions. Rather than aiming for the body without organs to clarify one's understandings, they created it in order to evoke questions and ongoing exploration. As such, the body without organs serves as a philosophical figuration rather than a metaphor. Elizabeth Adams St. Pierre distinguishes between philosophical figurations and metaphors, asserting: "A figuration is not a graceful metaphor that provides coherency and unity to contradiction and disjunction. . . . A figuration is no protection from disorder, since its aim is to produce a most rigorous confusion as it jettisons clarity in favor of the unintelligible."[67] Deleuze and Guattari aim for the body without organs to foster complex conceptions of humans and of life more broadly rather than simplified, stagnant, and clear ones.

How does the body without organs relate to material bodies? The body without organs is not a body but rather difference that can become a body. Colebrook summarizes, "The body without organs is the life we imagine as underlying our forms of organization."[68] Imagine the primordial stew composing the Earth in its early days of existence. Like the body without organs, the Earth consisted of chaotic collisions of nutrient-rich molecules. Just as early earthly organisms eventually organized and stagnated the intermixing molecules, human bodies organize particles within their bounds and beyond.[69] Since disorder constitutes a body without organs, and stability, structure, and hierarchies compose a body or organism, tension occurs between the body without organs and organized bodies. Existing in a continual state of process, the BwO resists not organs, but the "organization of the organs called the organism."[70]

Applying the practice of becoming-a-body-without-organs to the ontology above, I wonder: What would happen if, rather than using the four facets—cognition, embodiment, emotion, and sociality—of this ontology as an organizing structure, they served as elements of the difference out of which humans form? In other words, what if the four interconnected qualities functioned as a body without organs? Such action involves working backward from the organism to its constitutive diversity.

In addition to focusing on how integrated cognition, embodiment, emotions, and sociality differ and intermix over the course of a musical event, imagine if I had engaged the high school students in activities that challenged them to disorganize their typical self-conceptions. Maybe we could have reflected on what embodied-emotional reactions the students tended to experience while performing a given piece and intentionally tried to arouse markedly different ones; this might have included anything from changing dynamics to adding improvisations to digitally remixing the piece. Perhaps we also could have considered what social conditions and music-making would facilitate audience members' unexpected embodied-emotional experiences; maybe we could have altered their physical proximity to the performers, asked them to add rhythmic improvisations over certain melodies, or experimented with live tweeting responses to students' preplanned musical questions.

More broadly, teachers and students might ask: What happens if we attempt to resist all of the habits related to our cognition, embodiment, emotions, and sociality in order to make and experience music in previously unimagined ways? What new understandings and experiences will such experiments foster within familiar musical endeavors? What previously unimagined ways of being and becoming musical might they enable? What might we do to engage audience members and others with the cognitive, embodied, emotional, and social aspects of a musical endeavor in ways that challenge their existing conceptions, experiences, and limits?

Despite the possibilities enabled by becoming-a-body-without-organs, the process is problematic because it assumes a certain equality between those undertaking it. Rosi Braidotti critiques Deleuze and Guattari for asserting "a symmetry between the sexes, which results in attributing the same psychic, conceptual, and deconstructive itineraries to both."[71] In other words, Deleuze and Guattari imply that all humans can experience practices such as becoming-a-BwO in the same manner. Yet, the process of becoming-a-BwO presupposes the organization of the body, and bodies vary based on qualities such as class, gender, race, and sexual orientation. While each becoming-a-body-without-organs is a unique event, since marginalized individuals begin with bodies already etched with the violence of habitual unjust relationships, they will likely have markedly different experiences of becoming-a-body-without-organs than members of privileged groups.

Further compounding the problem is the fact that in most societies an able-bodied, heterosexual man serves as the majoritarian body. Since becoming-a-BwO involves moving away from the organization of the body and body-based hierarchies, the process in part undermines the notion of a single body serving as a norm from which all other bodies deviate. Yet, even though the "body" in a body without organs consists of ever-changing flows and intensities, speaking about a "body" in the singular can still invoke images of an ideal or normative body. While Deleuze and Guattari do not aim for their philosophical figuration to invoke corporality, I concur with Jorgensen and Job's assertion: "Once the body has been introduced, the reader has the freedom to interpret and critique the metaphor."[72]

Moreover, given that in many societies women serve as the primary caregivers for vulnerable bodies, Jorgensen and Yob argue that the concept of a BwO may suggest that women's "care of bodies with organs has been misguided."[73] It follows that using the process of becoming-a-body-without-organs as a means of countering cognitive-centric educational practices may have the opposite effect; emphasizing bodies without organs may diminish attention to humans' embodied nature. I offer that teachers and students might address these limitations by retaining the possibilities of becoming-a-body-without-organs while focusing on embodied, social, emotional narratives.

Emotional, Social, Embodied Narratives

Attending to individuals' narratives emphasizes the diversity and differing of each person's pasts and potential futures. Such action resists assuming that teachers and students becoming-a-body-without-organs have equivalent experiences. Wayne Bowman explains, "Little narratives recover concreteness, particularity, individuality, and situatedness."[74] An array of narratives, including those developed through contrasting experiences with privilege and marginalization, troubles both singular grand narratives and implied similarities among various stories.

Additionally, since narratives rely on the embodied-experiential construction of knowledge,[75] unlike the body without organs, they naturally foreground the importance of humans' noncognitive qualities. Despite this emphasis, because cognition plays a dominant role in contemporary education practices, focusing on "narratives" absent any qualities may still reinforce cognitive-centric understandings and practices. Specifically attending to the embodied, emotional, social aspects of one's narratives further highlights humans' often-relegated qualities.

In music education, honoring individuals' narratives can include changing questions like "How does focusing on different aspects of our current social interactions interconnect with our bodies and emotions and alter our musical experience?" to "How does focusing on different aspects of *your* current social interactions interconnect with *your unique* body and emotions and alter *your* musical experience?" While individual students' and teachers' stories may at times converge, starting from the assumption of difference rather than similarity avoids an "our" that neglects contrasting histories and divergent futures.

Students' social, embodied, emotional narratives might also constitute the core of musically educative projects and events. Take, for example, Brandon Magid's facilitation of "empathy concerts," in which students learned a song, of any genre, that they found particularly meaningful.[76] Students then performed the song at a public concert with the aim of having audience members empathetically engage with their unique self-expression. Juxtaposing a word like "empathy" with "concert" directs students' and teachers' attention to the embodied-emotional-social aspects of musical endeavors, subverting cognitive approaches to musical rehearsals and performances in the process.

Extending the idea of an empathy concert, students might re-create a classmates' chosen song. Through such endeavors, students might dialogue about why they originally selected their songs and how their meaning-making affected their musical interpretations. Students could then experiment with both re-creating their classmates' expressive decisions and reimagining the song through their own personal narratives. A reflective written or video journal over the course of the project could document students' changing musical understandings and self stories.

Deleuze, however, may find this emphasis on narratives problematic. In his writings about cinema, he argues against the narrative construction that guides most movies. Colebrook summarizes, "Deleuze will therefore object to narrative cinema, for narrative tends to begin with characters who act or move *because of the way they are*, whereas for Deleuze there are possible actions, movements, feelings and affects from which character is created."[77] In other words, those authoring cinematic narratives tend to treat humans as relatively unchanging, relying on the predictability for their plotlines.

In contrast, the concept of a body without organs challenges stable ways of being and preplanned trajectories. Individuals who perceive and experiment with embodiment, cognition, emotions, and sociality not as structuring elements but as chaotic intensities mirror Deleuze's ideas about cinematic characters who form from and alter through divergent possibilities. As such, placing social, emotional, embodied narrative formation in a productive tension with the process of becoming-a-BwO mitigates Deleuze's concerns about their potentially confining and stifling nature. In such instances, these narratives serve not to solidify experiences but to mobilize how focusing on one's changing, interconnecting embodiment, emotions, and sociality can foster previously unimagined narrative possibilities.

My own opening story about realizing that I was not alone in often having deep emotional experiences while engaging in artistic endeavors serves as one minor example of an embodied, social, and emotional narrative constructed with an awareness of the difference and differing indicative of becoming-a-body-without-organs. The tale highlighted not just a social-emotional moment but a rupture that altered my very understanding of the emotional-social potential of musical engagements. Likewise, such narratives can involve looking beyond joyful or sorrowful musical moments to instances enabling an expanded sense of what joy and sorrow could be and become. They might also include occurrences that disrupt how one conceives of their body's musical capacities and times when sharing a composition or improvisation creates previously unimagined empathy between individuals from contrasting social backgrounds. Such moments foreground not just emotions, sociality, and embodiment, but the changes to one's musical stories that a differing understanding of these qualities can enable.

While narratives of divergent possibilities align with Deleuze's assertions about cinema based on intensities and events rather than stable selves and trajectories, even the most transformative stories can stagnate and organize the self. Telling and retelling my color guard tale will inhibit my welcoming of further social, embodied, emotional narratives. Before moving creatively outward from this and the other stories presented here, consider how emotional, social, embodied narratives might inform the two ways in which individuals can become aware of their humanity discussed at the opening of this chapter: finding commonalities in experiences previously considered uniquely one's own and marking differences between humans.

Sharing social, embodied, emotional narratives enables an exploration of these possible similarities and differences while avoiding both assumed agreement between individuals' experiences and solidified conceptions of humans and human qualities. While one student might resonate with the embodied aspect of a teacher's or peer's story, another might perceive alignment with their musical portrayals of sociality or emotions. By moving from more ordered conceptions of humanity to more chaotic ones, teachers and students may find that the complexity of individuals' musical experiences serves as common ground that challenges superficial distinctions between "us" and "them."

In other words, teachers and students might come to understand that agreement can arise as much from similarities among individuals' musical experiences as from narratives of divergent embodied, cognitive, social, emotional differences and differing; we share the difference and differing of our musical experiences. In such instances, asking "Who are we?" becomes not about "we" versus "them" but about imaginative moments of connection and divergence, each valuable in its own right.[78] Yet, the practices described in this chapter largely neglect that humans' constant interactions with their multiple environments also inform, constitute, and potentially challenge one's narratives.

Notes

1. A version of this essay, with a slightly different title, altered headings, and various changes to content, was published as Lauren Kapalka Richerme, "Who Are Musickers?" *Philosophy of Music Education Review* 23, no. 1 (2015): 82–101.

2. "National Standards for Music Education," National Association for Music Education, accessed September 4, 2019, https://nafme.org/wp-content/files/2014/06/Archived-1994-Music-Standards.pdf.

3. The connection standard strands address sociality through the repeated use of words like "contexts" and "daily life." In addition to the two standards, MU:Pr5.1.7 and MU:Pr5.1.8, mentioning "emotional impact," one enduring understanding considers the "feelings that influence musicians' work. "National Core Arts Standards," National Coalition for Core Arts Standards, 2014, http://www.nationalartsstandards.org/.

4. Charles P. Schmidt and Stephen F. Zdzinski, "Cited Quantitative Research Articles in Music Education Research Journals, 1975–1990: A Content Analysis of Selected Studies," *Journal of Research in Music Education* 41, no. 1 (1993): 5–18. Schmidt and Zdzinski's findings demonstrate that cognition plays a central role in many of the most frequently studied topics in music education research while embodiment, emotion, and sociality remain largely unacknowledged.

5. June Boyce-Tillman, "Towards an Ecology of Music Education," *Philosophy of Music Education Review* 12, no. 2 (2004): 102–125. Wayne Bowman, "Cognition and the Body: Perspectives from Music Education," in *Knowing Bodies, Moving Minds: Towards Embodied Teaching and Learning*, ed. Liora Bresler (Boston: Kluwer Academic Publishers, 2004), 29–50; David J. Elliott and Marissa Silverman, "Rethinking Philosophy, Re-viewing Musical-Emotional Experiences," in *The Oxford Handbook of Philosophy in Music Education*, ed. Wayne D. Bowman and Ana Lucía Grega (New York: Oxford University Press, 2012), 37–62; Harold Fiske, "Engaging Student Ownership of Musical Ideas," in *The Oxford Handbook of Philosophy in Music Education*, ed. Wayne D. Bowman and Ana Lucía Grega (New York: Oxford University Press, 2012), 307–327; J. Scott Goble, *What's So Important about Music Education?* (New York: Routledge, 2010); David J. Elliott and Marissa Silverman, *Music Matters: A Philosophy of Music Education*, 2nd ed. (New York: Oxford University Press, 2015); Randall Pabich, "Learning to Live Music: Musical Education as the Cultivation of a Relationship Between Self and Sound," in *The Oxford Handbook of Philosophy in Music Education*, ed. Wayne D. Bowman and Ana Lucía Grega (New York: Oxford University Press, 2012), 131–146; and Iris Yob, "Cognitive Emotions and Emotional Cognitions," *Journal of Aesthetic Education* 32, no. 2 (1998): 27–40.

6. See, for example, Randall Allsup, *Remixing the Classroom: Toward an Open Philosophy of Music Education* (Bloomington: Indiana University Press, 2016); Cathy L. Benedict, "Naming Our Reality: Negotiating and Creating Meaning in the Margin," *Philosophy of Music Education Review* 15, no. 1 (2007): 23–36; John Kratus, "Music Education at the Tipping Point," *Music Educators Journal* 94, no. 2 (2007): 42–48; Thomas A. Regelski, "Music and

Music Education: Theory and Praxis for 'Making a Difference,'" *Educational Philosophy and Theory* 37, no. 1 (2005): 7–27; and Paul Woodford, *Democracy and Music Education: Liberalism, Ethics, and the Politics of Practice* (Bloomington: Indiana University Press, 2005).

7. In other words, I intentionally move between "embodied, emotional, social, cognitive" qualities in one sentence and "social, emotional, cognitive, embodied" qualities in a subsequent sentence.

8. In writing about this experience, I am not defending or advocating for the traditional American band model of music education. Yet, since such practices have had a profound impact on my own narratives as both student and teacher, they affect how I understand and act, including how I philosophize. The aspects of human ontology explored through this example apply to music teaching and learning of all kinds, and readers may find that other content and pedagogy enable them to explore the question "Who are we?" more deeply than that which I describe here.

9. George Lakoff and Mark Johnson, *Philosophy in the Flesh: The Embodied Mind and Its Challenge to Western Thought* (New York: Basic, 1999).

10. Ibid., 22.

11. Ibid.

12. Ibid., 20.

13. Wayne Bowman, "A Somatic, 'Here and Now' Semantic: Music, Body, and Self," *Bulletin of the Council for Research in Music Education*, no. 144 (2000): 54.

14. Ibid., 50.

15. Virginia Hoge Mead, "More Than Mere Movement: Dalcroze Eurhythmics," *Music Educators Journal* 82, no.4 (1996): 38–41.

16. Curwen developed the hand signs based on Sarah Glover's Norwich sol-fa method, from which he borrowed heavily, developed, and promoted as his own. Peggy D. Bennett, "Sarah Glover: A Forgotten Pioneer in Music Education," *Journal of Research in Music Education* 32, no. 1 (1984): 49–64.

17. Lois Choksy, *The Kodály Method: Comprehensive Music Education from Infant to Adult* (Englewood Cliffs, NJ: Prentice Hall, 1988).

18. Brigitte Warner, *Orff-Schulwerk: Applications for the Classroom* (Englewood Cliffs, NJ: Prentice Hall, 1991).

19. Wayne Bowman and Kimberly Powell, "The Body in a State of Music," in *International Handbook of Research in Arts Education:* Part 2, ed. Liora Bresler (Dordrecht, The Netherlands: Springer, 2007), 1091.

20. David Locke, "The African Ensemble in America: Contradictions and Possibilities," in *Performing Ethnomusicology: Teaching and Representation in World Music Ensembles*, ed. Ted Solis (Berkeley: University of California Press, 2004), 175.

21. Ibid.

22. Damasio distinguishes emotions and feelings, explaining that emotions are outwardly directed and public while feelings are inwardly directed and private. I maintain this distinction throughout this paper. Antonio R. Damasio, *The Feeling of What Happens: Body and Emotion in the Making of Consciousness* (Orlando, FL: Harcourt, 1999), 36.

23. Damasio, *The Feeling of What Happens*; Paul Ekman, "All Emotions Are Basic," in *The Nature of Emotion: Fundamental Questions*, ed. Paul Ekman and Richard J. Davidson (New York: Oxford University Press, 1994), 15–19.

24. Damasio, *The Feeling of What Happens*, 51.

25. Ekman, "All Emotions Are Basic," 18.
26. Lars-Olov Lundqvist, Fredrik Carlsson, Per Hilmersson, and Patrik N. Juslin, "Emotional Responses to Music: Experience, Expression, and Physiology," *Psychology of Music* 37, no. 1 (2009): 61–90.
27. Ibid.
28. Elliot and Silverman, "Rethinking Philosophy, Re-viewing Musical-Emotional Experiences," 52.
29. Damasio, *The Feeling of What Happens*.
30. Lakoff and Johnson, *Philosophy in the Flesh*, 4.
31. Peter Kivy, *Music Alone: Philosophical Reflections on the Purely Musical Experience* (Ithaca, NY: Cornell University Press, 1990); Jenefer Robinson, *Deeper Than Reason: Emotion and Its Role in Literature, Music, and Art* (New York: Oxford University Press, 2005).
32. Robinson, *Deeper Than Reason*, 411.
33. Kivy, *Music Alone*; see also Stephen Davies, *Musical Meaning and Expression* (Ithaca, NY: Cornell University Press, 1994), 312.
34. James Averill, "A Constructivist View of Emotion," in *Theories of Emotion*, ed. Robert Plutchik and Henry Kellerman (New York: Academic Press, 1980), 306–312.
35. Ibid.
36. Robinson, *Deeper Than Reason*, 411.
37. See for example, Paolo Fusar-Poli, Francesco Barale, Jorge Perez, Philip McGuire, Pierluigi Politi, Anna Placentino, Francesco Carletti, et al., "Functional Atlas of Emotional Faces Processing: A Voxel-Based Meta-Analysis of 105 Functional Magnetic Resonance Imaging Studies," *Journal of Psychiatry & Neuroscience* 34, no. 6 (2009): 418–432; Mark Coulson "Attributing Emotion to Static Body Postures: Recognition Accuracy, Confusions, and Viewpoint Dependence," *Journal of Nonverbal Behavior* 28, no. 2 (2004): 117–139; and Shunya Sogon and Makoto Masutani, "Identification of Emotion from Body Movements: A Cross-Cultural Study of Americans and Japanese," *Psychological Reports* 65, no. 1 (1989): 35–46.
38. Istvan Molnar-Szakacs and Katie Overy, "Music and Mirror Neurons: From Motion to 'e'Motion," *Social Cognitive and Affective Neuroscience* 1, no. 3 (2006): 236.
39. Ibid.
40. Pierre Bourdieu, *The Field of Cultural Production: Essays on Art and Literature*, trans. Randal Johnson (New York: Columbia University Press, 1993); Christopher Small, *Musicking: The Meanings of Performing and Listening* (Hanover, NH: University Press of New England, 1998).
41. Bourdieu, *The Field of Cultural Production*, 35. Bourdieu writes almost exclusively about artworks as stable entities, primarily referencing works of visual art and literature. Such a conceptualization is problematic because it neglects the evolving nature of artistic experiences. Small's emphasis on musicking helps to balance Bourdieu's limited view.
42. Ibid., 30.
43. Ibid., 215.
44. Small, *Musicking*, 131.
45. See, for example, Averill, "A Constructivist View of Emotion," 259; and Damasio, *The Feeling of What Happens*, 56.
46. Damasio, *The Feeling of What Happens*, 56.
47. Robinson, *Deep Than Reason*, 405.
48. Kathleen Higgins, "Refined Emotion in Aesthetic Experience: A Cross-Cultural Comparison," in *Aesthetic Experience*, ed. Richard Shusterman and Adele Tomin (New

York: Routledge, 2008), 110–111. Higgins notes that tranquility is sometimes included as a ninth *rasa*.

49. Kivy, *Music Alone*, 202. Kivy asserts that music can "embody" the "garden variety" emotions such as love, happiness, fear.

50. Elizabeth Gould, "Devouring the Other: Democracy in Music Education," *Action, Criticism, and Theory for Music Education* 7, no. 1 (2008): 29–44; Patricia O'Toole, "I Sing in a Choir but I Have 'No Voice!'" *The Quarterly Journal of Music Teaching and Learning* 4, no. 5 (1994): 65–76.

51. O'Toole, "I Sing in a Choir but I Have 'No Voice!'"

52. Gould, "Devouring the Other," 36.

53. Gilles Deleuze and Félix Guattari, *A Thousand Plateaus: Capitalism and Schizophrenia*, trans. Brian Massumi (Minneapolis: University of Minnesota Press, 1987), 249.

54. Ibid., 32.

55. Ibid., 32–33.

56. Ibid.

57. Like many of Deleuze and Guattari's concepts, "becoming" changes throughout their writing. Deleuzean scholar Todd May distinguishes between two uses of the term "becoming," the first referring to ongoing change and the instability of existence and the second denoting specific types of becomings, such as becoming-woman, becoming-animal, and becoming-imperceptible. Todd May, "When Is Deleuzian Becoming?" *Continental Philosophy Review* 36 (2003): 139–153.

58. Deleuze and Guattari, *A Thousand Plateaus*, 106.

59. For example, Deleuze writes, "The difference between minorities and majorities isn't their size. A minority may be bigger than a majority. What defines the majority is a model you have to conform to: the average European adult male city-dweller, for example. . . . A minority, on the other hand, has no model, it's a becoming, a process." Gilles Deleuze, *Negotiations: 1972–1990*, trans. Martin Joughlin (New York: Columbia University Press, 1995), 173.

60. Feminists such as Colebrook have problematized Deleuze and Guattari's notion of becoming-woman. I do not further address becoming-woman in this book. Claire Colebrook, "Creative Evolution and the Creation of Man," *The Southern Journal of Philosophy* 48 (2010): 109.

61. Gilles Deleuze and Félix Guattari, *Kafka: Toward a Minor Literature*, trans. Dana Polan (Minneapolis: University of Minnesota Press, 1986), 13.

62. Claire Colebrook, *Gilles Deleuze* (New York: Routledge, 2002), 136 (italics in the original).

63. For further discussion of becoming, see Lauren Kapalka Richerme, "A Deleuzian Reimagining of Susanne Langer's Philosophy: Becoming-Feeling in Music Education," *Music Education Research* 20 (2018): 330–341.

64. Deleuze and Guattari, *A Thousand Plateaus*, 43, 161.

65. Michael Peters, "Education and Philosophy of the Body: Bodies of Knowledge and Knowledges of the Body," in *Knowing Bodies, Moving Minds: Towards Embodied Teaching and Learning*, ed. Liora Bresler (Boston: Kluwer Academic, 2004), 25.

66. Elizabeth Grosz, *Volatile Bodies: Toward a Corporeal Feminism* (Bloomington: Indiana University Press, 1994), 172.

67. Elizabeth Adams St. Pierre, "An Introduction to Figurations—A Poststructural Practice of Inquiry," *International Journal of Qualitative Studies in Education* 10, no. 3 (1997): 280–281.

68. Claire Colebrook, *Understanding Deleuze* (Sydney, Australia: Allen & Unwin, 2002), xxi.

69. I adapted this explanation from Lauren Kapalka Richerme, "Difference and Music Education," in *Music Education: Navigating the Future*, ed. Clint Randles (New York: Routledge, 2014), 16–28.

70. Deleuze and Guattari, *A Thousand Plateaus*, 158.

71. Rosi Braidotti, *Nomadic Subjects: Embodiment and Sexual Difference in Contemporary Feminist Theory*, 2nd ed. (New York: Columbia University Press, 2011), 253.

72. Estelle R. Jorgensen and Iris M. Yob, "Deconstructing Deleuze and Guattari's *A Thousand Plateaus* for Music Education," *Journal of Aesthetic Education* 47, no. 3 (2013): 41.

73. Ibid.

74. Wayne Bowman, "Why Narrative? Why Now?" *Research Studies in Music Education* 27, no. 1 (2006): 9.

75. Barrett and Stauffer explain that narrative inquirers regard experience "as both essence of being and the source of knowing," elaborating, "How and what we understand ourselves and the world to be are embedded and embodied in experience." Margaret S. Barrett and Sandra L. Stauffer, "Resonant Work: Toward an Ethic of Narrative Research," in *Narrative Soundings: An Anthology of Narrative Inquiry in Music Education*, ed. Margaret S. Barrett and Sandra L. Stauffer (New York: Springer Science+Business Media, 2012), 4.

76. Brandon Magid, "Music & Meditation—Devising an Empathy Concert at Your School" (presentation, Big Ten Academic Alliance Music Education Conference, Ann Arbor, MI, October 10–12, 2018).

77. Claire Colebrook, *Deleuze: A Guide for the Perplexed* (New York: Continuum, 2006), 79 (italics in the original).

78. This does not mean that teachers and students should not talk about and challenge specific human differences, such as racist stereotypes. I return to this point in chapter 4.

3 Where Are We?

It might be said that there are two types of travelers: those who go to see things and those who go to experience places. The traveler who ventures to New York in order to see the sights differs from the individual who seeks to understand what it means for New Yorkers to commute, work, and spend time with family. Likewise, visitors to nearby towns or even parts of their own community who go solely for specific events and return directly home differ from those who seek the experiences of walking along random side streets or observing the distinctive nature of child-adult interactions in that location. The latter voyagers illuminate Tim Cresswell's contention: "Place is not just a thing in the world but a way of understanding the world."[1] While travelers rarely fit exclusively into one category—few go to New York without both taking in Times Square and considering the speed and style of transport—they may have a tendency to favor one way of perceiving, being, and becoming over the other. Engaging with the question "Where are you?" involves attending not only to the physical features of a location, but to the differing practices and values that diverse geographies make possible.

Music educators and students are travelers of sorts; they often perform and listen to music not originating in their hometowns, and they make composition decisions informed by their experiences with globalized popular music, movies, and video games. Yet, teachers' and students' musical "travels" frequently emphasize the musical equivalent of seeing things rather than experiencing places. They may engage with a song, compositional technique, or musical style without considering its historical and contemporary uses in its place of origin or how those in their own local musical communities engage with, alter, and draw inspiration from such music-making. Likewise, authors of standards and assessments in music and other subjects almost always emphasize universal content absent attention to students' and teachers' multiple contexts. They work from the assumptions that those in rural and suburban locations, each with a varying class and cultural constitution, should have the same musical wants, needs, and goals. As Sandra Stauffer summarizes, music education remains largely "placeless."[2]

Like those traveling primarily to see specific objects or events, students and teachers can certainly find learning about and making music apart from considerations of place meaningful. Yet, adventurers who return home with many photographs and few understandings about alternative ways of engaging in and with the world miss opportunities for individual growth. While they may know about other places, they miss gaining awareness about the possibilities that humans' divergent emplaced existences afford. Likewise, when teachers limit learners to the classroom, studio, or single stage, they neglect how other places do and might influence students' music-making throughout their lives. Placeless music education deprives students not only of specific knowledge and experiences but of the dispositions needed to foster ongoing relationships with members of differently located musical communities.

Exploring the question "Where are we?" involves conceiving of music teaching and learning environments as existing in ongoing integration with teachers' and students' multiple other physical and virtual locations. Such action complicates existing understandings and practices, revealing the often profound impact of place on musical traditions and innovations. Yet, if teachers and students wish to move beyond awareness of what is, then they might experiment with how music-making can alter their various environments, perhaps concurrently attending to how their own narratives might differ through their place-conscious travels. In such instances, walls and other physical and virtual divides become not barriers that impose and limit but openings that meaningful music-making might permeate.

Embracing Exclusions: Local, Global, and Glocal Places

Like the enumeration of human qualities in chapter 2, naming certain types of places inevitably restricts musical and educative experiences by omitting recognition of some locations while favoring others. Additionally, though one can delimit boundaries between certain locations, as multiply placed beings and becomings, humans can never completely disentangle the experience or influence of one environment from others. While I address intersections between music education and often excluded places, including local, global, and glocal ones, I posit these explorations not as a solidified framework but as a rhizomatic middle welcoming of further ruptures, connections, and wandering growth.

Local

Local environments can have marked effects on how individuals understand, interpret, and engage with music-making. For example, when teaching middle school students at a charter school in downtown Phoenix, Arizona, I used the viral video for the infamously simplistic and vacuous pop song *Friday* by Rebecca Black in order to facilitate a discussion regarding issues of musical quality.[3] Students' responses to the images took me by surprise; they immediately expressed concern that much of the video takes place in a car idling along the side of a street. I realized that most, if not all, of the students lived along narrow, bustling city streets, and stopping a car in front of their places of residence would likely have invited honks and other frustrated actions. Recalling the suburban Boston students who I taught previously, I speculated that few of them would have thought twice about a car halted on a street in a residential development.

The scenario caused me to consider how the Phoenix students also likely interpreted musical aspects of the song differently than their Boston counterparts. Some had already explained to me that their families often listened to mariachi music, and I knew firsthand that many of the nearby stores played Spanish-speaking radio stations. Alternatively, the Boston students expressed knowledge of traditional Irish music and classical music. My preparation for the *Friday* lesson, however, did not include considering that students' local environments might interface with their musical engagement let alone how such information could enrich my instruction.

By offering an explanation of existence as composed of differing and individual events, Gilles Deleuze suggests the need for increased attention to local happenings. Applying Deleuze's ideas to music education, Elizabeth Gould proposes "performative literacy," which she explains focuses on "local musics and people in social and educational contexts."[4] Similarly, Gould elsewhere envisions music teaching and learning occurring "all in relationship to the world" as it interfaces between schools and communities.[5] Music educators addressing culturally responsive teaching and culturally relevant teaching have posited related practices.[6] For example, Julia Shaw suggests that choral music educators might use repertoire that honors students' cultural heritage, work with musicians native to the cultures from which musical selections originate, allow students to serve as experts, and "discuss, interrogate, and delve deeply into related sociopolitical issues."[7] Recalling my problematic engagement with *Friday* provides possible extensions of such ideas.

If students' local environments affect not only in what practices they engage but the nature of their engagement, then attending to the local can also involve explorations of variations in musical style and significance. Augmenting Shaw's example, what if the teacher and students explored and perhaps problematized similarities and differences between choir arrangements of songs from their cultural heritage and local interpretations of such traditions? They might also examine how students and community members make meaning out of these songs. This could include interviewing locals about memories and current customs associated with particular musical practices. It could also involve online commentaries from community members, including of students' posted performances. In order to honor local customs and values, students and teachers might consider what musical, pedagogical, and performance-specific alterations they could make in light of such exchanges. They might also experiment with creating compositions incorporating elements of diverse local neighborhood traditions. Through such endeavors, the local becomes not just a source of knowledge and inspiration but an entryway for understanding the ongoing interplay of locations, music-making, and meaning-making.

In addition to reimagined content and pedagogy, embracing the local can include thinking creatively about when and how teachers and students share their work with their communities. Roger Mantie notes that, historically, leaders of the North American band movement paid noted attention to local circumstances. He writes: "Leaders of early bands, including professional bands, operated in response to the specific needs of time, space, and place. Even when employing the most draconian of methods, the goal was to play well for the sake of the audience and the event."[8] Mantie continues that this focus on place and audience reception shifted as bands sought legitimation through the Western art music tradition and institutions of higher education. Music educators and students might draw inspiration from these earlier musical endeavors by creating musical happenings with specific local audiences in mind. This does not mean that performances cannot challenge or extend audience preferences, but it problematizes events planned absent consideration of one's immediate community members, including those who may have felt excluded from past musical engagements.

Going further, Stauffer posits that teachers and students might engage with questions such as "What does the community tell me about how to serve or engage the marginalized?" and "How might the community help us?"[9] She provides the example of an Arizona educator who drew on community interests and knowledge to augment traditional music offerings with a mariachi ensemble that played at weddings, quinceañeras, funerals, and the grand opening of a 7-Eleven.[10] In such instances, the relationship between music education and local community becomes a two-way street; music educators and students learn from, interpret, and extend local music practices while simultaneously serving local community needs.

Yet, servicing existing needs emphasizes what is rather than what could be. Drawing on Deleuze's emphasis on creative potentialities, attending to the local might also involve imagining the role of music education in practices such as building a more inclusive community spirit or addressing local social or environmental problems. The two-way street extends outward in search of new happenings.

Global

Another group of locations often neglected by music education policymakers as well as those promoting practices attentive to students' immediate communities are what one might term "global places." While there exists no definitive boundary between the local and the global, global places generally exist beyond national borders. However, the term can also denote locations within one's country or region that reside a substantial physical distance away from teachers' and students' everyday geographic locations.

Since at least the 1967 Tanglewood Symposium, music educators have called attention to music and musical practices from different parts of the world.[11] In subsequent decades, authors created resources for teaching music-making ranging from djembe drumming to Javanese gamelan, and they continue to do so presently. Much of the rhetoric around teaching "multicultural music" or "world music," however, has focused on the musical practices themselves, only indirectly addressing global places.[12] Considerations such as the authenticity of teaching techniques and knowledge about the context in which native participants engage in certain music-making can provide teachers and students some information about diverse locations. However, without added attention, teachers and students may end up with few understandings about the local circumstances fostering and interfacing with such music-making.

The terms "multicultural music" or "world music" are themselves problematic because they position such endeavors in opposition to "typical" music-making—including Western classical music—that teachers generally deem "music" without a qualifying adjective. In Juliet Hess' words, engagement with "multicultural music" can serve as a "foray into the exotic where [teachers and students] may explore a musical culture and engage in relational social identity development while never leaving a Western European musical home."[13] Such language has the potential to propagate an "us" versus "them" mentality that can foster xenophobia and inhibit opportunities for mutual empathy, understanding, and shared explorations.

While still potentially divisive, using the terms "local" and "global" draws students' attention to their own emplaced nature, honoring that which makes their immediate communities unique. Such action also avoids hierarchical and solidified relationships between musical genres and practices. In any one location, some classical, hip-hop, and rock music-making is likely local while other practices within the same musical genre remain global. Additionally, one's distinction between local and global alters both as communities change and as individuals have new experiences. As educators and students expand their local engagements, they may find that some music they once understood as "global" also occurs locally.

Regardless of terminology, Joseph Abramo notes that attempts to teach "multicultural music" can propagate harmful stereotypes.[14] When a simple drumming pattern comes to represent "African" music, absent further investigation, students may perceive of the vast continent as a primitive, monolithic musical culture.[15] Hess explains that such a "performance of tolerance" allows for self-congratulation while potentially reinforcing the detrimental essentialization of people, music, and places.[16] By misrecognizing multicultural musical engagements as benevolent and apolitical, teachers and students aiming to celebrate diversity may actually bolster racist attitudes and notions of Western superiority.

Music educators can mitigate—although not completely eliminate—the possible adverse effects of teaching global musical practices through certain pedagogical decisions. For instance, similar to Shaw's suggestions regarding culturally relevant pedagogy, Mary Goetze encourages music educators engaging with unfamiliar global music-making to invite culture bearers into their classrooms.[17] Such individuals augment teachers' understandings not only of the selected musical practices but of how those in different places learn, value, and enact them. Yet, since culture bearers can themselves present essentialized versions of their cultures, Hess argues that teachers and students need to approach such engagements with critical awareness.[18] She continues that studying with multiple people—and I would add drawing on multiple divergent resources—fosters a fluid "kaleidoscope of sorts" rather than "a snapshot frozen in time."[19] Such action resists the tendency to minimize difference and complexity by treating single individuals or experiences as representative of an entire culture.

Given the ever-increasing opportunities made possible through the internet, music educators and students can directly interact with music makers in disparate locations through blogs, video and audio sharing, and what Marja Heimonen explains as "interactive, 'face-to-face' media connections."[20] Examples of this include Heidi Partti and Heidi Westerlund's research on an existing online classical-music composition community and Lauri Väkevä's assertions about the possibilities of extending popular music pedagogy to include online collaborative songwriting.[21] Additionally, perhaps drawing inspiration from music education researchers' explorations of informal online musical communities,[22] teachers and students in different countries might engage in musical exchanges and offer feedback on each other's performances, improvisations, and compositions. Augmenting these authors' ideas, they might simultaneously consider how various locations influence individuals' musical practices.[23] Beyond exchanges and collaboration, a globally focused music education attends to the different emplaced experiences of each participant.

Engaging with global music-making does not mean that teachers and students should treat globalization as an unquestioningly favorable process. Problematizing the unequal exchanges inherent in global capitalist systems, Deleuze and Guattari briefly note the existence of overarching movements within the world economy, positing four types of flows: matter-energy, population, food, and urban. They argue that global capitalism prohibits many beneficial flows, such as those that would eliminate human hunger across the globe.[24] Yet, Todd May draws on Deleuze's work to argue that globalized capitalism is not purely exploitative. He explains, "The axiomatic that binds us to the market also frees us from the oppression of traditional social codes. The question facing us now, the political question, is how to mobilize the deterritorialization that capitalism unleashes in the service of new ways of living together."[25] While globalized capitalist practices can subjugate individuals and inhibit the sharing of resources essential for survival and well-being, they may also spread thinking and action that challenge restrictive ways of being and becoming.

Acknowledging a related tension, Alexandra Kertz-Welzel addresses comparative music education practices, in which individuals borrow pedagogical techniques from those in other parts of the world. She argues that such action often fosters the standardization of music ensembles and teaching materials.[26] When considered critically, shared ideas, practices, and materials may prove meaningful in specific situations, but borrowing becomes problematic when driven primarily by the pursuit of profit.[27] Moreover, while cultural dissemination and hybridization via globalization can introduce artists and artistic practices to wider audiences,[28] they can also aid the reduction of cultural diversity, disproportionate allotment of intellectual rights, and hegemonic relationships between cultural industries and consumers.[29]

Given the problems and possibilities of globalization, part of embracing global musical places necessarily involves questioning one's own sense of belonging in the world. David Hansen explains a cosmopolitan education as one in which "students still live *in* their local world, but they are no longer merely *of* it."[30] He challenges teachers and students to see artistic contributions not only as *from* a specific society but as "bequeathed to persons everywhere."[31] While touring the National Museum of African Art in Washington, DC, I found myself struck by the difference such a reconceptualization can make. At first, I engaged with a set of intricately carved dark brown statues from Nigeria with a sense of awe; "Look at the stunning creations members of that society could produce," I thought. Given my white European heritage, I perceived the carvings as created by "others" unrelated to me. Yet, I recalled that, as citizens of the world, cosmopolitans understand global artistic practices as interlinked with their own ancestry. When I took a moment to reimagine the statues as pieces made by fellow humans and as part of our global humanity, I felt a new sense of pride in the capacities of my species.

This does not mean that I should appropriate the carvings as entirely my own or ignore the culture and context that created them. In such instances, cosmopolitan dispositions turn colonialist. Indeed, how the carvings I viewed got to America and the circumstances surrounding their display necessitate scrutiny. The global ultimately occupies a liminal space; it is part of our shared humanity yet not fully our own. Likewise, teaching and learning attending to the global occurs in a middle ground, resisting both appropriation and othering.

In short, globalization depends on the difference and differing central to Deleuze and Guattari's conception of existence. While this rhizomatic thinking and action can counter forms of oppression, when enacted uncritically, it may foster and propagate unethical processes.[32] A thoughtful welcoming of musical global places recalls Hansen's assertions about a teacher who "comes further *into* the world—as a listening, responsive figure—while becoming a representative and spokesperson *of* the world—as a knowledgeable figure for whom the world and its future matters."[33] Embracing global musical places necessitates age-appropriate explorations of the unceasing tension between potentially problematic impacts of globalizing forces and the musical potentialities and self-growth that they may facilitate.

While this book includes a few references to international authors, events, and personal experiences, I recognize that my own global perspectives remain limited.[34] My focus on North American music education researchers such as Gould and on my own Americanized narratives means that I have regrettably participated in the exclusion of global places. Despite my interest in world news and global musical and education practices, I rarely drew on such information while crafting my primary arguments for this text. This was in large part because I do not feel completely comfortable writing about that which I do not know firsthand. Yet, this unease will likely accompany most music educators' global engagements, and it should not serve as an excuse to avoid thoughtful explorations.

In asserting the value of embracing often excluded global places, I am as much writing for myself as for readers. I aim to include more substantial references to global places in future work and to address them more frequently in my undergraduate and graduate teaching. Rather than justifying hesitation, my discomfort indicates that I need to learn more, particularly through direct interactions with global music education researchers and teachers. Such undertakings, however, will never occur completely apart from local places that inform and in part constitute my evolving self.

Glocal

Think of a musical style or practice that has spread across the globe. Where did it originate and what local conditions enabled it to form and develop? Although music educators have attended to local and global places, the intersections of the two remain almost completely absent from the literature. Yet, contemporary life involves not just the local and the global but their evolving integration.

While genres of music such as hip-hop, jazz, prog rock, and reggae have spread throughout the world, they all have roots in localized musical practices. Boaventura de Sousa Santas writes, "Globalization presupposes localization," explaining, "There are no global conditions for which we cannot find local roots."[35] Conversely, when local practices become globalized, individuals and groups in other locations alter and transform them, often making a style distinct from that occurring in the place of origin.[36] As *Friday* spread throughout America and beyond, students interpreted it through ears attuned not just to popular music but to the musics of their home and local environments.

In the twenty-first century, asking "Where are we?" involves exploring "glocalization," the symbiosis of localizing and globalizing processes. Roland Robertson adapted the idea of glocalization from Japanese business jargon in the 1980s that addressed the "tailoring and advertising of goods and services on a global or near-global basis to increasingly differentiated local and particular markets."[37] Glocalization highlights both how localized practices become globalized and how globalized practices become localized. Robertson explains, "It is not a problem of *either* homogenization or heterogenization, but rather the ways in which both of these tendencies have become features of life across much of the late-twentieth-century world."[38]

Noriko Manabe's detailing of how Japanese youth alter the content and language conventions of American rap in order to make it their own provides an example of how musical glocalization occurs. She explains that in contrast with the commonplace American rap topics of poverty, discrimination, and identity, Japan's relative homogeneity in race and socioeconomic class led to rap about the "joys, sorrows, and banalities of middle class life."[39] Japanese rappers adapt American rap conventions, imbuing rap with subject matter relevant to local living conditions. Given the nature of Japanese syntax, those rappers also deviate from typical Japanese word ordering, often placing "a key word, such as the subject, at the end of the line" in order to enable the rhyming indicative of American rap.[40] Having encountered American rap through the global spread of recorded music, at the local level Japanese rappers reinterpret the practice of rap, including its subject matter and syntactical construction. This glocal Japanese rap may in turn become global as it flows to America and elsewhere via the internet and other avenues.

While authors generally conceive of glocalization as a process, music educators and students might use the term "glocal" to reference specific understandings about places. Given that the vast majority of locations throughout the world reside at the intersection of localizing and globalizing practices, when viewed from an omniscient perspective, one might deem all places glocal. However, this does not mean that humans necessarily perceive their multiple places as glocal. Imagine listening to an Afro-Cuban ensemble at a local performance venue. One audience member might conceive of the venue as primarily local, omitting the global locations that contributed to the ensemble's performance, while another listener might consider the place primarily global, imagining that their experiences mimic those had by individuals in the locations from which the music originated. Alternatively, a participant who authors the location as primarily glocal attends to the uniqueness of the local performance venue in integration with the global places that facilitate the development, spread, and reinterpretation of such music-making. Likewise, teachers and students embrace glocal places when they ponder and experiment with how local musical traditions influence a rock band's cover of a Beatles tune or a youth orchestra's engagement with a Piazzolla piece.

How might music educators and students create an educative experience centered on glocal places? One possibility might begin with students selecting a handful of global musical practices. They could then work in small groups to record how local music-makers—including themselves—attempt to re-create or extend such music-making. Looking across the project, they could analyze how local influences might have informed those interpretations and augmentations, including instances of stereotyping or other problematic qualities. Having crticially considered and refined their projects, students might use these glocal renditions as the basis of a performance centered on differences and similarities, including injustices, across the various places. Through such creative endeavors, teachers and students do not merely emphasize local, global, and glocal but produce and reimagine what "local," "global," and "glocal" are and can become.

Despite the possible advantages of naming these excluded places, marking distinctions between local, global, and glocal places can contribute to stagnant images of such locations. Welcoming some aspects of local, global, or glocal music-making inevitably excludes other viewpoints and experiences. This raises the question: What might assist music educators and students in conceiving of various places as multifaceted and constantly changing?

Moreover, while the distinction between local and global may demand more fluidity than designations such as "world music" or "multicultural music," it can still foster harmful identity politics. One can easily come to equate local with "good" or "safe," as opposed to the potentially dangerous global. Although teachers cannot necessarily eliminate the possibility of problematic value judgments, conceptualizing places as possibilities that humans unceasingly construct rather than as delimited points on the globe can challenge immobile boundaries and hierarchies.

Emphasizing Differing: Striated and Smooth Spaces and Places

Although humans tend to conceive of them as stable, places, like all of existence, continually differ. Consider how the town in which you now live has changed since you began residing there. Perhaps developers have added or demolished houses, shops, or entertainment centers, or maybe community members have altered facades, windows, roofs, or the grounds surrounding their residences. More subtly, a windy evening may have left debris on various surfaces, or the look of buildings may alter as the setting sun illuminates them with ever-changing orange hues. Cresswell explains, "Places are never complete, finished or bounded but are always becoming—in process."[41]

Through the interrelated concepts of "striated spaces" and "smooth spaces" Deleuze and Guattari emphasize this incompleteness, complicating common perceptions about humans' emplaced nature.[42] They explain striated spaces as sedentary, asserting that walls, enclosures, and roads between enclosures constrain and divide them.[43] In striated spaces, boundaries restrain movement, change, and variation, separating people, items, and ideas into predefined, closed locations. Conversely, Deleuze and Guattari posit smooth spaces as mobile environments that foster growth and lack limitations.[44] Smooth spaces favor heterogeneity and variability as well as openness and evolving events.[45]

Striated spaces and smooth spaces might facilitate an awareness of the differing occurring in local, global, and glocal places in three ways.[46] First, while never exclusively one or the other, the combination of striation and smoothness within a space in part depends on a location's physical properties. Deleuze and Guattari designate the city as "the striated space par excellence";[47] in cities, streets, highways, walls, canals, buildings, and other structures work to confine and control motion and difference. For example, physical boundaries and limited transportation options dissuade dwellers within specific city neighborhoods from forming relationships with those beyond certain borders. Likewise, classrooms physically separated from the rest of a school and community resist musical exchanges beyond their walls, and spaces divided within by structures such as music stands, desks, podiums, or carpet squares favor certain types of musical engagement while discouraging many others. While music educators and students may still smooth such environments, perhaps through the rearrangement of chairs or temporary abandonment of music stands, the eventual stagnation of new physical configurations may in turn striate them.

Conversely, Deleuze and Guattari posit the smoothness of spaces such as the desert, steppe, ice, and sea, noting that events, affects, and intensities rather than stable properties fill such locations.[48] The sea teems with events, such as waves and water swells, that continually move and change in magnitude. In contrast with highways and other divides that separate cities, waves propagate freely, intermixing and altering. In contemplating my own engagement with smooth musical spaces, the annual Lotus World Music and Arts Festival in Bloomington, Indiana, comes to mind.[49]

On a September Saturday afternoon, a relatively small, verdant community park near the town center hosts diverse musical practices, ranging from Mongolian folk music to Cajun swamp-pop. Interactive performances and dialogue occur at various locations, and audience-participants move freely throughout. Just as the intensity at one area reaches its peak, perhaps with attendees clapping an Afro-Caribbean clave rhythm and singing a call and response song, music in another section ebbs as performers stop playing and begin taking questions from the audience. The openness of the park facilitates the intermingling of people and practices, enabling continually changing musical events with varying energy levels.

Despite this tendency toward smoothness, the park still includes points of striation. Objects such as chairs and tents slow movement from one performance section to the next, and in some locations platforms and other structures separate performers from audience members. Moreover, the smooth space within the park depends on the physical boundaries that divide it from the surrounding streets and buildings. Without striated borders, smooth physical spaces risk spreading so thin that they lose their vibrant nature.[50]

Second, the concepts of striated and smooth spaces emphasize differing by illuminating how humans do what Andy Bennett calls "authoring" their locations.[51] While physical locations can lend themselves to certain practices—an open floor enables dancing and group activities more easily than rows of chairs—Deleuze and Guattari explain: "There are not only strange voyages in the city but voyages in place."[52] Humans can author a single location as a primarily stagnant, homogenous, striated space or as a primarily varying, heterogeneous, smooth space. For Deleuze and Guattari, this authorship occurs mainly through specific types of activity.

While striated spaces develop via repetition and movement along preplanned paths,[53] individuals foster smooth spaces by focusing on evolving "free action" and variable wanderings.[54] Musically educative practices that contribute to the formation of striated spaces might include duplicating the same scales, repertoire, listening exercises, or other musical endeavors day after day and moving through the same curricula, standards, and assessments year after year. Such repetition and predetermined motion bounds the meanings and actions that teachers and students deem possible within a given physical place. In contrast, consider the iconic scene in the movie *Wayne's World* when Wayne and Garth begin headbanging as Queen's "Bohemian Rhapsody" plays on the car radio. Rather than authoring their car as a primarily striated space by undertaking typically accepted practices such as casual conversation or quietly listening to music, Wayne and Garth smooth the car through their unpredictability and changing intensity. Similarly, music educators smooth classrooms when they welcome a student who unexpectedly brings in a composition or recording that ignites group exploration, or when they encourage students to invent musical practices that defy existing genres, labels, and divides between school and society.[55]

While Deleuze and Guattari focus on action, other philosophers have explained that humans author places through their assignment of meaning. For writers such as Edward Casey and Tim Cresswell, this meaning-making distinguishes "spaces" from "places."[56] Stauffer explains, "Places *become* places . . . in the lived experiences and interpretations of people who act and interact within them, and through the human meanings that are associated with them."[57] For instance, the concrete walls of a stadium transform into a meaning-laden place as concert goers assign the location various purposes. The space of a stadium in an aerial photograph contrasts the place of a stadium during a football game or the place of a stadium during a music festival. Drawing on the work of the aforementioned place philosophers, I use the terms "striated spaces" and "smooth spaces" when addressing a location's physical qualities, and "striated places" and "smooth places" when emphasizing humans' meaning-laden authoring, including through their actions.[58]

Deleuze and Guattari's assertion that striating and smoothing exist in ongoing integration serves as a third way in which these concepts emphasize differing. They explain, "Smooth space is constantly being translated, transversed into a striated space; striated space is constantly being reversed, returned to a smooth space."[59] Estelle Jorgensen and Iris Yob explain this juxtaposition as a dualism, and indeed it does involve two processes.[60] Yet, unlike prominent philosophical dualisms such as mind and body or Jorgensen's own distinctions, including between form and context and great and little music traditions,[61] Deleuze and Guattari emphasize the differing of each concept in integration with the other. In other words, instead of aiming for smoothing *or* striation or even smoothing *and* striation, Deleuze and Guattari highlight how both processes evolve in and through their context-specific meetings. Striating is intimately tied to specific smooth spaces and places; it occurs uniquely in integration with the changing particularities of a smooth location and vice versa.

This integration of smoothing and striation can refer to both physical spaces—lines of dunes temporarily striate the desert—and to places that humans author through meaning-laden practices. For example, I striated the high school classroom in which I taught by arranging the chairs into evenly spaced arcs and by engaging students in the same practices day after day and year after year. Students played many of the same warm-up exercises and repertoire as prior generations of band members, and they endowed concerts, competitions, and football games with meanings similar to those of their predecessors.

Conversely, students smoothed the room by moving their chairs closer to their friends during rehearsals and creating random groupings of furniture before and after school. They also undertook some previously unimagined actions and forms of authorship by playing recently composed pieces and by improvising, journaling, and utilizing contemporary technology. The students and I also smoothed the classroom through the practices needed for newly created electives, including music composition and beginner piano and guitar. Yet, I simultaneously striated these classes by stabilizing and limiting their curricula and by using familiar pedagogical practices and forms of assessment.

While some integration of smoothing and striation happens naturally in all teaching and learning situations, emphasizing differing can involve awareness of and experimentation with the ways in which striated spaces and places become smooth and vice versa. In retrospect, I might have worked with students to smooth the classroom by setting up composition stations or areas conducive to informal learning. We also could have sought to author a smoother classroom through practices that ruptured definitions of "band," "music composition," and "school music class" more broadly. This might have included a band centered on the exploration and preservation of local music traditions or a music composition class experimenting with thoughtfully hybridizing musical practices from multiple continents. In turn, we might have striated the classroom as these wanderings led toward a planned performance or other musical event.

When engaged in alongside embracing excluded places, including local, global, and glocal ones, emphasizing the differing integration of smoothing and striation resists the tendency to conceive of such locations as stagnant. In these moments, the global, local, and glocal transforms from a bounded geography defined by what each excludes to changing sites of possibility. The global opposes not the local but the immobility of colonialism, capitalism, and other hierarchies. Similarly, while local communities may harbor forms of global striating, such as retail or textbook monopolies, they can also promote smooth free actions, perhaps reenvisioning annual events to be more inclusive, participatory, and spontaneous. This goes as much for the local place of the collegiate school of music as it does for the elementary music classroom or town parade.

The idea that locations rely on the integration of smoothing and striation is not unique to Deleuze and Guattari. Cresswell writes, "Place as practice and practice as placed always relies on the symbiosis of locatedness and motion rather than the valorization of one or the other."[62] However, in contrast with Cresswell, Deleuze and Guattari insinuate the value of smooth places over striated ones.[63] Jorgensen and Yob treat this implied preference for smooth spaces as at odds with Deleuze and Guattari's assertion that their foremost interest lies in the ongoing symbiotic processes and combinations of smoothing and striating.[64] Alternatively, I interpret their extended attention to smooth spaces as a means of breaking from a Western intellectual tradition that has honored striation while largely ignoring smooth spaces and places.[65]

By emphasizing smoothing and minimizing striation, Deleuze and Guattari invert humans' habitual favoritism of the latter. They provide smoothing more attention not because they want to prohibit all striating, but because doing so fosters the relative parity needed for ongoing smoothing-striating processes. Absent significant attention to smoothing, teachers and students bounded by the primarily striated locations and forms of authorship permeating contemporary policy and practice cannot easily experiment with creative possibilities for intersections of the two.

Becoming-Nomad

Attending to smoothing and to the integration of smoothing and striation has the potential to inform not only spaces, places, and practices but teachers' and students' becomings. Like the body without organs, Deleuze and Guattari's philosophical figuration of a nomad complicates how teachers and students might alter through embracing exclusions and emphasizing differing.[66] They explain that by highlighting process, motion, and journeying rather than destinations, the nomad inhabits and extends smooth spaces.[67] For the nomad, "A path is always between two points, but the in-between has taken on all the consistency and enjoys both an autonomy and a direction of its own. The life of the nomad is the intermezzo."[68] While nomads journey from one fixed point or location to another, they reach those points only to leave them behind. In Gould's words, "Nomads move with [the desert], deterritorializing only to reterritorialize, arriving only to depart, using relays of potentialities."[69] Nomads challenge preset routes, cross boundaries into new locations, and reimagine possibilities for action and authorship within and among global, glocal, and local places.

Recall from chapter 2 Claire Colebrook's explanation of becoming-animal as a process through which one does not transform into an animal but rather senses the world as though they were an animal.[70] Becoming-nomad, then, involves entering into momentary relations with nomads, perceiving and feeling events as uncertain wanderings. Teachers and students who become-nomad relish the challenge of finding opportunities to amble within rigid physical spaces and education policy mandates as well as to travel away from those spaces; they view journeying not as a burden they tolerate, but as an often joyful occurrence that can integrate with their everyday decisions and imaginings.

Asserting that one can "become-nomad" necessitates understanding the nomad as minoritarian. In most contemporary societies, stability and settled conceptions of places constitute majoritarian identities and practices. People expect to travel again and again along the same paths to and from work, school, and stores, and they typically repeat the same repertoire of endeavors in largely unchanged residences each evening. Wandering along diverse avenues to and from known locations or engaging in markedly different practices from one day to the next remains rare and not generally valued in social, economic, and political spheres. Although music education ultimately involves the integration of smoothing and striation, given contemporary societal norms, the practice of becoming-nomad affords a counter to taken-for-granted habits that limit thinking, feeling, and action. Yet, what about those who wander out of necessity rather than choice?

While Deleuze and Guattari do not specifically describe images of nomads or nomadic peoples, the term "nomad" is problematic because it has the potential to reinforce colonialist stereotypes. Writing about Rosi Braidotti's extension of Deleuze and Guattari's concept of the nomad, Gould explains, "Post-colonial feminists argue that Braidotti's valorization of nomadism is ethnocentric as it emanates from a position of privilege as a white, academic feminist and does not take into account the realities of actual displaced persons, many of whom are non-white."[71] The practice of becoming-nomad has the potential to invoke images of exotic others who, unlike the one becoming-nomad, do not necessarily have the means to decide whether or not they desire to have such a lifestyle. Using the term "nomad" while neglecting the challenges that nomadic peoples face can undermine efforts to challenge oppressive institutions and regulations that may hinder their way of life and limit opportunities for change. Further addressing these issues necessitates added attention to Deleuze and Guattari's differentiation between nomads and other travelers.

Nomads, according to Deleuze and Guattari, are not just any individual who roams. While noting possible overlap, they distinguish between itinerants, migrants, and nomads, explaining: "The primary determination of nomads is to occupy and hold a smooth space."[72] Nomads do not just wander, but serve a specific function—extending smooth spaces—through their wandering. It follows that nomadic peoples do not necessarily act consistent with Deleuze and Guattari's concept of the nomad. For example, individuals who live in the smooth physical space of the desert and yet travel the same paths, stop at the same locations, and repeat the same practices year after year extend striated spaces rather than smooth ones. This distinction, however, does not eliminate the issue of privilege. Some individuals can choose whether or not to roam, but nomadic peoples, immigrants, migrant workers, and other marginalized individuals and groups may not necessarily have the economic, social, and political capital to enact an alternative lifestyle, and those who do may face discrimination through classism, racism, and xenophobia. Although teachers and students can acknowledge and aim to counter the unthoughtful valorization of nomadic individuals, the possibility of neglecting how they may contribute to and benefit from their circumstances will always lie latent when invoking this philosophical figuration.

This relates to a larger issue with the Deleuze and Guattari's writings about the nomad. Like most of Deleuze and Guattari's concepts, the nomad's abstract nature remains divorced from the different, differing material realities in which diverse teachers and students reside. Deleuze and Guattari conceive of the nomad in terms of function; they ask what a nomad does rather than how nomads make meaning out of their practices. Teachers and students can function like nomads—wandering among glocal, local, and global locations and altering classroom routines—without finding value or significance in their actions.

Additionally, absent recognition of individuals' divergent meaning-making processes, Deleuze and Guattari assume an equality among individuals' experiences of becoming-nomad. Gould's explication of "nomadic subjects" exposes the problematic effects of such uniformity. Drawing on Braidotti's adaptation of Deleuze and Guattari's writings, Gould details the plights of "individuals working as outsiders," including women university band directors as well as nonwhite and homosexual music educators.[73] Since such bodies deviate from those of the norm—white, heterosexual, male bodies—"their success depends on using their difference as a source of value."[74] In other words, because in and of itself the presence of women, nonwhite, and LGBTQ+ band directors does not challenge current structures and practices, merely welcoming them into existing systems is insufficient. When the dominant majority defines what "counts" and "holds value," minorities will always remain subjugated.

Instead, Gould posits the necessity of honoring and celebrating the thinking and action that, by nature of their outsider status, only such "nomadic subjects" can provide. The transgender educator contributes ways of perceiving, engaging with, and becoming through music teaching and learning that, because of the embodied, individual nature of human experience, remain partly outside the realm of possibility for those identifying with their assigned sex. Extending Gould's thinking, I argue that if humans construct and come to understand their lives through narratives, then considering how diverse individuals create meaning in and through becoming-nomad can mitigate the abstract and universal nature of such practices.

Narratives of Becoming-Nomad

Focusing not just on the process of becoming-nomad but on narratives of becoming-nomad acknowledges the varying and variable roles that students' and teachers' past, present, and potential future cognitive-embodied-emotional-social experiences do and might play in such action. Narratives of becoming-nomad also resist subsuming subjugated voices under single descriptions of the process or neglecting the divergent, differing meanings that individuals bring to and create through their wanderings. Deleuze and Guattari, however, generally disparage the practice of meaning-making, writing, for example, "We will never ask what a book means."[75] Yet, their disregard seems to stem from equating meaning with sign-value or signification,[76] suggesting that they find not meaning-making but stagnant meanings problematic.

Conversely, narrative philosophers tend to treat meaning production as continually changing. Jerome Bruner describes narratives as "impenetrable to both inference and induction, they resist logical procedures for establishing what they *mean*. They must, as we say, be *interpreted*."[77] Explaining how the meanings and interpretations ascribed to narratives change over time, Richard Rorty references T. S. Eliot's statement, "What happens when a work of art is created is something that happens simultaneously to all the works of art that preceded it."[78] The evolution of one's personal narrative does not just add to a cemented past but reconstructs the meaning of that past through meaning-making in the present. As such, since narrative meaning-making differs from the more stable meaning attached to a signifier or philosophical proposition, it does not exhibit the qualities that Deleuze and Guattari deem particularly problematic.

Part of considering narratives of becoming-nomad can involve teachers and students pondering how their global, local, and glocal environments interface with their current and potential future stories. They might ask: How does music-making inform the stories we as individuals and as a group tell about our multiple communities? What musical places are excluded from our current narratives, and what roles might they play in our future ones? How do we author various places as primarily smooth or striated, and how does and might our music-making contribute to such authorship? In what ways might creative musical experiments with and within various places make meaningful contributions to our individual and collective narratives?

Furthermore, teachers and students can raise what Stauffer and Barrett call "questions that are often left unasked" in order to foster opportunities for frequently silenced individuals to author locations in ways meaningful for their changing narratives.[79] Kevin Bradt explains the welcoming of excluded voices as central to narrative ways of knowing, writing: "Narrative epistemology continues to ask how the recovery of what has been missing, diverted, or suppressed from consciousness might yield different assumptions, perspectives, interpretations, and, hence, different conclusions from those of the prevailing and dominant models and paradigms of thought. Story, therefore, is not afraid of the discovery of the unexpected and unthinkable or the simultaneous existence of variations, anomalies, disparities, contradictions, or multiple alternative views."[80]

Extending Gould's assertions about women band directors and other nomadic individuals, facilitating narratives of becoming-nomad might involve placing special significance on the stories of minoritarian teachers, students, and local and global community members. For example, while students whose families move frequently may not desire to become-nomad by wandering to other locations within their own country, such individuals may find it meaningful to explore the music-making in their new place of residence or to learn about the musical practices of refugees or itinerate groups in other countries. Additionally, augmenting the example presented in the "Glocal" section, students might reflect on whose narratives they initially omitted from their small groups as well as how their own narratives altered over the course of the project. They might then ask those initially excluded persons to give input on their forthcoming musical event. Students and educators could also brainstorm how they might further smooth the physical environment of the musical event in ways that they and others would likely find meaningful.

If, as Bruner asserts, "We *become* the autobiographical narratives by which we 'tell about' our lives,"[81] then beyond considering how meaning-making influences and integrates with one's actions, becoming-nomad necessitates examining the very process of narrative construction. Rather than settled scripts, telling and retelling stories of one's life involves revision and re-creation.[82] While narratives do not form from scratch each time, "They get out-of-date, and not just because we grow older or wiser but because our self-making stories need to fit new circumstances, new friends, new enterprises."[83]

Despite this variability, Bruner argues that narratives remain situated in preset cultural conventions. These "forms of canonicity" enable individuals to recognize and interpret the breaches central to narrative plots.[84] Bruner explains, "It is our sense of belonging to this canonical past that permits us to form our own narratives of deviation while maintaining complicity with the canon."[85] In other words, perceived agency within narratives relies on the existence of preformed expectations regarding typical storylines.

This interplay of canon and autonomy can become problematic if it limits how individuals construct and understand their stories. As Wayne Bowman notes, since narratives can reinforce and legitimate potentially problematic parts of a status quo, "There is nothing inherently emancipatory about narrative."[86] For example, if cultural norms about what members of certain gender identities, races, or social groups can or should do inhibit one's narrative creation, then those narratives cannot serve as challenges to existing social conventions and institutions. Yet, Bruner does not problematize his statement: "Life narratives obviously reflect the prevailing theories about 'possible lives' that are part of one's culture."[87] In the midst of canonicity and bounded future possibilities, Deleuze and Guattari's philosophical figuration of the nomad offers an alternative way of conceptualizing how humans might produce and interrogate their own narratives.

Becoming-nomad through narrative construction involves challenging the need for any sort of canon or predetermined storyline. Like the rhizome, narrative formation can proceed from and through the middle without a linear structure, reused plot, or static locations. By transgressing standard narrative trajectories, nomadic teachers and students constantly work to free themselves from conventional visions of transformation, including those related to the ongoing construction of their multiple differing places. In such instances, narrative deviations—be they women band directors or a growing sense of responsibility to individuals in another part of the world—become not aberrations from a norm but unique offerings meaningful because they provide what norms cannot. This does not mean that individuals need to abandon all canonical narratives; Deleuze and Guattari still note the inevitable interplay of striated and smooth spaces. However, just as the nomad occupies and holds smooth space, those who become-nomad while constructing and reconstructing narratives favor free motion and creative, meaningful action.

Traveling—be it near, far, or within place—involves not just seeing things and experiencing places but writing and rewriting our own emplaced stories through our journeying. Becoming-nomad through narrative creation and narratives of becoming-nomad relate to the overarching practice of complicating. Attending to the possibilities of becoming-nomad while asking "Where are we?" complicates musically educative endeavors, emphasizing how these meaning-laden events do and might integrate with and influence one's evolving constructions of self and place. The process of complicating alone, however, does not consider the ethical implications of musically educative experiences.

Notes

1. Tim Cresswell, *Place: A Short Introduction* (Malden, MA: Blackwell, 2004), 11.
2. Sandra L. Stauffer, "Place, Music, Education, and the Practice and Pedagogy of Philosophy," in *The Oxford Handbook of Philosophy in Music Education*, ed. Wayne D. Bowman and Ana Lucía Frega (New York: Oxford University Press, 2012).
3. My work at the charter school was part of my responsibilities as a teaching assistant at Arizona State University. Students from a secondary general music class taught at the school as part of their required field experience. My supervisor, Evan Tobias, suggested that I lead a lesson on *Friday* while the undergraduate students observed.
4. Elizabeth Gould, "Music Education Desire(ing): Language, Literacy, and Lieder," *Philosophy of Music Education Review* 17, no. 1 (2009): 49. I further address Gould's writings about "performative literacy" in chapter 6.
5. Elizabeth Gould, "Women Working in Music Education: The War Machine," *Philosophy of Music Education Review* 17, no. 2 (2009): 129–130.
6. See, for example, Kate R. Fitzpatrick, "Cultural Diversity and the Formation of Identity: Our Role as Music Teachers," *Music Educators Journal* 98, no. 4 (2012): 53–59; Julia Shaw, "The Skin That We Sing: Culturally Responsive Choral Music Education," *Music Educators Journal* 98, no. 4 (2012): 75–81.
7. Shaw, "The Skin That We Sing," 78. Geneva Gay posits the need for "culturally responsive teaching," which she asserts involves "using the cultural knowledge, prior experiences, frames of reference, and performance styles of ethnically diverse students to make learning encounters more relevant to and effective for them." In addition to the "synergistic relationship between home/community culture and school culture" promoted by culturally responsive teaching, Gloria Ladson-Billings encourages "culturally relevant teaching," explaining the need for students to "recognize, understand, and critique current social inequalities."

Geneva Gay, *Culturally Responsive Teaching: Theory, Research, and Practice* (New York: Teachers College Press, 2010), 31; Gloria Ladson-Billings, "Toward a Theory of Culturally Relevant Pedagogy," *American Educational Research Journal* 32, no. 3 (1995): 471.

8. Roger Mantie, "Bands and/as Music Education Antinomies and the Struggle for Legitimacy," *Philosophy of Music Education Review* 20, no. 1 (2012): 75.

9. Sandra L. Stauffer, "Placing Curriculum in Music," in *Music Education for Changing Times: Guiding Visions for Practice*, ed. Tomas A. Regelski and J. Terry Gates (New York: Springer, 2009), 180.

10. Ibid.

11. Allen Britton, Arnold Broido, and Charles Gary, "The Tanglewood Declaration," in Documentary Report of the Tanglewood Symposium, ed. Robert A. Choate (Washington, DC: Music Educators National Conference, 1968).

12. See, for example, Carlos Abril, "Music That Represents Culture: Selecting Music with Integrity," *Music Educators Journal* 93, no. 1 (2006): 38–45; Mary Goetze, "Challenges of Performing Diverse Cultural Music," *Music Educators Journal* 87, no. 1 (2008): 23–25, 48; and Carol Scott-Kassner and Mary Goetze, "The Struggle for Authenticity and Ownership: A Brief Overview of the Past and Future in Multicultural Approaches to Music Education," *The Mountain Lake Reader* (2006): 8–15.

13. Juliet Hess, "Performing Tolerance and Curriculum: The Politics of Self-Congratulation, Identity Formation, and Pedagogy in World Music Education," *Philosophy of Music Education Review* 21, no. 1 (2013): 73.

14. Joseph Abramo, "Mystery, Fire and Intrigue: Representation and Commodification of Race in Band Literature," *Visions of Research in Music Education* 9/10 (2007): 1–23.

15. Ibid., 5.

16. Hess, "Performing Tolerance and Curriculum," 77.

17. Goetze, "Challenges of Performing Diverse Cultural Music," 25.

18. Hess, "Performing Tolerance and Curriculum," 77.

19. Ibid., 83.

20. Marja Heimonen, "Music Education and Global Ethics: Educating Citizens for the World," *Action Criticism and Theory for Music Education* 11, no. 2 (2012): 73–74.

21. Heidi Partti and Heidi Westerlund, "Envisioning Collaborative Composing in Music Education: Learning and Negotiation of Meaning by Operabyyou.com," *British Journal of Music Education* 30, no. 2 (2013): 207–222; Lauri Väkevä, "Garage Band or GarageBand®? Remixing Musical Futures," *British Journal of Music Education* 27, no. 1 (2010): 59–70.

22. See, for example, Janice Waldron, "User-Generated Content, YouTube and Participatory Culture on the Web: Music Learning and Teaching in Two Contrasting Online Communities," *Music Education Research* 15, no. 3 (2013): 257–274; and Janice Waldron, "YouTube, Fanvids, Forums, Vlogs and Blogs: Informal Music Learning in a Convergent On- and Offline Music Community," *International Journal of Music Education* 31, no. 1 (2013): 95–105.

23. See further development of these ideas in Lauren Kapalka Richerme, "A Feminine and Poststructural Extension of Cosmopolitan Ethics in Music Education," *International Journal of Music Education* 35, no. 3 (2017): 414–424.

24. Gilles Deleuze and Félix Guattari, *A Thousand Plateaus: Capitalism and Schizophrenia*, trans. Brian Massumi (Minneapolis: University of Minnesota Press, 1987), 468.

25. Todd May, *Gilles Deleuze: An Introduction* (Cambridge, UK: Cambridge University Press, 2005), 147–148.

26. Alexandra Kertz-Welzel, "Lessons from Elsewhere? Comparative Music Education in Times of Globalization," *Philosophy of Music Education Review* 23, no. 1 (2015): 48–66.

27. Ibid.

28. See, for example, Murray Forman, *The 'Hood Comes First: Race, Space, and Place in Rap and Hip-Hop* (Middletown, CT: Wesleyan University Press, 2002), 21.

29. See, for example, S. Ambirajan, "Globalisation, Media and Culture," *Economic and Political Weekly* 35, no. 25 (2000): 2141–2147; Alexandros Baltzis, "Globalization and Musical Culture," *Acta Musicologica* 77, no. 1 (2005): 137–150; and Adam Hochschild, "Globalisation and Culture," *Economic and Political Weekly* 33, no. 21 (1998): 1235–1238.

30. David T. Hansen, *The Teacher and the World: A Study of Cosmopolitanism as Education* (New York: Routledge, 2011), 105 (italics in the original).

31. Ibid.

32. For a detailed exploration of ethics, see chapters 4 and 5. Summarizing Deleuze and Guattari's writings, Alberto Toscano explains, "It is the capacity to conjugate and control flows without the introduction of a transcendent agency (a totalizer) that makes the capitalist axiomatic the most formidable apparatus of domination." Alberto Toscano, "Axiomatic," in *The Deleuze Dictionary*, ed. Adrian Parr (Edinburgh: Edinburgh University Press, 2005), 18.

33. Hansen, *The Teacher and the World*, 21 (italics in the original).

34. I would like to thank Lauri Väkevä for bringing this very important point to my attention.

35. Boaventura de Sousa Santos, "Globalizations," *Theory, Culture & Society* 23, nos. 2–3 (2006): 397.

36. See, for example, Jennifer Lena, *Banding Together: How Communities Create Genres in Popular Music* (Princeton, NJ: Princeton University Press, 2012).

37. Roland Robertson, "Glocalization: Time-Space and Homogeneity-Heterogeneity," in *Global Modernities*, ed. Mike Featherstone, Scott Lash, and Roland Robertson (London: Sage, 1995), 28.

38. Ibid., 27 (italics in the original).

39. Noriko Manabe, "Globalization and Japanese Creativity: Adaptations of Japanese Language to Rap," *Ethnomusicology* 50, no. 1 (2006): 4.

40. Ibid., 8.

41. Tim Cresswell, "Introduction: Theorizing Place," in *Mobilizing Place, Placing Mobility: The Politics of Representation in a Globalized World*, ed. Ginette Verstraete and Tim Cresswell (New York: Editions Rodopi, B. V., 2002), 18.

42. Bennett explains that individuals "author" the places in which "collective identities are lived out." Andy Bennett, *Popular Music and Youth Culture: Music, Identity and Place* (New York: Palgrave, 2000), 64.

43. Deleuze and Guattari, *A Thousand Plateaus*, 381.

44. Ibid., 474–500.

45. Ibid.

46. As with the terms "cognitive," "embodied," "emotional," and "social" in chapter 2, in order to avoid a static hierarchy, I randomly mix the ordering of "global," "glocal," and "local." One might argue that individuals should value their local neighbors and countries more than global ones, and in chapter 5 I explain that this may at times be ethically appropriate. However, continually reordering these terms emphasizes that one location need not always take preference over the others.

47. Deleuze and Guattari, *A Thousand Plateaus*, 481.
48. Ibid., 382, 479, 481. Deleuze and Guattari explain that intensities, such as speed, are not composed of addable and displaceable magnitudes. They write, "Speed is not the sum of two smaller speeds." Intensities cannot divide without changing in nature each time. They also emphasize the relationship between intensity and difference, asserting "intensity is itself a difference" (ibid., 483).
49. See http://lotusfest.org/festival-main.
50. Deleuze and Guattari demonstrate this interconnectedness through the example of the striated spaces marked by agricultural grids and the smooth crop spaces lying within the grids. The grids mark boundaries within which the crops must reside; within those limits, the vegetation can grow freely. Deleuze and Guattari, *A Thousand Plateaus*, 384.
51. Bennett, *Popular Music and Youth Culture*, 64.
52. Deleuze and Guattari, *A Thousand Plateaus*, 493.
53. Ibid., 397, 480.
54. Ibid., 397, 478.
55. See, for example, Elizabeth Gould, "Dancing Composition: Pedagogy and Philosophy as Experience," *International Journal of Music Education* 24, no. 3 (2006): 197–207.
56. See, for example, Edward Casey, "How to Get from Space to Place in a Fairly Short Stretch of Time: Phenomenological Prolegomena," in *Senses of Place*, ed. Steven Feld and Keith Basso (Santa Fe: School of American Research Press, 1996), 13–52; Cresswell, "Introduction: Theorizing Place;" and Cresswell, *Place: A Short Introduction*.
57. Stauffer, "Place, Music, Education, and the Practice and Pedagogy of Philosophy," 436 (italics in the original).
58. This does not mean that individuals necessarily find these actions "meaningful." However, the meanings ascribed to individual places promote certain actions with and within them while dissuading others; even breaking from expected actions in a given location involves a meaning-laden choice.
59. Deleuze and Guattari, *A Thousand Plateaus*, 474.
60. Estelle R. Jorgensen and Iris M. Yob, "Deconstructing Deleuze and Guattari's *A Thousand Plateaus* for Music Education," *Journal of Aesthetic Education* 47, no. 3 (2013): 53.
61. Estelle Jorgensen, *In Search of Music Education* (Urbana: University of Illinois Press, 1997), 72–76.
62. Cresswell, "Introduction: Theorizing Place," 26.
63. Jorgensen and Yob, "Deconstructing Deleuze and Guattari's *A Thousand Plateaus* for Music Education," 47.
64. Ibid.
65. Deleuze and Guattari assert that the tree metaphor, which they associate with striation, has long dominated Western thinking, influencing members of scientific fields, such as botany and biology, as well as writers of topics ranging from theology to philosophy. Deleuze and Guattari, *A Thousand Plateaus*, 18.
66. As noted in chapter 2, Elizabeth Adams St. Pierre distinguishes between philosophical figurations and metaphors, explaining metaphors as providing coherency and clarity and philosophical figurations as intentionally complicating and confusing. Elizabeth Adams St. Pierre, "An Introduction to Figurations—A Poststructural Practice of Inquiry," *International Journal of Qualitative Studies in Education* 10, no. 3 (1997): 280–281.
67. Ibid., 380.

68. Ibid.
69. Gould, "Women Working in Music Education," 137.
70. Claire Colebrook, *Gilles Deleuze* (New York: Routledge, 2002), 136.
71. Elizabeth Gould, "Nomadic Turns: Epistemology, Experience, and Women University Band Directors," *Philosophy of Music Education Review* 13, no. 2 (2005), 156.
72. Deleuze and Guattari, *A Thousand Plateaus*, 410.
73. Gould, "Nomadic Turns," 158.
74. Ibid., 156.
75. Deleuze and Guattari, *A Thousand Plateaus*, 4.
76. See, for example, ibid., 4, 89.
77. Jerome Bruner, *Acts of Meaning* (Cambridge, MA: Harvard University Press, 1990), 60 (italics in the original).
78. Richard Rorty, "Analytic Philosophy and Narrative Philosophy," draft of lecture (University of California, Irvine: Richard Rorty Papers, 2003), 31.
79. Sandra L. Stauffer and Margaret S. Barrett, "Narrative Inquiry in Music Education: Toward Resonant Work," in *Narrative Inquiry in Music Education: Troubling Certainty*, ed. Margaret Barrett and Sandra Stauffer (New York: Springer Science+Business Media, 2009), 19.
80. Kevin M. Bradt, *Story as a Way of Knowing* (Kansas City, MO: Sheed and Ward, 1997), 106.
81. Jermone Bruner, "Life as Narrative," *Social Research* 71, no. 3 (2004): 694 (italics in the original).
82. See, for example, Walter R. Fisher, *Human Communication as Narration: Toward a Philosophy of Reason, Value, and Action* (Columbia: University of South Carolina Press, 1987); and Amia Lieblich, Rivka Tuval-Mashiach, and Tamar Zilber, *Narrative Research: Reading, Analysis, and Interpretation* (Thousand Oaks, CA: Sage, 1998).
83. Jerome Bruner, *Making Stories: Law Literature Life* (Cambridge, MA: Harvard University Press, 2002), 65.
84. Jerome Bruner, "The Narrative Construction of Reality," *Critical Inquiry* 18 (1991): 20.
85. Ibid.
86. Wayne Bowman, "Why Narrative? Why Now?" *Research Studies in Music Education* 27, no. 1 (2006): 9, 11.
87. Bruner, "Life as Narrative," 694.

4   Considering Deleuzian Ethics

WHILE FEW TEACHERS engage in overtly unethical behaviors, such as verbal abuse or having inappropriate relations with students, even mundane decisions can have notable ethical consequences. The choice to perform almost exclusively the music of white male composers or to foster or inhibit students' musical creativity, for instance, can have long-term impacts on students' self-esteem, dispositions, and future aspirations. Additionally, students miss engaging in valuable ethical decision-making processes when they leave music education endeavors without considering how entryways into classical music may exclude some individuals, popular music business practices can further economic inequalities, and engagements with local and global musical practices can promote varying levels of empathy, colonialism, and xenophobia. Given that contemporary education policymakers tend to emphasize success in the global marketplace while limiting attention to complex issues such as equity and civic responsibility, the need for students to develop the dispositions needed for more ethical practices has become increasingly critical.

Ethical deliberations demand not only distinguishing between "ethical" and "unethical" but between "more ethical" and "less ethical." Is it more ethical to devote class time to a group composition assignment or to let students develop their own projects? Is it more ethical to spend three months exclusively on popular music or to divide the time between different forms of musical engagement? How will varying instructional practices affect the ethical possibilities of the same musical content for different individuals at specific times and places? Considering to what extent certain practices may be more ethical resists the tendency to justify one's work as "ethical enough."

Reflecting on my own Pre-K–12 and collegiate teaching, I see many points when I might have openly acknowledged the ethical nature of everyday questions and actions. Although one middle school student's asking if Tchaikovsky was gay or another's assumption that all indigenous peoples play drums presented opportunities for thoughtful ethical conversations, my curt responses deadened those moments. Furthermore, I might have planned musically educative endeavors centering on ethical quandaries, perhaps facilitating units or musical events around topics such as vulnerable populations or environmental conservation. Yet, I am perhaps most struck by how my everyday actions—my unwillingness to listen to a student's ideas or to spend extra time welcoming someone from another country—may have impacted students' own valuations of everything from critical thinking to kindness toward immigrants. Replicating my own problematic behaviors, the students I taught may now vote a certain way in part because they do not feel empowered to question a prominent individual's advice or because they have not taken the time to dialogue with someone who they deem "other." While probably not attributable to any one teacher's actions, students' ethical dispositions inevitably develop through daily observations and engagements.

Over at least the last two millennia, philosophers have articulated contrasting schools of ethical thought. The actions of those abiding by these different systems can diverge markedly.[1] For instance, while individuals strictly following Kant's ethics may argue that there exists a duty to tell the truth even if doing so may cause harm, those attending to authors broadly defined as "consequentialist ethicists" determine "right" ethical action by examining outcomes.[2] Yet, music education writers such as Randall Allsup and Bennett Reimer have posited the need for more ethical practices without explicitly noting the frameworks or ideals underlying their calls.[3] When writers do name or imply a specific ethical position or author, such as David Elliott and Marissa Silverman's reliance on virtue ethics or Paul Woodford's use of Deweyan ethics, they rarely acknowledge any drawbacks of their selected lines of thinking.[4] Since the advantages of specific ethical practices exist inseparably from their risks, music educators might benefit from calls for added attention to ethics or morals that clarify accompanying assumptions and limitations.

Given the substantial and longstanding nature of the debates between advocates of various ethical schools of thought, it is beyond the scope of this text to claim certain ethical practices as somehow superior to all others. However, as noted in chapter 1, contemporary music educators face pervasive ethical dilemmas related to mass standardization and career-centric rationale. Since the troubling of stagnant hierarchies and singular life trajectories plays a key role in Gilles Deleuze's philosophizing practices, teachers and students may find his writings particularly meaningful for ethical deliberations surrounding such issues. Articulating how Deleuzian ethics can challenge the structures and ideologies that limit and confine minoritarian voices and music-making, Elizabeth Gould and David Lines have begun this timely work.[5] Building on their thinking, I explore the problems and possibilities of considering Deleuze's ethics in music education.

An Overview of Deleuzian Ethics

While the political overtones of Deleuze's writings imply a certain ethical stance, he makes few direct references to ethics. However, throughout his work he creates concepts that foster and at times demand a specific ethical orientation.

Examining both Deleuze's writings and those of scholars who investigate his ethics reveals three key aspects: attending to context, welcoming complexity, and imagining creative potentialities.

First, like Randall Allsup and Heidi Westerlund's Deweyan-based "situational ethics,"[6] Deleuze's ethics are specific to individual contexts and occurances. Writing about the rupturing of the rhizome, Deleuze and Guattari assert the need to look beyond dualisms and dichotomies, including that of good/bad. They explain, "Good and bad are only the products of an active and temporary selection, which must be renewed."[7] One may deem an action "good" in one context or time period and the same action "bad" under contrasting circumstances.

Similarly, writing about Foucault, Deleuze distinguishes between morals and ethics: "The difference is that morality presents us with a set of constraining rules of a special sort, ones that judge actions and intentions by considering them in relation to transcendent values (this is good, that's bad . . .); ethics is a set of optional rules that assess what we do, what we say, in relation to the ways of existing involved. We say this, do that: what way of existing does it involve?"[8] For Deleuze, ethical thinking and action do not involve adhering to rules or principles applicable in all circumstances, but rather deliberating with respect to specific times and places. While morality serves to judge life in the abstract, Deleuzian ethics involve decisions and actions about ways of existing in and with the world.[9]

A music educator working from moral grounding would evaluate the badness of behaviors apart from pondering a student's home life or interactions preceding the incident, while one working from ethics would take such considerations into account. More broadly, music educators attending to the contextual nature of acting more ethically would not begin from remembrances of their own music education or from recollections of what worked in other teaching and learning scenarios. Instead, they would consider and dialogue with others about possible ethical paths in integration with understandings about the unique students, locations, and local and global happenings at hand.

This openness to the opportunities latent in each moment reveals a second aspect of Deleuze's ethics: welcoming complexity. John Rajchman writes that instead of "purity and piety in identification" Deleuze's ethics involve seeking "a complexity and a dignity in our manners of being."[10] To understand good and bad as ephemeral constructs that forego preset rules and principles necessitates embracing diversity and plurality rather than succumbing to the efficiency of clear answers. Yet, rather than a static mosaic, Deleuze understands complexity as existing in constant motion.

In Deleuze's terms, each situation becomes an "event," a creative moment of change generated by ever-varying forces. Acting ethically involves not just contemplating events, but making "thinking its own event by embracing the rich chaos of life and the uniqueness and potential of each moment."[11] Emphasizing becoming over being, Deleuzian ethicists seek the points of rupture that constitute everyday life yet often remain obscured by the automation of habit. In this sense, the music educator and students who deliberate and revise their ethical trajectories over time act more ethically than those who unwaveringly aim for specific ends.

Third, Deleuze argues for an ethics highlighting creative futures, favoring previously unimagined possibilities rather than repetition of existing action. While most ethical theories attend to the future, at least in part, unlike those focused on specific ends or ideals, Deleuze envisions futures consisting of divergent, continually changing potentialities. Ronald Bogue summarizes that Deleuze posits "a view through the present and toward the future, one that envisions nothing specific in that future, but that trusts in the possibilities immanent within the real to produce something genuinely new."[12] In other words, Deleuzian ethicists imagine how ethical actions might impact the future without narrowing or confining visions of that future.

This emphasis on divergent futures in part aligns with Allsup and Westerlund's assertions about the role of imagination in situational ethics.[13] Yet, Allsup and Westerlund focus on how teacher-student dialogue promotes such imagining. This suggests that while imagination deviates from existing social actions, it derives in and through them. Alternatively, Deleuze posits that the nature of existence is fundamentally creative. Although dialogue may contribute to how one embraces this creativity, dialogue absent a Deleuzian understanding of existence severely limits students' and teachers' potentialities. John Marks explains that by resisting limited ethical visions of the status quo, Deleuze "conceives of society as experiment rather than contract."[14] Free-flowing spaces ripe for new actions and changing self-constructions facilitate the creativity needed for ethical imaginings.

Possibilities of Deleuzian Ethics

By foregrounding specific circumstances, Deleuzian ethics offer teachers and students an alternative to normalizing educational practices that erase differences between and within individuals. When considered through Deleuze's writings, even seemingly straightforward scenarios, such as two students cheating on a test, may necessitate divergent ethical treatment. What if one student—an English language learner—spent hours studying for the exam but still feared it impossible to pass without cheating, while the other student simply viewed cheating as preferable to studying at all. Certainly, acting ethically involves assigning consequences to each student, but while some ethical schools of thought would demand identical treatment of both individuals, Deleuzian ethics favor perceiving each situation as its own "event" worthy of unique ethical thought.

Moreover, those making decisions about the goals of music education and the types of musical engagement welcomed into schools can consider the particulars of evolving people and places. Should students at a predominantly Hispanic school spend years learning European music history and only a month investigating the cultural heritage of their direct ancestors? Is it "right" for show choir students from a wealthy school to compete directly with those from a community with scarce resources? While Deleuzian ethicists would shun easy answers to such inquiries, their engagement with them challenges the assumed goodness of standardized educational practices and outcomes.

Emphasizing context and complexity, however, is not unique to Deleuzian ethics. Consider, for example, theories subsumed under the category of "virtue ethics," on which music educators such as Wayne Bowman and Thomas Regelski have drawn directly and that Elliott and Silverman suggest through their terminology.[15] Such practices generally involve developing the character of ethical actors so that they promote individual and collective human flourishing within a specific set of circumstances. What, then, do Deleuzian ethics add to such discussions?

While not necessarily in direct opposition to the philosophies of authors such as Bowman, Elliott and Silverman, and Regelski, Deleuzian ethicists place greater emphasis on difference and differing. For example, Gould uses Deleuze's ethics to illuminate the problematic assumptions underlying social justice enacted through democracy. While such deliberations generally involve attending to context and complexity, Gould argues that abstract principles such as justice and equality rely on "materializations of assimilation and domination."[16] She continues that when music educators address "others," including other musics and students, they often do so by treating them as innocuous in one of two ways: as similar to existing norms or as different but in need of assistance. In both cases, teachers and students do not value the strange in its own right, including as a potential "danger" that may challenge existing practices.[17] Educators may, for instance, depoliticize jazz history or assimilate students' interest in rap under the broad category of "popular music." Simply attending to the complicated nature of specific circumstances can still reinforce the tyranny of majoritarian ways of being.

In contrast, Gould calls for an ethics composed "of difference, fields of difference," in which music educators "have nothing to think but difference itself."[18] Imagining ethical practices that begin from and work within difference, Deleuzian music educators foster scenarios in which differences become something other than deviations from a norm. For example, rather than making choices about performance attire based on the preferences of the majority, as Woodford's Deweyan-based democratic ethics would suggest,[19] music educators and students might start their ethical considerations with the perspectives of those who dress in ways counter to accepted norms. In agreement with Cathy Benedict's call for teachers to see ourselves as "Others,"[20] such action blurs the boundaries between norm and deviation, challenging the everyday hierarchies that produce seemingly natural thought processes and habits.

Teachers drawing on Deleuze's ethics also question the predetermined expectations they may have for students' futures as well as encourage students to challenge and reimagine the visions that they hold for themselves. Todd May and Inna Semetsky explain that for Deleuze an "ethical education" does not mean learning a set of stable identities but rather abandoning "asking who it is that we should be" in favor of wondering "who it is that we *might* be."[21] For example, while some would automatically praise the ethics of a teacher who provides more assistance to a violin student who has not had private music lessons than to one with such access, a Deleuzian ethicist might question the assumptions underlying such action. Do both students want to learn the violin? Are there other musical practices that either might find more personally meaningful? In what ways does learning the violin in the current manner serve to normalize and assimilate each student's becoming-other, in the process denying them opportunities to bring their own ideas and experiments to their music making?

This does not mean that a teacher who provides extra assistance should not undertake such endeavors. However, it complicates the ethical nature of practices that may at first glance appear unquestionably honorable. By considering students—and I would add teachers—what Deleuze calls "people-to-come," Petra Hroch explains learning "as a process of transformation, the process of students' coming to think differently, thereby becoming-other in the process, and supporting thinking differently from the norm, producing a diverse range of critical and creative ideas, and experiencing the joy of expressing one's capacities."[22] Attending to individuals' emerging interests, changing aims, and creative futures, Deleuzian ethicists welcome journeying along paths that teachers and students can never fully anticipate in advance.

Combining such thinking with Deleuze's emphasis on context means that teachers and students engaged in ethical deliberations necessarily innovate in integration with understandings about their own and others' complex material realities. Hroch implores educators to think about "people-to-come" in connection with spatial and temporal milieus. She writes: "Opening up the notion of subjectivity means that our relations to our environs—the earthly environment, as well as the social, cultural, and political ecology—are open to question, critical interrogation and creative reconceptualization."[23] As such, another feature of Deleuzian ethics is the interrogation of assumptions that underlie not just individual actions but the systems and institutions that enable and reinforce such situations. It follows that Deleuze's ethics directly challenge the mass standardization and career-centric rationale for education in more substantial ways than schools of thought such as virtue ethics.

Recalling the case of the two cheating students, a Deleuzian ethicist might spend less time considering necessary consequences and more time contemplating how the practice of testing might limit students' developing potentialities. Such music educators might ask: To what extent do my current assessments facilitate or bound students' individual growth in varying directions? When might these practices benefit specific students' current and potential future becomings, and when might they cause harm? What alternative practices might I, students, and others imagine? While dialogue can contribute to such envisionings, they can also develop through personal reflection and creative artistic endeavors. In the words of poststructuralist author Jean-François Lyotard: "The artist has a professional duty to bear witness that *there is*, to respond to the order to be."[24]

Because music educators engaging with Deleuzian ethics refuse to perceive music education as an apolitical practice that silently reinforces current norms and ways of being, they explore places of unknown possibility rather than start from a desire to replicate previous "successes" or perennial aims. When teachers encourage students to take responsibility for ethical deliberations, students can come to understand that decisions ranging from selecting repertoire to deciding where and how they perform to determining boundaries for a music composition project involve multiple layers of consideration. As such, they resist simplistic "right" and "wrong" ethical answers.

More broadly, the diverse needs and desires within and between contemporary local and global communities necessitate ethical practices that go beyond what currently exists to experiment with what might become. In a time when populations believe that single actions such as Brexit or building a wall along the Mexican-American border will have a marked impact on complex problems related to immigration, employment, and wage growth, an emphasis on the complicated nature of social issues and the dangers of limited alternatives is sorely needed. While not a panacea, practicing ethics sensitive to context while embracing complexity and promoting imaginative possibilities may encourage students to develop dispositions crucial to engaging with challenges the teachers of today cannot foresee. Such action facilitates students' eventual teaching, parenting, and coexisting with their own "people-to-come."

Potential Limitations of Deleuzian Ethics

Despite these possible benefits, Deleuze's ethics are potentially limiting because they can tend toward relativism. Focusing on differences and potentialities can lead one to the untenable position of valuing difference and creativity in and of themselves. Consider the extreme example of a student who asserts the transformative power of composing music with racist or homophobic lyrics. While one might argue that such lyrics infringe on other students' becomings, Deleuze's ethics do not overtly assist teachers and students in distinguishing where one human's possibilities end and another's begin.

Although Deleuze proffers no direct defense of the critique that his writings may lead to relativism, he at times suggests that not all thinking and action holds equal ethical merit. For example, his assertions about becoming-minoritarian imply the ethical nature of practices that subvert dominant norms and challenge hegemonic systems. In music education, this might include engaging with non-Western musical practices, seeking alternative, nonstandardized pedagogical tactics, or composing songs that give voice to marginalized individuals. Moreover, one can complicate and dive deeply into multiple perspectives and yet still judge a certain course of action "right" or "wrong" or more or less ethical. As Rosi Braidotti explains, one need not equate complexity with boundlessness, or human multi-facetedness with relativism.[25]

Yet, even if not completely relativistic, Deleuze's ethics may provide music educators minimal assistance in navigating commonplace dilemmas. Should a teacher allow a student to sit in the corner and play rock guitar every day simply because they claim to find no value in any other musical styles or practices? Should a teacher enable a motivated, accomplished classical trumpet player who dislikes improvising to go practice on their own while the rest of the ensemble improvises? Do teachers have any obligation to encourage students who enjoy composing on GarageBand to try other software or to sing or play a nonvirtual instrument? Should teachers foster students' individual musical and educative experiments to the exclusion of developing learning experiences centered on social justice topics? Deleuze's ethics demand that teachers and students attend to context and embrace complexity when undertaking such deliberations, but his writings omit the necessity of balancing competing processes and aims.

More problematically, focusing on creative futures can leave current forms of oppression unacknowledged. Writing broadly about poststructuralism, Linda Alcoff argues that by making gender and other qualities invisible, such writers undercut their ability to counter dominant structures and practices.[26] Honoring the difference and differing of each student can minimize opportunities to name and challenge overarching hegemonic systems. For instance, while a unified music composition project will almost certainly squelch some students' interests and ideas, the process may have a greater impact beyond the classroom than thirty unique social justice endeavors.

Likewise, Braidotti critiques Deleuze for neglecting any sort of clear political project.[27] To be clear, Deleuze's writing is overtly political; the word "capitalism" appears in the subtitle of his most cited book, *A Thousand Plateaus: Capitalism and Schizophrenia*, and coauthor Félix Guattari had a long-standing history of political activism, particularly involving defending gay rights. In the text, Deleuze and Guattari write negatively about the "State apparatus," including capitalism, and incite readers to challenge it through radical actions that unsettle existing political institutions.[28] In agreement with Gould's assertions regarding the problems of democratic action, including the potential disregard of minoritarian viewpoints,[29] I posit that music educators and students need not let contemporary political institutions and processes limit their ethical imaginings. Artistic endeavors can certainly contribute to creative visions for politics and civic life that defy current practices. However, like Braidotti, I worry that primarily seeking societal change outside of existing political institutions minimizes opportunities for other potentially more ethical alternatives.

Deleuze's ethical-political writings are troubling not because they omit political action, but because they may diminish attention to the skills and dispositions, such as compromising and sustaining grassroots organizations, that facilitate change within contemporary democratic systems. Additionally, ethical practices that omit or undermine the need for shared endeavors and cohesive political actions can do a disservice to individuals and groups working for change through such processes. Since many music educators throughout the world have their endeavors funded by democratic governments, including via public schools, state-based and national institutions of higher education, and government-sponsored arts grants, it is troubling to assert an ethical philosophy that substantially undermines these programs. Does this mean that music educators should abandon Deleuzian ethics altogether?

Arendtian Judging

Hannah Arendt's writings may serve as a starting place for a process-based ethical approach that aligns with much of Deleuze's ethics while avoiding his tendency toward relativism and neglect of political action. A German-born political theorist who escaped Europe during the Holocaust, Arendt (1906–1975) eventually become an American citizen. Her body of work deals largely with authority, totalitarianism, and the nature of freedom. Rejecting overarching ethical criteria and rules, Arendt argues that such dictates serve as crutches and limit one's capacity to think critically in relation to unique circumstances.[30] Instead, she posits the ethical possibilities of the complex, evolving process of judging.

For Arendt, judgment in the political sense shares similarities with Immanuel Kant's writings about aesthetic judgment.[31] Kant argued that aesthetic judgments reside in a middle ground between mandate and opinion. For example, saying that I find a musical performance beautiful differs from saying that my favorite instrument is the cello; the former implies that I desire, although do not demand, that others will agree with my evaluation, while the latter carries no expectation of agreement. Kant clarifies that aesthetic judgments do not subsume beauty under a concept or limited set of criteria; arguing about the beauty of an experience need not build on propositional logic or other systematic forms of thinking. People can accept that others disagree with them about the beauty of a given musical performance, but they expect that, rather than pure caprice, their evaluations rely on reasons that one can articulate if pressed. In contrast, those expressing preference for a certain instrument generally expect neither the need to justify their selection nor agreement from others.

Applying such thinking to political judgments, Arendt asserts that, like aesthetic judgments, arguments may produce agreement, but they need not do so. Instead, by engaging with contrasting viewpoints, humans come to understand the world that they have in common.[32] The world that any one human knows is not common because it only accounts for that individual's perceptions and socially constructed understandings. Conversely, "We have the world in common *because* we view it from different perspectives."[33]

When humans share their understandings about specific situations and experiences, their diverse viewpoints enable multifaceted conceptions of a collective reality. Similar to Gould's assertions about the ethical possibilities of dissensus, in which individuals honor differences and welcome critical dissent,[34] working within this constellation of perspectives curtails the subjugation or neglect of minoritarian voices. Such action contrasts forms of democracy in which the majority can simply vote against those in fewer numbers without ever trying to understand their perspectives. By embracing the plurality of the common world in which humans reside, teachers and students can resist the problems of both predetermined rules and consensus-based approaches. Yet, because constructing a common world involves viewpoints other than one's own, it resists the tendency toward narcissism and complete relativism.

Arendt posits imagination as the faculty that facilitates deep engagement with the diverse viewpoints constituting the common world. She explains that imagination enables individuals to create a dialogue of understanding by distancing that which we find close to us while simultaneously bridging the abyss of that which we find remote.[35] Imagination facilitates the letting go of one's own perspective and the temporary adoption of other perspectives. Arendt writes, "While I take into account others when judging, this does not mean that I conform in my judgment to their's [sic]. I still speak with my own voice and I do not count noses in order to arrive at what I think is right. But my judgment is no longer subjective either, in the sense that I arrive at my conclusions by taking only myself into account."[36] Imagination neither transcends perspectives in search of pure objectivity nor resigns one to their own inevitably limited perspective.[37]

Artistic practices may facilitate this imagining of multiple viewpoints. Maxine Greene writes that the ongoing process of self-creation involves "hearing different words and music, seeing from unaccustomed angles, realizing that the world perceived from one place is not *the* world."[38] Although Greene does not cite

Arendt in relation to this statement, she references Arendt's common world on the following page, suggesting a possible connection with her ideas. Working within these multifaceted viewpoints, individuals can make ethical judgments with the intent of securing agreement from others, while simultaneously acknowledging that they may not receive it. An example from my own teaching experience illustrates what happens when a teacher does not engage in such action.

In my first year as a high school band director, I honored the long-standing tradition of playing Leroy Anderson's "Sleigh Ride" at the annual December concert. In the following year, I decided that I lacked the time to polish the piece along with our other demanding repertoire and chose not to include it on the program. Many students complained, and I told them that I would hold one after school rehearsal in which I would allow the sophomores, juniors, and seniors to try playing the piece. This meant practicing the parts on their own and coming prepared to put them together quickly. While I have no doubt that some students did practice, at the rehearsal the technical passages lacked clarity, the counter-melodies were inaccurate, and the students could just barely make it through the entire piece without stopping. Their playing came nowhere close to meeting my standards for an acceptable performance, and I told them that they could not perform it at the concert. The students, particularly the seniors, expressed extreme frustration and disappointment, and some of them treated the repertoire we did perform with noted disdain from that day forward. Following the concert, band members still moaned about my decision, and I even got complaints from a couple of parents. Many relationships needed mending.

In recalling this story, I find myself most saddened not by the outcome, but by my own decision-making process. In choosing not to play the piece, I thought primarily about my own aims for the band program and about how embarrassed I would feel to perform a piece sloppily. I gave minimal consideration to the meanings that students ascribed to performing the piece and essentially no consideration as to what my actions might mean for parents and other community members. At the time, my process seemed ethical; I wanted the students to value hard work and high-quality musical performances, and I wanted class time devoted to deep engagement with unfamiliar music. Yet, in retrospect, I find my deliberations problematic because I neglected to imagine the situation through students', parents', and community members' perspectives and to take those views into account when judging possible courses of action.

Since one's understandings of the common world develop not in the abstract but in relation to specific situations, the process of judging varies from one instance to another. As such, judging involves ongoing considerations not only about what action to take but about the process of judgment itself.[39] Linda Zerilli explains that for Arendt, "There can no more be *the* final or conclusive argument for the equality of the sexes than there can be *the* final and conclusive argument for the beautiful. Every political or aesthetic argument must be articulated in relation to a set of particulars."[40] The reasons for certain judgments and criteria for judging resist stagnation, instead evolving over time with respect to specific contexts.

To illustrate further this point, Arendt distinguishes between determinant judgments, which subsume the particular under a general rule, and reflective judgments, which derive the rule from the particular.[41] Zerilli explains: "Arendt's point is not to contest the idea that we often do subsume particulars under rules (e.g., 'this is a war'), but rather to foreground the features of judgment that characterize it as critical value judgment (e.g., 'this war is unjust'). The act of mere subsumption that is at stake in a determinative judgment, though far from easy, is not fully reflective and critical, for it mobilizes particulars to confirm the generality of concepts. Lost is the particularity of the particular itself, the 'this' that refers to this war and to no other."[42] In other words, avoiding the generalities of determinant judgments such as "war is bad," Arendt favors reflective judgments enabled by sustained consideration of why "*this* war is bad." To give a music education example, rather than asking why engaging with popular music or using Orff pedagogy is "good" or "bad" in the universal sense (a determinant judgment), teachers inspired by Arendt might consider the ethical value of such practices when taught in a particular way for a certain group of students at a given time and place (a reflective judgment). Likewise, in the "Sleigh Ride" situation, my imagining and judging would have occurred differently had I been teaching other students or even the same students under contrasting circumstances.

Deleuzian Potentialities and/of Arendt's Ethics

Arendt's emphasis on the particularities of reflective judgments is reminiscent of the context-based aspect of Deleuze's ethics. By foregrounding the specificity of reflective judgment (e.g., "this musically educative endeavor is good for these students at this time and place") over the generalization and categorization of determinative judgment (e.g., "this musically educative endeavor is always good"), Arendt demonstrates alignment with Deleuze's assertions about the temporal nature of "good" and "bad." For Arendt and Deleuze, ethical deliberations continually evolve in integration with lived experiences and can never precede a specific set of circumstances.

Additionally, both Arendt and Deleuze envision an ethics that challenges norms and welcomes diversity. By attending to the multiple perspectives needed to construct a common world, Arendt's process of judging involves embracing complexity rather than simple or singular answers. Such action shares similarities with Deleuze's emphasis on ethics as a multifaceted endeavor that resists reduction to clear principles or directives. In short, Arendt and Deleuze seek to complicate ethical quandaries, troubling streamlined, efficiency-oriented practices in favor of evolving critical reflection.

Despite this overarching alignment, Arendt's and Deleuze's ethics diverge on a couple of substantial issues. While Arendt asserts the possibility of creating a common world by imagining a situation through diverse viewpoints, Deleuze's attention to unceasing differing resists such action. Deleuze would likely find the common world problematic because it serves as a structure that solidifies what he conceives of as a fundamentally chaotic existence. Furthermore, since attention to certain perspectives automatically relegates or omits others, such selection contradicts the unending welcoming of exclusions central to Deleuze's philosophizing.

However, absent striving for a common world, a Deleuzian ethicist may work from their own singular perception of a context without considering any others. I could (and did) make an ethical decision about not playing "Sleigh Ride" absent marked attention to students' and/or community members' viewpoints. Aiming for a rich constellation of perspectives also fosters opportunities for collaborative group political action largely absent from Deleuze's ethics.

One perspective central to Deleuze's ethics but addressed only obliquely by Arendt is the need to consider previously unimagined potentialities, focusing on becoming rather than being. Zerilli argues that the imaginative process enabling Arendt's practice of judgment involves not just that which already exists but aspects of a world that might come into existence. When embraced freely, imagination is "productive and spontaneous not merely reproductive of what is already known, but generative of new forms and figures."[43] While such assertions align with Deleuze's ethical potentialities, without added attention, those imagining existing scenarios through multiple perspectives may end up emphasizing life as it is rather than experimenting with what it might become.

The imagining of specific scenarios through diverse individuals' current perceptions becomes problematic if it primarily tends toward the replication of existing institutions. For instance, while Arendtian imagining and judging may have played a meaningful role in my "Sleigh Ride" deliberations, helping me decide whether or not to allow students to play the piece, drawing on Deleuze's ethics could have inspired further possibilities. Rather than asking "To play or not to play?" the students and I might have creatively imagined how, when, and where we might engage with the piece. We also might have deliberated the limits of treating "Sleigh Ride" as a "piece" rather than as changing musical practices, or considered if we should remain within the confines of a "band." Although Arendt's proposed processes may also foster engagement with such questions, Deleuze's creative, potentiality-based ethics encourages them to the forefront.

Considering

Inspired by Arendt's and Deleuze's writings, I posit that "considering" might serve as a process that can inform music educators' ethical practices. Arendt notes that in Kant's notion of aesthetic judgment, "We are considerate in the original sense of the word, we consider the existence of others and we must try to win their agreement."[44] Drawing on this explanation of considering others and on Deleuze's philosophical practice of creating new concepts, I put forth my own practice of considering. Considering involves Arendt's process of judging—and by extension the faculty of imagination—in ongoing integration with a welcoming of Deleuzian potentialities.

Positioning Arendt's and Deleuze's ideas in a productive tension, I offer two qualifications about the practice of considering. First, while those considering retain Arendt's striving toward a common world, they acknowledge the limits of such action. Imagining multiple perspectives temporarily ossifies those perspectives and omits additional viewpoints. Although teachers and students cannot avoid these tendencies, ongoing attention resists making them permanent. Such action might include constantly pondering how one's imagined perspectives may have differed and contemplating the individuals' perspectives currently excluded from their imaginings.

Second, the practice of considering involves taking account of individuals' perspectives both as they are and as they might be. Intermixing Deleuze's emphasis on imaginative possibilities with Arendt's practice of judging involves treating judging as a creative act that seeks points of rupture and departure. In such instances, those judging refuse confinement within current systems and viewpoints, instead favoring the unsettled and unexpected.

In short, considering draws on the complexity and process-orientation of both Deleuze's and Arendt's ethics. In agreement with Arendt, considering involves imagining situations from multiple perspectives and making a judgment. Doing so challenges the tendency toward complete relativism inherent in Deleuze's ethics. Additionally, while teachers and students may use considering to critique and radically undermine existing political institutions, attending to the common world can facilitate thoughtful collective action within existing democratic political institutions more so than Deleuze's ethics alone.

On the other hand, recalling Deleuze's ethics, those considering more ethical paths accentuate the temporary, changing nature of imagining. They also conceive of judging as a creative, potentiality-producing practice. Perhaps inspired by inventive artistic practices, teachers and students can reimagine Arendtian ethical endeavors as rhizomatic processes with increased potential to break from rather than re-create past judgments and judging processes.

Envision what might have happened had I embraced the practice of considering when confronted with the high school students' request to play "Sleigh Ride". I could have asked: How did and might playing "Sleigh Ride" contribute to individual students' identities and becomings? What meanings might audience members find in the song? To what extent would students, administrators, and audience members care about the quality of the performance? How might playing or not playing "Sleigh Ride" contribute to the school and local community as it currently existed and what it might become? I also might have tried to develop a critical distance from which I could reflect on my own relationship with the song. What meaning did I find in the song? Did it represent a school tradition of which I was not a part? How might playing or not playing the song contribute to my changing interpersonal relationships and musical and educative becomings? This imagining and distancing alone, however, omits the differing potentialities central to Deleuze's ethics.

Since my proposed ethical philosophizing vibrates amid the meeting of Arendt's and Deleuze's assertions, part of considering would involve creative experiments with alternative ways that the students and I might have engaged with "Sleigh Ride" as well as with other musical practices. Might student leaders have arranged sectionals and additional rehearsals during which they worked on the song? What if the students used technology to create a mash-up or composition inspired by "Sleigh Ride"? Could the students and I have encouraged the audience to learn the melody or rhythms to "Sleigh Ride" and to take an active role in the performance? How else might we have included other students or community members in the winter concert? At what other events and in what alternative places might we have performed or engaged with the song? Was "band" as I saw it really serving the students' and community's needs—including those of students not currently participating in the group—and what other options might I and others imagine?

From this constellation of viewpoints, I could then make a judgment, perhaps encouraging students and community members to do the same. While others may not agree with my decision, I would make it in the same way that I would call a musical event "beautiful"—with a willingness to explain my judgment and the hope that I could convince others of it. However, this judging would not strictly follow along Arendt's ethical framework. In addition to remaining receptive to the notion that my judgment needed revision, I would consider how creative ethical potentialities might continually stretch, open, and transform my imagining and judging processes.

I will never know what would have happened had I considered these and other questions when making a decision about the song. Yet, regardless of the outcome, I would almost certainly have felt better about the process that enabled it. However, I wonder: What problems might the process of considering still hide?

Notes

1. See, for example, Marcia W. Baron, Philip Pettit, and Michael Slote, *Three Methods of Ethics: A Debate* (Malden, MA: Blackwell, 1997); Tom L. Beauchamp, *Philosophical Ethics: An Introduction to Moral Philosophy*, 3rd ed. (Boston: McGraw Hill, 2001); John Deigh, *An Introduction to Ethics* (Cambridge, UK: Cambridge University Press, 2010); and Noel Stewart, *Ethics: An Introduction to Moral Philosophy* (Cambridge, UK: Polity Press, 2009).

2. Baron, Pettit, and Slote, *Three Methods of Ethics*.

3. Randall Allsup, *Remixing the Classroom: Toward an Open Philosophy of Music Education* (Bloomington: Indiana University Press, 2016); Bennett Reimer, *A Philosophy of Music Education: Advancing the Vision*, 3rd ed. (Upper Saddle River, NJ: Prentice Hall, 2003).

4. David J. Elliott and Marissa Silverman, *Music Matters: A Philosophy of Music Education*, 2nd ed. (New York: Oxford University Press, 2015); Paul Woodford, *Democracy and Music Education: Liberalism, Ethics, and the Politics of Practice* (Bloomington: Indiana University Press, 2005).

5. Elizabeth Gould, "Social Justice in Music Education: The Problematic of Democracy," *Music Education Research* 9, no. 2 (2007): 229–240; David Lines, "Deleuze and Music Education: Machines for Change," in *Cartographies of Becoming in Music Education: A Deleuze-Guattari Perspective*, ed. Diana Masny (Rotterdam: Sense, 2013), 23–33.

6. Randall Allsup and Heidi Westerlund, "Methods and Situational Ethics in Music Education," *Action, Criticism, and Theory for Music Education* 11, no. 1 (2012): 124–148.

7. Gilles Deleuze and Félix Guattari, *A Thousand Plateaus: Capitalism and Schizophrenia*, trans. Brian Massumi (Minneapolis: University of Minnesota Press, 1987), 10.

8. Gilles Deleuze, *Negotiations: 1972–1990*, trans. Martin Joughin (New York: Columbia University Press, 1995), 100.

9. John Marks, "Ethics," in *The Deleuze Dictionary*, ed. Adrian Parr (Edinburgh: Edinburgh University Press, 2005), 85.

10. John Rajchman, *The Deleuze Connections* (Cambridge, MA: MIT Press, 2000), 96.

11. Cliff Stagoll, "Event," in *The Deleuze Dictionary*, ed. Adrian Parr (Edinburgh: Edinburgh University Press, 2005), 88.

12. Ronald Bogue, *Deleuze's Way: Essays in Transverse Ethics and Aesthetics* (New York: Routledge, 2007), 11.

13. Allsup and Westerlund, "Methods and Situational Ethics in Music Education," 140–143.

14. Marks, "Ethics," 85.

15. Wayne Bowman, "Music as Ethical Encounter," *Bulletin of the Council for Research in Music Education*, no. 151 (2000): 11–20; Thomas A. Regelski, "The Good Life of Teaching or the Life of Good Teaching?" *Action, Criticism, and Theory in Music Education* 11, no. 2 (2012): 42–48; Elliott and Silverman, *Music Matters*.

16. Gould, "Social Justice in Music Education," 236.

17. Ibid., 238.

18. Ibid.

19. Woodford, *Democracy and Music Education*.

20. Cathy Benedict, "Defining Ourselves as Other: Envisioning Transformative Possibilities," in *Teaching Music in the Urban Classroom*, Vol 1, *A Guide to Survival, Success, and Reform*, ed. Carol Frierson-Campbell (Lanham, MD: Rowman & Littlefield Education, 2006), 3–13.

21. Todd May and Inna Semetsky, "Deleuze, Ethical Education, and the Unconscious," in *Nomadic Education: Variations on a Theme by Deleuze and Guattari*, ed. Inna Semetsky (Rotterdam, The Netherlands: Sense, 2008), 150 (italics in the original).

22. Petra Hroch, "Deleuze, Guattari, and Environmental Pedagogy and Politics: *Ritournelles* for a Planet-Yet-to-Come," in *Deleuze and Guattari, Politics and Education: For a People-Yet-to-Come*, ed. Matthew Carlin and Jason Wallin (New York: Bloomsbury Academic, 2014), 57.

23. Ibid., 58.
24. Jean-Francois Lyotard, *The Inhuman*, trans. Geoffry Bennington and Rachel Bowlby (Stanford, CA: Stanford University Press, 1991), 88, 97 (italics in the original).
25. Rosi Braidotti, *Transpositions: On Nomadic Ethics* (Cambridge, UK: Polity Press, 2006), 20.
26. Linda Alcoff, "Cultural Feminism versus Post-structuralism: The Identity Crisis in Feminist Theory," *Journal of Women in Culture and Society* 13, no. 3 (1988): 420.
27. Braidotti, *Transpositions*, 267.
28. Deleuze and Guattari, *A Thousand Plateaus*, 351–422.
29. Gould, "Social Justice in Music Education."
30. Linda Zerilli, "Toward a Feminist Theory of Judgment," *Signs* 34, no. 2 (2009), 309.
31. Linda Zerilli, *Feminism and the Abyss of Freedom* (Chicago: University of Chicago Press, 2005), 133.
32. Ibid., 140.
33. Ibid. (italics in the original).
34. Gould, "Social Justice in Music Education." Gould takes the idea of dissensus from Ewe Ziarek, *An Ethics of Dissensus: Postmodernity, Feminism, and the Politics of Radical Democracy* (Stanford: Stanford University Press, 2001).
35. Hannah Arendt, *Essays in Understanding, 1930–1954*, ed. Jerome Kohn (New York: Harcourt Brace, 1994), 323.
36. Hannah Arendt, "Some Questions of Moral Philosophy," in *Responsibility and Judgment*, ed. Jerome Kohn (New York: Schocken Books, 2003), 140–141.
37. Linda Zerilli, "We Feel Our Freedom: Imagination and Judgment in the Thought of Hannah Arendt," *Political Theory* 33, no. 2 (2005): 175.
38. Maxine Greene, *Releasing the Imagination: Essays on Education, the Arts, and Social Change* (San Francisco: Jossey-Bass), 20 (italics in the original).
39. Zerilli, *Feminism and the Abyss of Freedom*, 145.
40. Ibid., 144 (italics in the original).
41. Hannah Arendt, "Imagination," in *Lectures on Kant's Political Philosophy*, ed. Ronald Beiner (Chicago: University of Chicago Press, 1982), 83.
42. Zerilli, "Toward a Feminist Theory of Judgment," 312.
43. Zerilli, "We Feel Our Freedom," 163.
44. Arendt, "Some Questions of Moral Philosophy," 142.

5 Reconsidering Considering

While my story in chapter 4 about considering multiple perspectives when confronted with band students who wanted to play "Sleigh Ride" may at first appear straightforward, its potential limitations necessitate investigation. For example, when I imagined the students' and community members' perspectives, how did I know that I was not making inaccurate assumptions or bending their views to meet my own desires? Given that I never fully located the one who considers, including in relation to those they imagine, how the considering process affects those who undergo it remains unclear.

My "Sleigh Ride" story is also problematic because I treated the process of considering as primarily cognitive, neglecting how humans' sociality, emotion, and embodiment integrate with and inform all thinking. If imagining another's perspective involves one's own embodied-social-emotional reactions to that viewpoint, then the imaginer may miss how these qualities might inform another's perspective. Such action can further cognitive-centric worldviews, limiting understandings of and possibilities for the emotional-embodied aspects of ourselves and others. Furthermore, my inattention to my own embodied emotions caused me to portray my processes of imagining and judging as relatively easy, involving neither apprehension nor discomfort. Yet, critically reflecting on one's past actions in order to consider more ethical paths forward often invokes feelings of vulnerability that teachers may seek to avoid.

Focusing on a single instance of considering may also dissuade readers from imagining countless additional possibilities for the process. While my "Sleigh Ride" tale revealed how one might draw on a combination of Hannah Arendt's and Gilles Deleuze's writings when confronted with a specific dilemma, it left many assumptions about band, music, teaching, and learning unquestioned. If, as Arendt suggests, acting ethically involves more than just "the refraining from doing wrong, which may mean the refraining from doing anything," the roles that considering might play in music education practices ranging from what constitutes "accepted" music-making to determining who has access to various forms of music education necessitate attention.[1]

Locating the I Who Considers

Given that the band students openly shared their pointed opinions with me about playing "Sleigh Ride," my story did not fully address how to imagine divergent viewpoints absent such information. Arendt suggests that direct dialogue can inform the imagining of others' perspectives.[2] Yet, she neither overtly calls for dialogue nor critiques imaginings occurring without it.

Moreover, Arendt explains that judgers' imaginings may deviate from the actual viewpoints of those they seek to understand. Writing about representing to oneself the perspective of an individual living in a slum, she explains: "The judgment I shall come up with will by no means necessarily be the same as that of the inhabitants whom time and hopelessness may have dulled to the outrage of their conditions, but it will become an outstanding example for my further judging of these matters."[3] This example illuminates possible advantages of surmising rather than asking about others' perspectives. Although some individuals facing dire circumstances may have little trouble expressing their hardships, as noted by writers such as Paulo Freire and Albert Memmi, hegemonic relationships often foster varying levels of acceptance and desensitization.[4] Since those currently enduring oppressive circumstances may have habituated to their situations, imagination absent dialogue enables outsiders to see problems more readily and to consider others' plights anew. Such action, however, carries its own risks.

Judging based on what one believes another thinks and feels rather than seeking out what they actually experience can foster inaccurate understandings. While someone imagining living in a slum might get a broad sense of such persons' situations, they inevitably miss many nuances. I wonder: What do individuals conceive of as the worst and best parts about their circumstances, both day-to-day and long term? What systems and individuals contribute to their predicaments? What are their hopes and aspirations? Such answers will likely vary, even between those experiencing similar circumstances, as well as change over time. While imagining without dialogue may cause one to judge certain situations as troubling, it often inhibits specific, multifaceted understandings that can inform decisions about future action.

Furthermore, particularly with less overt forms of oppression, imagining without dialogue can encourage people to miss or dismiss problematic occurrences. It is not hard to think of individuals who, even when they purportedly "put themselves in another person's shoes," still defend sexist, racist, or homophobic jokes or minor instances of bullying, arguing that they personally "have a tough skin." In such moments, imagining may do little to change their minds. While Arendt suggests that imagining involves perceiving the world as another does rather than as the imaginer would in that position, absent dialogue, such understandings may remain elusive.

My "Sleigh Ride" tale is also problematic because it primarily honored the voices of the students who complained. In neglecting to ask other students and parents for their thoughts, I omitted many other possibly divergent perspectives. Thoroughly examining everyone's viewpoints before making any judgment, however, is often impractical. Although one cannot reasonably expect that I should have talked with every band student and parent before making a decision, I wonder what might have happened if I had made a concerted effort to discuss students' and others' desires and motivations prior to the "Sleigh Ride" incident. Such understandings could have made my imagining process more accurate and detailed, perhaps ultimately altering my judgment.

Building on these ideas, I posit an extension of Arendt's conception of imagination, arguing that teachers and students might view it as an iterative process that includes dialogue whenever possible. In other words, while imagining how individuals might understand a given circumstance can serve as a useful and sometimes necessary starting point, the practice of considering involves seeking out a plurality of actual voices that one can use to inform their ethical deliberations. This does not mean that teachers and students must agree with or placate all individuals with whom they speak. However, just as imagining necessitates distance from one's own perspectives, considering requires listening openly, temporarily suspending assumptions. While most situations will necessitate imagining some perspectives from reasoned conjecture alone, educators and students who invite diverse input over time can draw on those understandings interactions when confronted with new scenarios.

Conceiving of imagining as an ongoing process means understanding the "I" that imagines and subsequently judges as existing in constant flux. Yet, despite Arendt's assertions about the contextual nature of judging and the evolution of the very criteria for judgment, she does not articulate how the processes of imagining and judging change those who undertake them. Arendt's statements about using Shakespeare's characters as examples of heroes and villains reveal her assumption that humans are relatively stagnant beings, at least in comparison with Deleuze's conception of existence. She writes: "We judge and tell right from wrong by having present in our mind some incident and some person, absent in time or space, that have become examples."[5] To return again and again to the same example implies that it remains good or bad despite one's changing imaginings and judgments. It also omits how the selection of examples alters the I who draws on them. While not overtly contradicting Arendt, conceiving of Deleuzian difference and differing as underlying instances of imagining and judging highlights how teachers and students change through their ethical considerations.

This may seem like an obvious point; clearly humans continually change over time. You are not the same person as when you started this paragraph, chapter, or book. Yet, there exists a difference between approaching life as an I who goes moment to moment and week to week largely unchanged and the uncertainty, difference, and differing that constitute an ephemeral I. Stated differently, the extent to which an individual understands themself as primarily consistent or changing can inform how they engage with everyday labels and practices. Approaching the "Sleigh Ride" incident with a mainly stable sense of self would have encouraged me to engage with students' concerns through my existing definitions of "band" and "music education," as well as with personal pride that would likely have dissuaded significant changes to my practices. Alternatively, imagining the students' perceptions of "Sleigh Ride" with an openness to my own differing and to the ephemeral and variable nature of my musically educative goals would not only have informed my decision-making, but potentially altered my sense of self as an educator and music maker.

Drawing on Deleuze, my proposed process of considering necessitates experiencing I as constantly changing. Imagining fundamentally alters the I who then judges, and judging in turn alters the changing I who then imagines. Conceiving of life as unstable, however, does not mean instantly abandoning one's values. Teachers and students should not equate a welcoming of alternative possibilities with relativism or the negation of prior learnings. Metaphorically, rather than adding another piece atop one's existing "self" block tower, experiencing I as differing involves incorporating newfound blocks into continually evolving arrangements.

In summary, imagining and judging are not clear, predictable, and universal but rather different for each individual and differing in integration with our changing selves over time. Just as one can never fully construct a common world, the I who considers remains in constant motion and therefore not completely locatable. I can no longer look back on that winter concert with the pride and enthusiasm that I felt in the moment; I am no longer that teacher.

Beyond Cognition

Another assumption underlying Arendt's writings is that imagining is a primarily cognitive endeavor. She asserts the need for "thinking in examples" and making diverse individuals' positions "present in my thought."[6] Likewise, Arendt explains imagination as having "an image in my *mind* of something that is not present,"[7] and elsewhere she states that through the imagination, common sense "can think . . . in the place of everybody else."[8] However, Arendt hints at how human qualities beyond cognition might inform ethical processes. When using the example of imagining oneself living in a slum, she writes: "I arrive at this notion by representing to myself how I would feel if I had to live there, that is, I try to think in the place of the slum-dweller." Although her use of the word "feel" in the first part of the sentence suggests that imagination involves emotion, the phrase "to think" emphasizes cognition.

Similarly, Arendt clarifies the role that the sensory plays in judging. She asserts that unlike thinking, judging does not leave the world of appearances but "retires from active involvement in it to a privileged position in order to contemplate the whole."[9] While this statement suggests that judging may involve embodied perception, it propagates a mind-body dichotomy. Furthermore, in *The Life of the Mind* Arendt writes that in order to think, philosophers must "blind" themselves to the sensory, adding, "While you are thinking, you are unaware of your own corporality."[10] At minimum, such arguments imply a conception of human ontology that favors cognition over and apart from humans' other qualities.

In addition to contradicting recent neuroscience research,[11] separating cognition from humans' sociality, embodiment, and emotions can limit the richness of one's imaginings. When individuals consider how others think about an issue or situation but omit how they feel, imaginers may more easily misunderstand or write off their perceptions. For instance, without recognizing the emotional attachment underlying the high school students' desire to play "Sleigh Ride," in imagining their viewpoints, I may still have trivialized their request.

Deleuze's overarching philosophical project troubles cognitive-centric understandings of existence. According to Deleuze and Guattari, while scientists think through functions and philosophers create concepts, artists compose sensations.[12] Sensations, along with the related concepts of affects and percepts,[13] distinguish artistic endeavors from other activities.[14] While such arguments are still problematic because they suggest a discipline-specific divide between thinking and feeling, Deleuze attends to emotion much more than Arendt.

Although Deleuze does not apply the ideas of sensations, affects, and percepts directly to ethical endeavors, Ronald Bogue proffers such a connection. Noting that Deleuze's ethics demand attentiveness, Bogue explains one's ethical obligation as "to affect and be affected, to suspend, as much as one can, the categorization and comprehension of the other, and then open oneself to the undetermined, hidden possible worlds that are expressed in the affective signs of the other."[15] Stated differently, Deleuzian ethics involve not just intellectualizing the world from diverse perspectives but *sensing* it through open encounters with difference.

Drawing on Bogue's interpretation of Deleuze's ethics, I propose an extension of my Arendtian-inspired process of imagining that involves sensing others' perspectives. For instance, the affect arising when teachers welcome the pain or joy in a student's eyes and body integrates with the student's surrounding words and silences. This holistic experience informs ethical judgments. Although thinking always occurs separate from embodied-emotional experiences, attending to sensing emphasizes noncognitive qualities.

Yet, just as one can never completely know another human's thought processes, music educators and students can never fully understanding one another's embodied-emotional sensations. Addressing the related experience of empathy, Sarah Ahmed elaborates on this point.[16] She argues that empathy serves as a reminder about the flesh that physically bounds one body from the next. Describing her mother's debilitating illness, Ahmed explains her mother's pain as "shrouded in mystery," adding, "I lived with what was, for me, the unlivable."[17] While Ahmed could sense her mother's predicament, she could never fully experience her suffering. She summarizes, "In this way empathy sustains the very difference that it may seek to overcome: empathy remains a 'wish feeling,' in which subjects 'feel' something other than what another feels in the very moment of imagining they could feel what another feels."[18] Humans' separate bodies ensure that fully shared embodied-emotional experiences remain elusive. This disconnection should not dissuade teachers and students from considering the affective qualities of others' perspectives, but they might acknowledge the inevitable limits of such action.

I wonder: What might such ethical sensing look and sound like in a music teaching and learning setting? Writing about assessments that draw on critical theory and involve forms of resistance, Brent Talbot and Hakim Williams describe a project called "constructive controversy."[19] A teacher facilitating this educative experience presents a controversial issue, such as the historical, agenda-driven meanings surrounding songs such as "La Cucaracha" or "This Land Is Your Land." The class then discusses the issue and students select the side that they most strongly support. Subsequently, the teacher asks the students to compose a new song or to arrange an existing protest song in order to argue convincingly for the *opposite* side. Talbot and Williams summarize that this endeavor "encourages students to step into the 'other' perspective which is so often easily/readily demonized."[20]

While Talbot and Williams do not assert it directly, it follows that composing or arranging music centered on a perspective antithetical to one's current views usually involves imagining the embodied-emotional aspects of that position. Teachers might enhance this empathetic tendency by drawing explicit attention to the feelings underlying contrasting viewpoints, perhaps asking: What embodied-emotional reactions do you think those with different perspectives feel when interfacing with this issue? How might those embodied emotions inform your composition or arrangement? Rather than solely *thinking* about the world through another's perspective, those imagining might resist—as best as possible—their own embodied-emotional-social reactions, aiming instead to *sense* others' situations. Such action facilitates motion toward the construction of a more detailed and multifaceted common world.

While empathy can facilitate ethical thinking and action, sensing, as described here, is undertaken with the purpose of contributing to ethical practices. This raises the question: What is the relationship between sensing and judging? Arendt cautions against equating the presence of particularly ardent feelings or certain types of feelings with more or less ethical actions. She argues that feelings offer no indication of right and wrong, explaining that they may result more from a sense of conformity or nonconformity than from judgment.[21] Providing the example of a conflict between old and new habits, Arendt asserts that imagining the potential rejection of the familiar may arouse feelings of guilt, regardless of whether judging reveals the new habits as more ethical.[22] For Arendt, judgment is not the same as identification, recognition, or empathy and must be distinguished from them.[23]

Readers may interpret my own utilization of the term "considering" as foregrounding cognition while minimizing attention to humans' integrated emotions, bodies, and sociality. While a term like "sensing" shares greater alignment with Deleuzian ethics than considering, in agreement with Arendt, I posit that emotions alone cannot serve as reliable indicators of "good" or "bad"; primarily sensing another's perspective may lead to hasty and limited judgments. I have chosen to use the term considering with the qualification that considering relies on a conception of humans as embodied-cognitive-emotional-social beings.

In short, sensing another's situation offers insights critical for imagining a common world. However, if the empathy aroused limits or overtakes one's ability to imagine a plurality of other social-embodied-emotional-cognitive perspectives, then it may foster problematic judgments. The experience of imagining another's embodied-emotional-social-cognitive perspective should complicate and inform rather than simplify or dictate the process of judging. Since considering demands substantial emotional-cognitive-embodied-social investment, its potential effects on those who undertake it necessitate further investigation.

Reimagining the Ethical Self

It is perhaps clichéd to say that ethical action demands some degree of selflessness. The morality of most religions rests on varying notions of self-sacrifice, and almost all ethical schools of thought argue for the moderation of self-interest in exchange for either specific obligations or overarching considerations such as collective flourishing. Likewise, drawing on Kant, Arendt explains: "Egoism cannot be overcome by moral preaching which, on the contrary, always sends me back to myself"; rather, judging demands plurality, in which the self regards itself not as the whole world but as a citizen of the world.[24] In other words, conceiving of oneself as intertwined with a global humanity necessitates resisting narcissism in favor of concern for all individuals.[25] Going further, Arendt posits that judging inhibits the domination of one's self-interest by demanding "certain sacrifices," including the "denial of selfishness."[26] While I concur that ethical practices necessitate avoiding egocentrism, I worry that unchecked self-sacrifice can prove detrimental to one's well-being.

When the students in my undergraduate and graduate classes and I discuss ethical issues such as classism and discrimination, they often express feeling overwhelmed and powerless. While few students outright resist or disregard the need to take such issues seriously, they articulate concern about how they can balance the demands of teaching with the need to consider more ethical practices. Although there clearly exists no easy solution to such worries, part of addressing them might involve reconceptualizing one's music educator self.

Acting more ethically necessitates turning away from past practices and the accompanying self who enacted them. Deviating from one's prior conceptions of what music education is and should be, and likewise what defines a "good" music educator or music student, troubles one's existing identity. When individuals conceive of themselves largely as stagnant, whole beings, even small changes to their selves can feel overwhelming.

Deleuze's understanding of existence, including humans, as constituted by difference and differing provides an alternative. Favoring a conception of life as an unending string of "ands" rather than a single "I," Deleuze and Guattari pose the possibilities of reaching "not the point where one no longer says I, but the point where it is no longer of any importance whether one says I."[27] Stated differently, I suggests a completed, largely unchangeable being while "and . . . and . . . and . . ." emphasizes unceasing variability and the potential to live otherwise.

Music makers who conceive of themselves as fluctuating connections may find making changes to their self-understandings easier than those wedded to more stable identities. For instance, the educator who conceives of their Kodály pedagogies as an "and" may readily welcome "ands" related to informal or project-based learning, even if they challenge existing practices. Conversely, educators stating "I, a Kodály educator" imply resistance to alteration. They may incorporate hip-hop or a song about injustice into their practices, but their goals and values, including ethical ones, remain largely unchanged. While experiencing oneself as difference and differing does not automatically foster more ethical teaching and learning practices, it may lessen one's initial apprehension about taking such action.

Reimagining one's self is not a purely cognitive exercise. Brené Brown explains that specific feelings of vulnerability arise from situations invoking "uncertainty, risk, and emotional exposure."[28] Since imagining the world through the emotional-social-cognitive-embodied perspective of another individual involves letting go of one's immediate embodied-emotional-cognitive-social state, such action may foster the emotional exposure and absence of grounding that can cause one to feel vulnerable. Likewise, because judging necessitates a continually changing set of criteria responsive to imagining processes, it demands an openness to risk and instability that tends to coincide with experiences of vulnerability.

Since humans often deem vulnerable experiences uncomfortable, students and teachers may try to resist practices that invoke them, including ethical considerations and actions. Arendt, however, does not provide readers assistance in interfacing with the social-embodied-emotions that may arise through imagining and judging. Moreover, the cognitive centrism pervading contemporary education discourse encourages teachers and students to treat the emotional exposure that may accompany changing self-conceptions with suspicion. Brown argues that individuals may dismiss vulnerability as weakness when "we realize that we've confused *feeling* with *failing* and *emotions* with *liabilities*."[29] If the process of considering more ethical paths forward often causes individuals to feel vulnerable, then teachers and students need not only awareness and acknowledgment of that potential but also ideas about how to respond in such moments.

Deleuze's emphasis on human qualities beyond cognition, described in the previous section, offers an alternative to avoiding or distrusting the emotional-laden aspects of one's own ethical practices. Building on these ideas, I posit that individuals might welcome the feelings that arise when engaged in the practice of considering. For example, in my own teaching, I know that augmenting existing curricula with ethically aimed discussions around topics such as white privilege, heteronormativity, and discrimination often makes me feel vulnerable. While in my early teaching endeavors I tried to hide and move quickly past such feelings, more recently, I have worked to embrace them and to in part share them with students.[30]

Before engaging with what I deem difficult topics, I make it a habit to look into all students' eyes and to take a deep breath, in the process reassuring myself that my emotional exposure is normal and perhaps useful to our deliberations. I also try to use the word "vulnerable" throughout our discussions and to let silence uncomfortably endure until I or others muster the courage to speak. Yet, I cannot say that I find such action easy, and my comfort level varies based on factors such as my life outside of teaching and my degree of success at building a good rapport with individuals in a given class. Even now, recalling and writing about vulnerable experiences makes me feel unsettled and anxious.

I have also learned that assuming others simultaneously share my vulnerability is problematic and intertwined with my own privilege. A student recently told me that my expressing of my own unease about social justice–related topics in part undermined the voices of those who felt comfortable openly addressing such issues. Welcoming and acknowledging one's own vulnerability is not in itself ethical, and such action necessitates added attention to immediate circumstances. However, because undertaking more ethical practices demands changed self-conceptions, embracing feelings of vulnerability opens up the possibility for such action.

While developing a conception of one's self as fluid and emphasizing the role of human qualities beyond cognition may assist teachers and students in considering more ethical paths forward, such actions do not eliminate the potential problems of unbridled selflessness noted at the start of this section.

Teachers—myself included—at times risk their future capacity to make meaningful, musically educative contributions by not attending to their own survival. Some burn out and leave the profession, some become cynical, some neglect relationships with friends and family, some engage in other self-destructive behaviors such as drug use; the list does not end there. Yet, neither Arendt nor Deleuze addresses this potentially serious limitation, and calls for more ethical thinking and action in music education often omit the ethics of caring for oneself.[31]

Although the topic of teachers' self-care demands its own book, I briefly offer that the practice of considering involves balancing imaginative ponderings about more ethical practices with concerns about our own survival as educators and as socially situated individuals with lives beyond the classroom. Such a conception reminds me of something that, referring to part of the mandatory preflight instructions, my mentor Steve Seidel once said: "We need to secure our own oxygen masks first before assisting others."[32] He continued that while he always had a negative gut reaction to the thought of helping himself first, arts educators need to take such advice seriously. Just as those who initially neglect to put on their own oxygen masks risk passing out before getting the chance to assist others, music educators who consistently forgo their own personal, artistic, and educative needs and desires may never realize their full potential as teachers.[33]

Broadening the process of considering to include accounting for one's own yearnings does not mean neglecting that all educative practices propagate certain ethical positions and norms, including potentially harmful ones. Attending to oneself is not a license for disregard, complacency, or selfishness. However, in first securing our personal oxygen masks, we acknowledge our vulnerability, admitting that if we do not attend to our own needs and desires—including integrated social, emotional, cognitive, and embodied ones—we may not survive let alone flourish within this profession. By adopting a conception of existence that centers instability and emotion, teachers and students might engage in the practice of considering in ways that, rather than denying our humanity, seeks empowerment in and through it.

Narratives of Considering

My "Sleigh Ride" example demonstrates how teachers might use the process of considering when confronted with specific dilemmas, but they can also consider more ethical paths forward as a part of their ongoing planning and reflection. Although a given situation demands imagining the perspectives of those immediately and tangentially involved, considering possible overarching changes to curricula, pedagogy, and other aspects of teaching and learning necessitates attending to a wider array of viewpoints. These include the perspectives of diverse students, colleagues, community members, and revered pedagogues and musicians, including those who replicate long-standing musical traditions as well as those who promote alternative practices. Yet, absent attention to individuals' divergent, evolving stories, teachers imagining multiple perspectives may end up relying on limited grand narratives.

In order to resist perceiving the viewpoints of the majority as universal, teachers might imagine their current and potential future work through the perspectives of those from contrasting socioeconomic backgrounds, races, genders, sexual orientations, home environments, citizenships, and spiritual beliefs, as well as of people with different cognitive, physical, emotional, social, and developmental needs, to name a few. In addition to dialogue, teachers and students might deepen their understandings about such differences and differing by reading narratives by and news stories about various individuals and groups. They could also engage with academic literature exploring divergent individuals' stories centered on topics ranging from bullying to persons with disabilities to immigration. Artistic endeavors created by or otherwise involving various people and groups can also serve as rich sources of information.

Teachers, however, are not the only ones who might engage in the process of considering. In her limited writings on education, Arendt argues that while educators have typically tried to protect children from the world, they might instead prepare them "for the task of renewing a common world," including the "chance of undertaking something new, something unforeseen by us."[34] Arendt, however, stops short of seeing schools as political, arguing that they offer a middle ground between the political public realm and the nonpolitical private realm;[35] children can only fully participate in the political upon having gone through a certain developmental and educational trajectory that transitions them into the "state of adulthood."[36] Gert Biesta problematizes this position, explaining that individuals do not learn to judge so that they can exist politically but rather through judging they bring the political into existence.[37] He argues that schools provide an ideal place for engaging with practices such as imagining and judging both because students may not necessarily learn these processes elsewhere and because, given that questions about "togetherness-in-plurality" permeate students' lives inside and outside of school, teachers can never fully teach apart from them.[38]

If we as individuals and as a music-education community believe that part of our responsibility includes assisting students in developing the ethical dispositions and thought processes needed for twenty-first-century life, then we might involve students in considering more ethical paths forward, including those that elude our own imaginings. Envision, for example, students generating a list of the most pressing problems facing their school and local community. Having decided on a couple of key issues, the students might find or create music representing competing sides of the debate. They might also involve history, science, or other classes in providing supporting information. Having imagined diverse, feelingful perspectives, they might make a judgment about how they could use artistic endeavors to foster a more ethical course of action. Key considerations might include: In light of this project, what are the limits of the musical practices with which I have the most familiarity? What music teaching and learning decisions might have the most substantial effect on the ethical aspects of my own and others' narratives and narrative construction?

Subsequently, the students might brainstorm a list of potential content, and in the spirit of Arendtian judgment, attempt to convince one another and their teacher of the value of particular options. While Arendt, like Elizabeth Gould, reminds readers about the problems of pure consensus,[39] engaging students in such inquiries can inform teachers' own imagining and judging as well as develop students' ethical capacities. Such practices also honor the attention to complexity and differing that are key to Deleuze's ethics and yet largely missing from contemporary political rhetoric. Although I ultimately conceive of considering not as an exercise but as a way of being in the world, guiding students through the process fosters actions and dispositions that can transfer to life beyond the classroom.

Given the globally connected nature of contemporary life, aiming to construct a common world also involves imagining one's work through at least a couple of nonlocal perspectives. Emphasizing the global voices with which one already has familiarity, however, can stifle alternative imaginings. Looking to current events can encourage teachers and students to consider previously omitted global perspectives as well as foster broader awareness about those circumstances.

Judith Butler explains the interconnection between local experiences and global attentiveness. While every event takes place in a certain location and involves specific people whose bodies face real risks, "What is happening 'there' depends on the event being registered in several 'elsewheres.'"[40] Significant global news media attention to killings of journalists or religious genocides may alter local governments' responses. Conversely, a lack of such exposure can embolden those pondering similar atrocities. Music educators and students who use global narratives to inform their construction of the common world play a small role in the acknowledgment that may encourage others to make more ethical choices. Butler summarizes that without global ethical recognition and response, "something of the reality of the event is lost."[41]

When music educators and students contemplating more expansive changes feel overwhelmed, they might consider how even seemingly small actions can facilitate more ethical teaching and learning experiences. For example, Ahmed writes about the ethical nature of bearing witness to her mother's pain, thereby giving it the status of a shared event rather than a private burden.[42] In alignment with Deleuze's emphasis on embracing that which societies exclude, I wonder: What opportunities do teachers and students have to give voice to silent suffering or subjugation? While such action might eventually include creating curricula centered on these topics, it can start with the recognition of a single person's story, be it that of a student, local or global community member, or historical musical figure. By demonstrating the possibilities of breaking from one's engrained habits, undertaking small changes can assist teachers and students in overcoming a sense of powerlessness. Yet, since considering is an unending process, it would be problematic for a music educator to claim that these minor changes are enough.

Music educators, myself included, cannot continue to exclude certain individuals, such as those of low socioeconomic status, from teaching and learning endeavors.[43] The profession also cannot continue to emphasize Western-centered solo and ensemble competitions to the detriment of other forms of music-making. Considering small changes cannot give way to complacency or limited visioning. Inspired by Deleuze's unceasing welcoming of diverging potentialities, including those that may initially seem unfeasible, teachers and students might consider what ethical actions they deem most crucial for challenging the extreme self-interest and ungrounded fear of difference all too pervasive in twenty-first-century societies.

What Problems Remain?

At this point, the considering of more ethical paths forward may appear relativistic. Indeed, the process of considering avoids stagnant or solidified definitions of "ethical" or "more ethical," instead leaving such designations in the hands of individual teachers and students. Yet, seeking to imagine others' social-cognitive-embodied-emotional perspectives as accurately as possible and using that information to judge avoids the complete relativism of capricious choices made absent critical reflection.

Additionally, when dialogue or other interactions make teachers and students aware of inaccuracies in how they perceived another's viewpoint, the process of considering necessitates that they alter their judgments in light of that information. Such action resists a laissez-faire approach in which one may work from self-interest while purportedly understanding different perspectives. Furthermore, when teachers or students deem certain practices "more ethical" than alternative ones, they do so with the willingness to try convincing others of their positions. Articulating and defending the emotional-embodied-social-cognitive rationale behind one's decisions eliminates the complete relativism of choices made simply because "I thought it was more ethical."

Another possible concern about the process of considering may involve the significance granted to varying viewpoints. Should teachers really assign the same value to perspectives of students with whom they have direct contact as to those of individuals from another country? Should they consider the viewpoints of administrators who have the ability to terminate their employment with the same severity as those of local community members? The answer in both instances is clearly "no"; imagining one's work through diverse viewpoints does not mean automatically attributing equal weight to each.

In writing about cosmopolitan ethics, Kwame Anthony Appiah argues that although all humans have obligations to those throughout the world, people will feel a greater sense of duty toward those within their own families, neighborhoods, and nations.[44] Likewise, I posit that while still taking into account as many different perspectives as possible, teachers and students might grant more importance to the viewpoints of those closest to them. Imagining different perspectives resists addressing current students' needs in ways that harm or inhibit those in one's local and global communities. However, teachers and students necessarily devote themselves mainly to those they can most directly assist, including local individuals who may often go unnoticed.

Proximity, however, need not serve as the only criterion for balancing multiple perspectives; one's future survival also demands serious attention. For example, in the case of administrators and policies, if teachers decide that one more ethical path forward will likely cost them their jobs, then they may certainly feel justified in preserving their livelihoods by avoiding that option. This does not mean that teachers should always refrain from engaging in subversive action or raising their voices in dissent; however, they should not feel obligated to sacrifice their ability to continue teaching. The significance of engaging with multiple viewpoints comes from the awareness of the complex ethical implications of specific choices and from the potential imaginative alternatives that various perspectives can inspire.

An additional possible critique of considering is that focusing on a process rather than on the judgments themselves does not go far enough in addressing current critical ethical problems, such as the exclusion and subjugation of certain ways of being musical or the divisive rhetoric aimed at transgendered persons, immigrants, and many others. Indeed, there is a part of me that wanted to use this chapter as a platform for sharing my own judgments in the hope of posing serious challenges to existing practices and ultimately seeking agreement from readers. Just contemplating such action, however, causes me to feel extremely vulnerable. This exposure and uncertainty arises from fear that my judgments might alienate some readers by going too far and others by not going far enough. While I can never fully distinguish these feelings from other rationale, I also resist posing more specific directives for other reasons.

Since judgments always depend on specific circumstances, my own judgments do not automatically transfer to other contexts. While I could make broad statements against limited views of musicality or forms of discrimination, those vague declarations may not necessarily incite the ethical journeying most meaningful for individual teachers and students. In contrast, offering readers a process for ethical decision-making may encourage critical thinking about the interplay between ethics and the context-specific narratives that constitute and surround all humans.

Furthermore, Deleuze's ethics involve thinking and sensing in possibilities rather than in directives. In addition to implying that I have ethical "answers"—which I do not—telling readers what they should or even could do, rather than opening up space for them to experiment with what they *might* do, would restrict ethical action to that which I or others have already envisioned.[45] Instead, positing considering as a creative and evolving process enables possibilities for a renewed sense of personal ethical responsibility as well as for innovative paths that extend rhizomatically—moving in diverse directions along unplanned routes—from individual and collective narratives.

In summary, I constructed the practice of "considering" by intersecting Deleuze's and Arendt's process-based ethical philosophies. Considering maintains Deleuze's focus on the complex, differing, and potentiality-driven nature of ethical engagements while avoiding his tendency toward relativism and resistance to working within existing political systems, including democracy. While considering relies on Arendt's proposed processes of imagining and judging, consistent with Deleuze's writings, it simultaneously involves understanding the common world as an unreachable limit and resisting stagnant conceptions of the self who considers. Additionally, I detailed the possibilities of sensing, as opposed to just contemplating, others' situations as well as of welcoming the embodied-emotional experiences, including vulnerability, that accompany more ethical practices.

Considering necessitates balancing what is with what might be, intermixing the constraints of the here and now with previously unimagined potentialities, including those fostered through attending to often omitted narratives. By embracing rather than avoiding this complexity and uncertainty, I think that teachers and students can develop dispositions important for ethical decision-making throughout their lives. However, given the limits of my own narratives, I will have to let you be the judge of that.

Notes

1. Hannah Arendt, "Some Questions of Moral Philosophy," in *Responsibility and Judgment*, ed. Jerome Kohn (New York: Schocken Books, 2003), 142.
2. Ibid., 141.
3. Ibid., 140.

4. Paulo Freire, *Pedagogy of the Oppressed*, trans. Myra Bergman Ramos (1970; repr., New York: Continuum, 2000); Albert Memmie, *The Colonizer and the Colonized* (Boston: Beacon Press, 1965).
5. Arendt, "Some Questions of Moral Philosophy," 145.
6. Ibid., 146, 141.
7. Ibid., 139 (italics mine).
8. Ibid., 140.
9. Hannah Arendt, *The Life of the Mind* (San Diego, CA: Harcourt, 1971), 94.
10. Ibid., 84, 85.
11. See, for example, Antonio R. Damasio, *The Feeling of What Happens: Body and Emotion in the Making of Consciousness* (Orlando, FL: Harcourt, 1999); and George Lakoff and Mark Johnson, *Philosophy in the Flesh: The Embodied Mind and Its Challenge to Western Thought* (New York: Basic, 1999), 22.
12. Gilles Deleuze and Félix Guattari, *What Is Philosophy?* Trans. Hugh Tomlinson and Graham Burchell (New York: Columbia University Press, 1994), 197–198.
13. Affects and percepts are related to affections and perceptions. Using the example of one's nostrils recoiling from the smell of cheese, Colebrook defines affections as what happens to us as a result of an event. Alternatively, what one receives, such as the odor of the cheese, constitutes a perception. While affects and percepts are prepersonal, meaning they do not come from a particular individual's or group's point of view, affections and perceptions reside in perceivers. Claire Colebrook, *Gilles Deleuze* (New York: Routledge, 2002), xix–xx, 21–22. For additional discussion of Deleuze's aesthetic philosophy, see Lauren Kapalka Richerme, "A Deleuzian Reimagining of Susanne Langer's Philosophy: Becoming-Feeling in Music Education," *Music Education Research* 20 (2018): 330–341.
14. Through the ideas of sensations, affects, and percepts, Deleuze and Guattari articulate how artistic experiences relate with human feelings while not necessarily evoking particular feelings. Colebrook summarizes: "Imagine a painting that just *is* terrifying or depressing; we may not be depressed or terrified when we view it but it presents the 'affect of depression or terror.'" Through their potential to foster deepened awareness and understandings of the possibilities for human emotion, artistic endeavors can enhance participants' engagements with the feelingful aspects of their own and others' lives. I further address Deleuze and Guattari's writings about the relationship between the arts and emotion in the "Limitations" section of chapter 6. Colebrook, *Gilles Deleuze*, xx (italics in the original).
15. Ronald Bogue, *Deleuze's Way: Essays in Transverse Ethics and Aesthetics* (New York: Routledge, 2007), 12–13.
16. Sara Ahmed, *The Cultural Politics of Emotion* (New York: Routledge, 2004), 29.
17. Ibid.
18. Ibid., 30.
19. Brent Talbot and Hakim Mohandas Amani Williams, "Critically Assessing Forms of Resistance in Music Education," in *Oxford Handbook of Philosophical and Qualitative Perspectives on Assessment in Music Education*, ed. David J. Elliott, Marissa Silverman, and Gary McPherson (New York: Oxford University Press, 2019), 83–100.
20. Ibid.
21. Arendt, "Some Questions of Moral Philosophy," 107.
22. Ibid.
23. Linda Zerilli, "Toward a Feminist Theory of Judgment," *Signs* 34, no. 2 (2009), 313.

24. Arendt, "Some Questions of Moral Philosophy," 142–143.

25. This idea may extend to animals and to the earth's existence more broadly, but Arendt does not make such links explicit.

26. Arendt, "Some Questions of Moral Philosophy," 141.

27. Gilles Deleuze and Félix Guattari, *A Thousand Plateaus: Capitalism and Schizophrenia*, trans. Brian Massumi (Minneapolis: University of Minnesota Press, 1987), 3.

28. Brené Brown, *Daring Greatly: How the Courage to Be Vulnerable Transforms the Way We Live, Love, Parent, and Lead* (New York: Gotham, 2012), 34.

29. Ibid., 35 (italics in the original).

30. See further explanation of the problems and possibilities of welcoming vulnerable experiences in Lauren Kapalka Richerme, "Vulnerable Experiences in Music Education: Possibilities and Problems for Growth and Connectivity," *Bulletin of the Council for Research in Music Education*, no. 209 (2017): 27–42.

31. See, for example, Randall Allsup, *Remixing the Classroom: Toward an Open Philosophy of Music Education* (Bloomington: Indiana University Press, 2016); Patrick Schmidt, "Ethics or Choosing Complexity in Music Relations," *Action, Criticism, and Theory for Music Education* 11, no. 1 (2012): 149–168; and Paul Woodford, *Democracy and Music Education: Liberalism, Ethics, and the Politics of Practice* (Bloomington: Indiana University Press, 2005).

32. This is a paraphrase from a statement Seidel made at the Harvard Graduate School of Education Finding Voice Conference, Cambridge, MA, in October, 2011.

33. In making this analogy, I do not mean to promote paternalistic attitudes toward students or others; those we teach are rarely helpless, and educating should not be conceived of as "saving" the destitute.

34. Hannah Arendt, *Between Past and Future: Exercises in Political Thought* (New York: Viking, 1968), 196.

35. Gert Biesta, "How to Exist Politically and Learn from It: Hannah Arendt and the Problem of Democratic Education," *Teachers College Record* 112, no. 2 (2010): 563.

36. Ibid., 558. As noted by writers such as Judith Butler, Arendt's distinction between public and private is extremely problematic. Butler, *Notes Toward a Performative Theory of Assembly* (Cambridge, MA: Harvard University Press, 2015), 44–45.

37. Biesta, "How to Exist Politically and Learn from It," 571.

38. Ibid., 571–572.

39. Elizabeth Gould, "Social Justice in Music Education: The Problematic of Democracy," *Music Education Research* 9, no. 2 (2007): 229–240.

40. Butler, *Notes Toward a Performative Theory of Assembly*, 104–105.

41. Ibid., 105.

42. Ahmed, *The Cultural Politics of Emotion*, 29.

43. See, for example, Kenneth Elpus, "Music Teacher Licensure Candidates in the United States: A Demographic Profile and Analysis of Licensure Examination Scores," *Journal of Research in Music Education* 63, no. 3 (2015): 314–335; and Kenneth Elpus and Carlos Abril, "High School Music Ensemble Students in the United States: A Demographic Profile," *Journal of Research in Music Education* 59, no. 2 (2011): 128–145.

44. Kwame Anthony Appiah, *Cosmopolitanism: Ethics in World of Strangers* (New York: W. W. Norton, 2006), 158.

45. I in no way mean to undermine the work of other philosophers and critical theorists who assert more detailed critiques and positions. Such practices hold value and may inform the process of considering.

6 Musically Connecting With

In the summer of 2007, I found myself sitting surrounded by mosquito netting on a cot in rural Ghana while using my flashlight to read Roger Scruton's *Culture Counts: Faith and Feeling in a World Besieged*. While Scruton's defense of the superiority of "high culture" may have resonated with me had I read his words in the Massachusetts house I shared with four music performance majors, I experienced cognitive dissonance as the intricate Ewe drumming patterns from a nearby village penetrated the night air, mixing with my contemplation of his text. In those moments, the idea of understanding the complex Ewe musical practices—not to mention the rich participatory musical way of life embraced by almost every member of the village—as somehow inferior to my own Western classical musical upbringing could not have seemed more absurd. While my experiences in Ghana did not make me want to abandon other forms of music-making, they engendered awareness about the limits of my prior practices and their accompanying philosophies.

Over the past few decades, the question "What are musical endeavors good for?" has served as the bedrock for various music education inquiries, particularly those of pragmatist philosophers.[1] Wayne Bowman explains that pragmatists resist objectivity, uniformity, stagnation, and predictability, arguing that meaning and value do not preexist but rather derive from human action.[2] In posing the question "What are musical endeavors good for?" these writers generally emphasize the process of engaging with it rather than specific answers. What Ewe drumming or Western classical music-making is "good for" will vary based on individuals' determinations at specific times and places.

While I agree that music-making and music education are not ultimately "good for" something once and for all but "good" in relation to particular situations, I wonder: Might they also be "good for" some temporarily agreed upon purposes? In his 2010 book *What's So Important about Music Education*? J. Scott Goble poses one such possibility: that music education is good for understanding how "particular musical practices influence the social and political balance of the nation" and for supporting our own and others' psychosocial equilibration through the learning of multiple musical traditions.[3] Music educators and students may draw inspiration from Goble's assertions—indeed, his ideas may have assisted me in articulating the value of my Ghanaian musical experiences— but they are limiting because they foreground existing musical traditions while excluding or minimizing musical alteration, innovation, and hybridization.[4] Additionally, Goble's focus on relationships between musical endeavors and national sociopolitical realms may stifle attention to local and global musical spheres as well as interactions between them.[5]

In contrast with Goble's limited ascription of import, writers have explained music as "good for" an expansive range of purposes. For example, the authors of documents accompanying the American National Core Music Standards argue that the arts serve as: communication; creative personal realization; culture, history, and connectors; means to well-being; and community engagement.[6] While music educators and students may benefit from exploring and experimenting with these diverse purposes, the broadness of such lists may inhibit them from clearly articulating the significance of their work. Additionally, a vast range of purposes provides little insight into why teachers and students might decide to favor certain musical and pedagogical practices over others. Given these limitations, asking "What are music endeavors good for?" demands investigations expansive enough to encompass a wide range of contemporary music-making, yet narrow enough to inform both discourse and practice.

Positing music as good for one or more purposes, however, risks codifying and delimiting thinking and action. Although not denying divergent possibilities, asserting music as good for something inevitably minimizes attention to potential alternative functions. Yet, the absence of such positioning and its accompanying debates may dissuade music educators and students from examining the assumptions underlying their work, including those related to the Eurocentric proclamations of writers such as Scruton. Given this tension, I offer the following inquiry not as an answer but as a single, necessarily limited possibility; it serves not as a stable endpoint but as a variable middle from which additional wanderings might flourish.

Encounters with Deleuze's Artistic Philosophizing

Extending the work of pragmatist philosophers, I examine the question "What are musical endeavors good for?" My exploration burgeons from Gilles Deleuze and Félix Guattari's concept of the "refrain," which they relate directly to artistic function. Before engaging with this concept, I situate it within their writings about immanence.

Immanence

Similar to concepts such as a body without organs and smooth spaces, which I discussed in chapters 2 and 3, respectively, immanence involves the ongoing uncertain process of differing. However, unlike the other aforementioned concepts, immanence highlights ephemeral meetings and changing relations.

Immanance involves "only speeds and slowness between unformed elements, and affects between nonsubjectified powers."[7] For example, in my opening story, immanence might include the fluctuating interplay between my recollections of prior musical endeavors, the Ewe drumming permeating the evening air, and my developing understandings of Scruton's book. In those fleeting moments, these disparate qualities and experiences existed in a continually varying state of interconnection, altering each other in the process; my interpretation of the philosophy and appreciation of my previous music-making developed in and through the process.

Deleuze and Guattari contrast immanence with transcendence. Transcendence "organizes and develops forms (genres, themes, motifs) and assigns and develops subjects (personages, characters, feelings)."[8] Stated differently, transcendence involves distinct entities and planned systems, foregrounding boundaries and divisions rather than variable forces and ongoing motion. In transcendent relationships, ideas, things, or qualities exist ordered and complete; their interactions change neither their nature nor their hierarchical positions. I in part experienced transcendence as I solidified my categories and orderings of "classical music" and "Ewe drumming" as well as noticed differences between various Ewe performances. In such instances, I understood my experiences as bounded and separate from each other, rather than as existing in a state of changing interconnection.

Comparing immanence and transcendence, James Williams summarizes that while immanence designates "a relation 'in' something," transcendence references "a relation 'to' something."[9] "Relations in" involve varying, permeable flows, while "relations to" occur through comparisons of solidified entities. Focusing on the complex interplay of my changing self in interaction with Ghanaian musical traditions evoked immanent "relations in," but when I used Scruton's words to compare Western classical music and Ewe drumming, I created transcendent "relations to." In the latter instance, I tried to solidify the music, distinguishing it from my immediate circumstances in order to contrast it with another delimited set of ideas and practices.

Initially, it may seem as though value judgments distinguish immanence from transcendence, and indeed Deleuze and Guattari note that transcendence often implies aiming for specific ends.[10] Transcendence, however, also occurs through the categorizing absent value-laden language. For instance, the authors of music standards, curricula, and assessment documents often emphasize "relations to" without necessarily promoting a distinct hierarchy. They separate practices, such as listening, creating, and performing, and classes, such as music technology and ensembles, from each other and from other forms of musical engagement.[11] These practices and classes relate *to* each other rather than differ in integration *with* each other. Conversely, conceiving of listening, creating, and performing as connective, changing relations that blur preset boundaries between them would involve relations of immanence.

A multitude of "relations in" forms what Deleuze and Guattari term a "plane of immanence," which they directly associate with artistic endeavors.[12] By emphasizing divergent motion and flows, individual writers each lay out their own plane of immanence. Deleuze and Guattari contrast the plane of immanence laid out by novelist and poet Heinrich von Kleist with those of authors Johann Wolfgang von Goethe and Georg Friedrich Hegel. They explain that Kleist's use of "catatonic freezes and extreme velocities" differs from Goethe's and Hegel's emphases on "harmonious development of Form and a regulated formation of the Subject, personage, or character."[13] In short, Kleist's plane of immanence develops differently from those of Goethe and Hegel and cannot be subsumed by them.

Suggesting that the same holds true for musical planes of immanence, Deleuze and Guattari write: "When Boulez casts himself in the role of historian of music, he does so in order to show how a great musician, in a very different manner in each case, invents a kind of diagonal running between the harmonic vertical and the melodic horizon. And in each case it is a different diagonal, a different technique, a creation."[14] Stated differently, Jennifer Higdon creates one harmonic-melodic sound plane while Miles Davis forms another, and one cannot explain or evaluate Higdon's inventions in terms of Davis's and vice versa. While I problematize Deleuze and Guattari's use of terms such as "great musician" below, these statements exemplify their emphasis on artistic immanence—the relations within each composer's array of creations that make their practices unique—rather than transcendence—relating one composer to another or to a preset standard of greatness. However, this does not mean that a composer's plane of immanence exists in complete isolation.

In addition to the continually changing relations within a single plane of immanence, Deleuze and Guattari explain that individual planes of immanence transform as concepts flow between them and as they connect with problems and events.[15] Beyoncé's plane of immanence may alter as it integrates with those of rappers and country-music artists as well as with situations such as instances of racism and police brutality. During each encounter, different musicians and events do not just relate "to" each other but evolve "in" and through their engagements.

The Deleuzian Refrain

Through their concept of the "refrain," Deleuze and Guattari provide further insight into the relations within and between varying artistic planes of immanence. Although, like most of their concepts, the refrain defies clear definition, they tend to emphasize its territorializing nature. The refrain defines a territory by developing chaotic elements into organized "motifs and landscapes."[16] In other words, the refrain consists not of stagnation but of the temporary ordering of forces. Elizabeth Gould summarizes: "Like the chorus of a song (the return of familiar musical material), the Deleuzian refrain constitutes a moment of stability in chaos."[17] The chorus of a song has an order and predictability that, while not stationary, contrasts the variability of each verse.

Applying such thinking to music education, Gould explains that the Deleuzian refrain includes the sites to which music returns, including national anthems and other compositions serving specific purposes,[18] as well as "the territories of genre and stylistic practices and conventions on which music performances and compositions stabilize."[19] Similarly, she argues that music educators create territories through repeated pedagogies and curricula, including the concepts and performance skills that structure practice.[20] The refrain forms when music educators rely on preset processes and ends, closing off alternative possibilities and imaginings.

Although Deleuze and Guattari describe the refrain as "the block of content proper to music,"[21] they do not equate the refrain with "music" itself. Instead, they posit the refrain as a "problem" that music confronts,[22] explaining it as "a means of preventing music, warding it off, or forgoing it."[23] Returning to Gould's examples, while Deleuze and Guattari use terms like "melody" or "rhythm" to describe certain playings of scales, etudes, and common tunes,[24] because of their repetitive, territorialized nature, they would likely not deem them "music." Further understanding the refrain necessitates perceiving its territorializing function as but one of its interconnected processes.

At the broadest level, Deleuze and Guattari describe the refrain as having three simultaneous or mixing aspects: a center, a territory, and an opportunity for escape.[25] More specifically, they write that, like a black hole, a refrain possesses: (1) a stable central point; (2) a defined yet partly chaotic territory around that point; and (3) opportunities for exit.[26] Elizabeth Grosz reinterprets this explanation using the more familiar terminology of homes, yards, and ways out. She explains the three components of the refrain as: "First, a point of order or inside—a home, nest, or space of safety that filters out or keeps the forces of chaos temporarily at bay; . . . second, a circle of control that defines not only a safe inside but also a malleable or containable outside, and terrain to be marked, a field to be guarded; . . . third, a line of flight to the outside, a movement or migration, transformation, or deformation."[27] The refrain includes a stable home, a mostly predictable yard, and a gateway allowing for departures. As such, while the refrain consists of territorializing forces, it simultaneously reveals spaces for escape and deterritorialization.[28]

From these openings—the breakaway from the black hole or the way out of the yard—"Music takes up the refrain, lays hold of it . . . in order to take it somewhere else."²⁹ In escaping the refrain, music does not separate from the refrain but rather transforms the refrain through its unpredictable motion. Deleuze and Guattari explain, "Music is a creative, active operation that consists in deterritorializing the refrain."³⁰ Music not only resists the territorialization of the refrain, it appropriates the refrain's content in order to release it from existing limits. For example, at the micro level, a jazz improviser might free the notes in a given chord or scale from their circumscribed relations, perhaps deterritorializing the refrain of a dominant seventh chord through the addition of a sharp eleventh. The dominant seventh chord functions as a stable home while the sharp eleventh escapes its boundaries, transforming the dominant seventh chord in the process. More broadly, music occurs when individuals use notes, rhythms, and expressivity to defy the yard's preset forms and commonplace interpretations by experimenting with the previously unheard.

Despite this emphasis on breakaways from familiar yards, Deleuze and Guattari mirror their assertions about the constant transversal of striated and smooth spaces detailed in chapter 3 by articulating the interplay of territorializing and deterritorializing forces.³¹ Even for territorial motifs, "It is not one *or* the other, fixity or variability; certain motifs or points are fixed only if others are variable, or else they are fixed on one occasion and variable on another."³² Just as an escape cannot happen absent a bounded home or yard, deviation becomes apparent only when contrasted with predictability. Ordered key changes enable the improviser to create rupturing flows, and the predictability of many popular songs highlights the deterritorializations of innovators such as Kendrick Lamar.

While Deleuze and Guattari at times attribute a deterritorializing function only to specific types of musical engagement, elsewhere they explain that even a certain sequence of sounds has the potential to both territorialize and deterritorialize. Using the example of a Beethoven melody, they argue that despite its transformative potential, when used as a "signature tune," it can "develop its force into a sickly sweet ditty."³³ A Beethoven tune played at a public festival may deterritorialize participants by encouraging them to reflect on their humanity, but when adapted to underscore a tagline in a commercial, it might serve to territorialize listeners' preferences and economic decisions.³⁴ Deleuze and Guattari tend to use the refrain and its accompanying relations when addressing music in the abstract. However, through their Beethoven example, they suggest that the value of a given artistic endeavor may depend in part on its functions within a specific context.

To illustrate this point further, take my experiences at a jazz club in New Orleans. The musicians began with the territorialized refrains of well-known tunes. Yet, they soon found open gateways enabled by extended solos and their interactions with each other and the audience. The piano player transitioned from a stride bass style into quotations from Liszt's *Hungarian Rhapsody No. 2 in C-sharp minor*, while the trumpet player held up an extra cowbell for the drummer to use in his improvisations. The audience responded at various points with clapping, singing along, calls for "more cowbell!" and requests for "When the Saints Go Marching In," to which the musicians eventually responded. While the same tunes played in a different context might have served a primarily territorializing function, the night transformed the boundaries I had previously used to delimit jazz and possible audience-performer interactions.

Moreover, Deleuze and Guattari hint that, just as music deterritorializes the refrain, musical practices can challenge solidified ways of being.[35] John Rajchman summarizes that for Deleuze, "[Artworks] are not there to save us or to perfect us (or to damn or corrupt us), but rather to complicate things, to create more complex nervous systems no longer subservient to the debilitating effects of clichés, to show and release the possibilities of a life."[36] For example, music-making that protests injustices or coheres marginalized communities deterritorializes the refrain of soundscapes celebrating the status quo. Those who use musical experiences to flee territorialized assumptions and habits may return to their everyday encounters with transformed perspectives and practices. Through this continual escaping and returning, the Deleuzian refrain emphasizes the fleeting nature of one's current musical home.

What Is Music-making Good For?

While not necessarily converging on a single response, Deleuze's writings suggest that musical endeavors are in large part "good for" the challenging and reimagining of territorialized ways of being. Such rationale already guides some current musical experiences, including educative ones. Gould provides the example of engaging with the historiographies and associated musics of slaves who deterritorialized African work songs and reterritorialized them to express their experiences of forced labor. She asserts that such action exceeds "received narratives of slavery, resistance, and oppression."[37] When teachers and students look for moments of rupture in well-worn, one-sided stories and focus on the differing relations within or between specific musical genres and practices, they deterritorialize the experiences that have constituted the refrain of music education.

Despite these deviations, transcendent relations and the process of territorialization continue to hold a central place in contemporary music education practices. Teachers plot out the territories of standardized curricula, bounded assessments, and repeated performance practices, and they rely on "accepted" repertoire, classes, pedagogical methods, and audience-performer interactions. Gould summarizes, "Delineating these territories for students is what music educators 'do.'"[38]

More subtly, even philosophers who have deterritorialized then-current music education practices by challenging limited understandings about content and pedagogy have a tendency to propagate transcendent "relations to" while neglecting immanent "relations in." Estelle Jorgensen, for instance, posits a "dialectical view," in which she uses pairs of terms to pose "questions and challenges" that music educators can adapt in light of specific situations.[39] These dialectical relations include experiences such as "making" and "receiving," "pleasure" and "understanding."[40] Describing each term in great detail, Jorgensen clearly distinguishes it from its partner experience. Similarly, Bennett Reimer proposes a "synergistic approach" between understanding music as form, as practice, and as social agency.[41] Through this synergism, he suggests that educators "recognize sufficient overlaps among seemingly contending views to allow a more inclusive position to be attained."[42]

While neither Jorgensen nor Reimer asserts one experience or understanding as necessarily superior to the others, their delimitation of terms such as making and receiving or form and practice emphasizes relations to. The positioning of these various ideas draws attention to how they differ from each other—even in moments of overlap—rather than how they might integrate and evolve over time. Each concept becomes a territory, a yard one may traverse or even redraw, but not escape.

Drawing on Jacques Derrida's work, Patrick Schmidt makes a similar point. He argues that because dialectical frameworks foreground synthesis, they "do not account for or value the surpluses, differences, and ramifications generated by actions, interactions or texts."[43] What happens when neither making, receiving, nor a synthesis of the two encapsulates the totality of one's musical experiences? How does focusing on making alter and perhaps delimit one's understandings of what receiving is and could be, and vice versa?

In contrast, emphasizing immanent relations in involves looking for fluidity between such concepts as well as attending to their ongoing diversifying. Practice does not just "overlap" with social agency but continually alters in interaction with it and with other ideas and problems. Deterritorializing music and music education also involves asking what such labels exclude and how emphasizing specific categories might inhibit previously unimagined variability.

In making these observations, I am not asserting that transcendent relations and territorialization should play no role in music teaching and learning. As Deleuze and Guattari note, a territory "not only ensures and regulates the coexistence of members of the same species by keeping them apart, but makes possible the coexistence of a maximum number of different species in the same milieu by specializing them."[44] Since divisions ensure the continuation of certain differences, absent labels such as creating, performing, pleasure, and understanding, music educators might undertake deterritorialized music-making that unthoughtfully propagates a limited array of aims and practices, thus concurrently inciting reterritorialization. Yet, because transcendent territorialized relations remain the norm in music education, music educators and students might benefit from imagining the possibility of immanent, deterritorialized relations. Prior to exploring such action, I attend to the problems of Deleuze's artistic writings.

Limitations

One pervasive limitation is the favoring of Western art music over other forms of musical engagement. Deleuze and Guattari draw extensively on the Western musical canon, referencing the work of Beethoven, Debussy, and Schumann, as well as on then-contemporary composers, including Boulez, Cage, Messiaen, and Varèse, but they rarely acknowledge any other musical practices. When they do briefly mention "folk and popular" songs, including lullabies and drinking, work, and military songs, they explain them as refrains, implying that they cannot perform the deterritorializing function indicative of "music."[45] Likewise, they directly distinguish children's songs from music, writing, "Animal and child refrains seem to be territorial: therefore they are not 'music.'"[46] Without further explanation, why folk, popular, and children's songs cannot incite the deterritorialization indicative of music remains unclear. More troublingly, by deeming certain practices as territorial absent attention to their function, Deleuze and Guattari imply stagnant forms of being, contradicting their own emphasis on becoming.

A related problem is that Deleuze and Guattari almost exclusively address completed works of art, largely omitting artistic processes. There are some rare exceptions; for instance, they note that a Chopin rubato will occur differently with each playing.[47] However, such statements still emphasize musical products—in this case a Chopin piece—while neglecting music-making absent such boundaries. Although Deleuze and Guattari's writings do not preclude the possibility that music performers, listeners, DJs, or others could create their own planes of immanence, their singular focus on completed artworks may dissuade readers from attending to such potentialities.

Gould, however, provides an extension of Deleuze's writings about the refrain that takes into account diverse artistic practices and does not limit deterritorialization to those with specialized training.[48] In agreement with Gould, I propose an expansion of Deleuze's writings that neither limits music to specific genres or musical practices nor excludes the engagement of children and other individuals. Such a conception highlights how artistic practices vary in integration with the world rather than the persistent qualities of solidified creations.

Another limiting aspect of Deleuze's artistic philosophizing is his neglect of human embodiment. He and Guattari write as though humans' minds could create and evaluate music absent one's individual embodied experiences.

Additionally, they overtly minimize the role of emotions in artistic experiences, positing prepersonal, autonomous "affects"—which they directly distinguish from an individual's "feelings"—as one of the forces constituting a "work of art."[49] While Deleuze and Guattari hint at the role emotions and feelings may play in music creation, at one point noting that sadness can "become sonorous,"[50] they provide no further insight about such possible relationships.[51]

Despite this lack of attention, Grosz interprets Deleuze and Guattari's statements about artistic deterritorializations as implicating humans' bodies. She writes that in breaking from the refrain, "Music opens up and transforms us, making of both our bodies and of the earth itself a new site of becomings."[52] Likewise, building on Deleuze and Guattari's work, Gould asserts that deterritorializing the refrain includes "emotional dimensions."[53] Drawing on Grosz and Gould, I posit an extension of Deleuze's writings about immanence and deterritorialization that emphasizes the embodied-emotional aspects of artistic experiences.

A related, potentially problematic aspect of Deleuze's artistic philosophy involves the role of meaning-making. While Deleuze articulates possible relationships between artistic endeavors and other aspects of everyday experience, by omitting how humans do and might endow such events with significance, his philosophizing risks becoming an intellectual exercise disconnected from evolving emotional-embodied-social experiences of music-making. Using Deleuze's work to propose more active and connective music education practices, David Lines notes in passing the problematic effects of teaching and learning focused on "'excellence' at the expense of 'significance.'"[54] Building on Lines' thinking, I integrate Deleuze's writings about immanence and deterritorialization with the meaning-laden process of forming musical connections.

Connecting figures prominently into Deleuze and Guattari's concept of the rhizome. Articulating the first of six principles of the rhizome, they write: "Any point of a rhizome can be connected to anything other, and must be."[55] Just as a botanical rhizome will connect with anything—be it plant or plastic—that surrounds it, rhizomatic musical practices involve forming connections within and across categories, structures, people, and places.[56]

While the rhizome in part inspired my interest in the process of connecting, its abstract nature parallels that of the refrain and deterritorialzion. Deleuze and Guattari detail how the rhizome functions while omitting how diverse individuals might make meaning out of such happenings. Given this serious limitation, I abandon Deleuze and Guattari's rhizomatic connectivity, instead using the term "connection" as it relates to humans' social-embodied-emotional experiences.

In common usage, the word connection implies a meaning-laden process that humans generally deem important. Brené Brown explains, "Connection is the energy that is created between people when they feel seen, heard, and valued."⁵⁷ In artistic endeavors, I offer that in addition to occurring between participants, this energy can form between a single person and a musical process, product, or other event. By using music-making to connect with parts of their selves that may often lay hidden, individuals can feel valued—or can come to value themselves—even when making music alone.

George Lakoff and Mark Johnson's work provides insight into why diverse individuals might deem connective experiences significant. They argue that the abstract idea of connection derives from humans' embodied experiences.⁵⁸ For example, babies need physical connections with caregivers in order to develop, and those of all ages need social connections in order to survive.⁵⁹ Connective experiences have contributed to humans' well-being over time and across cultures.

This does not mean that disconnection never holds value or that all connections are ethical. Yet, Lakoff and Johnson's work highlights why humans in diverse places tend to perceive connective experiences as important. In contrast with the abstract process of deterritorializing, connecting emphasizes the meaning-laden nature of music-making endeavors.

Good for Connecting

Forever limited by our distinct bodies and yet conjoined in our common humanity, I suggest that humans' music-making often stems from a desire to connect. Stated differently, music-making is and might be "good for" forming connections, both to ourselves and to our multiple environments. I traveled to Ghana because I sought a sense of connection to music makers outside of the traditions I already knew and to the curious and expressive parts of myself that my music-making up until that point had left unexplored. Likewise, individuals may join musical groups, attend musical events, and engage in solo musical endeavors in order to experience the connectivity with aspects of themselves and others that such endeavors can foster.

Connecting can involve deterritorializing as well as the territorializing, transcendent relations to as well as immanent relations in. Students can form meaningful, changing connections that challenge existing undertakings and habits as well as meaningful, relatively stagnant connections that reinforce preset boundaries and aims. To illuminate further these important differences, I draw on Deleuze and Guattari's assertions about transcendence and immanence in order to distinguish between what I term "connecting to" and "connecting with."⁶⁰

Connecting to and Connecting With

"Connecting to" implies the meeting of largely stagnant entities indicative of transcendent relations and territorialization. Just as connecting an interlocking block to other blocks forms a new territory within physical space, connecting to another individual during a musical endeavor involves reinforcing existing identities and focusing on the resultant outcomes of the engagement. For example, I might connect to another singer as I interpret my preformed emotional portrayal of a musical line as syncing with theirs, forming a sound "superior" to that of our last attempt. In such instances, I perceive my own identity, conception of "music," and musical values as remaining essentially unchanged.

In contrast, "connecting with" involves relations of immanence and the process of deterritorialization, in which individuals alter in and through their meeting. Such interactions trouble preset boundaries, including definitions of self and musical understandings. Perhaps when hearing another instrumentalist perform a musical phrase, I experience myself connecting with differing understandings of their emotions or of my own evolving expressive potential. I am no longer a delimited self but rather interacting flows. In such instances, meaning and value reside primarily in the connective relations themselves, rather than in a resultant system, divide, or hierarchy. Similarly, recall the practices of becoming-nomad and becoming-bodies-without-organs from chapters 2 and 3, respectively. Since becoming-other involves deterritorialization, when deemed meaningful by those engaging in them, such experiences involve connecting with.

Few musical engagements involve solely connecting to or connecting with, and it is possible to experience both at the same time. For instance, while engaged in Ewe drumming, I might focus on mimicking the master drummer's tone quality (connecting to) and simultaneously become aware of my changing self and musical understandings (connecting with). Additionally, there exists no clear, quantifiable divide between connecting to and connecting with, and such designations always depend on one's time, place, and prior experiences. While one musician may conceive of themselves as connecting to another, focusing on a specific distinction or goal, the latter musician could experience the same event as connecting with by attending to how they differ through the process. In such moments, the second person would also resist stagnant terms such as "musician," sensing themselves not as an individual entity but as change and difference.

Examples of Musical Connecting

While not prominent in music-education discourse, the practice of connecting—although not necessarily connecting with—has received marked attention. In the "Philosophical Foundations and Lifelong Goals" section of the framework accompanying the 2014 American National Core Arts Standards, the authors use "The Arts as Culture, History, and Connectors" as one of five headings.[61] Their subsequent explanation suggests both immanent connections formed by "integrating meaning across a variety of content areas" and transcendent connections created by cultivating "habits of searching for and identifying patterns, relationships between the arts and other knowledge."[62] In the former, the arts serve to set connective relations into motion (connecting with), while in the latter, connections form between distinct entities (connecting to).

Music-education philosophers have also indirectly addressed possibilities of connecting with. Describing an event involving participants from diverse religious and musical backgrounds, June Boyce-Tillman writes, "The interconnections in the central section of Space for Peace were intense and as the piece moved forward participants became more skilled at creating complex interrelationships."[63] Boyce-Tillman's explanation of evolving relations that resisted preformed trajectories suggests an emphasis on immanence rather than transcendence. Since the participants' changing interplay of experiences was immanent only to itself, the event might have fostered the attention to personal and interpersonal differing indicative of connecting with.

More specifically, Estelle Jorgensen and Iris Yob assert a link between Deleuze's ideas and Jorgensen's metaphor of music teaching and learning as like a web and connectivity.[64] While Jorgensen focuses this "picture" of music education on physical and technological connections, including those made possible by the internet, she acknowledges the potential of musical connectivity based on individual curiosities, explaining, "Students in the connectivity model are liberated to follow their own interests and talents."[65] Jorgensen elaborates that the interconnectivity of contemporary societies enables possibilities for "individually tailored programs of study" that learners construct in relation with their prior experiences.[66] Since such teaching and learning enables unique wanderings adaptable for diverse students, it implies the favoring of variable connecting with over connecting to preset musical practices and goals. Jorgensen's remaining discussion, however, highlights the conceivable benefits and problems of connectivity as a means of music instruction rather than as a purpose of music education.

More similar to my conception of connecting with is what Gould terms "performative literacy." Drawing directly on Deleuze's writings, Gould explains performative literacy as a "music education of connections," elaborating that it includes "all configurations involving students, teachers, musics, schools, and communities—in terms of desire."[67] Gould's emphasis on "musical and educational relationships, interactions, and ethics in shifting relations" aligns with the immanent aspects of connecting with.[68] Yet, my proposed practice of connecting with diverges from Gould's assertions about performative literacy in three important ways.

First, Gould provides desire a central role in performative literary, clarifying that desire does not involve fulfilling a need or come from a position of lack, but rather serves as a productive "positive possibility."[69] While I concur that desire can incite the forming of musical connections with, such experiences can also occur in integration with individual and group needs and wants. For example, students may feel an emptiness that they address by musically connecting with their emotions, or they may find that musically connecting with peers or those of different ages fulfills a part of their sociality that feels lacking absent such encounters.

Second, Gould focuses on the need to break with musical and educational norms, seeking "moments and spaces of resistance and revolution."[70] Teachers and students may experience connecting with through such events, which align closely with Deleuze's provocative philosophical project, but they can also foster connecting with through more subtle forms of deterritorialization. Imagine two students who compose and then perform a vocal duet. They may connect with each other and their classmates as their self-understandings change in and through their musical engagements. Such events may deterritorialize students' music-making without necessarily confronting resistance or inciting revolution.

Finally, if music educators and students share a concern for making their work viable in the sociopolitical sphere, then their terminology should resonate with various stakeholders. Since Gould writes that she created performative literacy as "a site in and through which music subject positions may be claimed," she did not necessarily select her language with political stakeholders in mind.[71] However, how music educators form their practices within the profession inevitably informs their discourse with other stakeholders.

The term performative literacy is troubling because music educators and policymakers often use the word "literacy" in conjunction with Western notation and terminology; for example, "artistic literacy" appears throughout the Eurocentric framework accompanying the 2014 American National Core Arts Standards.[72] Touting the possibilities of performative literacy within and beyond the music education community may have the problematic effects of minimizing or excluding music-education practices not reliant on Western notation or of encouraging the colonization of such music-making through it. Additionally, because education leaders often value music literacy far less than language literacy, such terminology may encourage them to relegate music education, rather than to explore its other aspects and potential purposes.

Given Lakoff and Johnson's assertions about the common and generally positively understood human embodied experience of connection, the term "connecting with" might serve as both a philosophical position and a meaningful way of communicating with various stakeholders. In other words, in asserting that musically educative endeavors are good for connecting with, I offer that this purpose could inform both the profession's practices and its discourse at large.

Music-making, however, is but one of many ways in which humans can connect with themselves and others, and such events are neither stagnant nor standardized. While sociocultural webs influence one's musical meaning-making, to expect that all individuals, even within a certain social group, will experience a sense of musical connection during a specific event neglects each person's unique past, present, and potential future experiences. Further investigating how connecting with might influence music teaching and learning demands attention to individuals' narratives as well as to their narrative construction processes.

Narratives of Connecting With

Since humans' narratives exist in a state of constant flux, what a given student finds meaningful on one day may not hold the same value at subsequent times. Likewise, a teacher cannot guarantee that students who do not find composing a hip-hop song, improvising, or listening to a piece by Caroline Shaw connective in one moment will never value such experiences. Humans' continually changing narratives mean that experiences of musically connecting with integrate with and in part constitute individuals' evolving senses of self. This idea echoes Randall Allsup's statement: "We are simultaneously made and remade by the music we make."[73]

In addition to involving immediate meaning-making, musically connecting with ourselves and others informs what one subsequently finds meaningful. The student who experiences a sense of connection through a mariachi performance or music-composition project cannot help but bring that meaning-making to future musical experiences. As such, teachers can experiment with content and practices that, while perhaps not fostering an immediate sense of connection, students may later deem meaningful. Rather than asking "*What* experiences might facilitate musical connecting with?" music educators sensitive to their own and students' changing narratives might question "*When* might certain experiences facilitate musical connecting with?"

While connecting to and connecting with may explain why people often engage in musical endeavors, emphasizing the deterritorializing aspect of connecting with encourages individuals to welcome deviations to their existing narratives. Such action aligns with the reflective practices often foregrounded by those asserting humans' narrative construction of reality. Kevin Bradt explains, "Knowledge through story-based epistemology asks us ... to examine the *a priori* categories used to defend the prevailing dominant versions of social reality as if they were the *only* ones imaginable."[74] Narratives situate one's self within past experiences and a historical-cultural milieu, but their unfinished nature provides grounds for diverse departures and unexpected wandering. When teachers and students let go of their preconceptions in favor of imaginative physical, social, and emotional differing, they foster narratives that connect with relations rather than identities.

Gould specifically hints at what such a potentiality-driven music education might include: "[A perfomative literacy] curriculum focuses on local musics and people in social and educational contexts, using pedagogical approaches that not only account for difference but are inhered in and as difference as they elide power relations characteristic of the teacher/student dyad, enabling teaching and learning among people and in places as appropriate and necessary within and (often) with-out schools and schooling. Pedagogy, then, occurs everywhere and is understood in an expansive materialist, feminist sense."[75] While these ideas provide important inspiration, Gould does not offer further elaboration, perhaps in part because doing so would constrain applications of her philosophizing. Similarly, Lines briefly notes the possibilities of art responsive to the "resonances of daily life in communities," including critical reflections on local, national and global cultures.[76]

Building on Gould's and Lines's work, I posit that, growing from their unfinished individual narratives, students and teachers might form musical connections within three planes of immanence: self, local, and global. In naming these different planes, I acknowledge that I have demarcated and territorialized musical endeavors; although such action does not preclude other relations in, it inevitably emphasizes these named relations while temporarily minimizing attention to unnamed ones. Not naming any planes of immanence, however, can encourage teachers and students to propagate existing practices, missing opportunities for diverse, perhaps previously unimagined wanderings.[77] Given this tension, I posit these three planes of immanence not as a solidified framework but as a fluid middle ripe for extension, adaptation, and experimentation. While I now explore potential evolving relationships within each plane of immanence, since Deleuze asserts that concepts move between planes and that planes continually intersect and morph, these connections need not remain isolated from each other or from other planes, problems, and experiences.

Musically Connecting with Self and Places

Drawing on the conception of humans explained in chapter 2, in the self plane of immanence, individuals can use music to connect with their different, differing qualities, including cognition, emotion, embodiment, and sociality. While individuals might perceive musical connections as forming *to* a stable self, conceiving of humans as multiplicities involves understanding connections as occurring *with* one's continually changing qualities.

As noted in chapter 2, Deleuze and Guattari write that "heterogeneous terms in symbiosis" constitute multiplicities.[78] Since embodiment, cognition, sociality, and emotion function in ongoing integration, humans can never connect with one absent the other three. Yet, working within such awareness, teachers and students can primarily focus on the differing of a single quality.

Connecting with one or more of humans' integrated qualities necessitates not only that humans attend to those qualities, but that they make meaning out of such action. While a teacher might complicate a student's understandings by, for instance, asking the student to focus on their emotions while creating music, the student will only experience a sense of connection if they find significance in such action. Since meaning derives from students' narratives, teachers necessarily take those stories into account when making decisions about content and pedagogy.

For example, in addition to asking students to attend to their changing emotions while making or listening to certain music, a teacher might encourage them to reflect on and experiment with how their emotions relate to their lives outside of the classroom, including what they might take away from such experiences. Students could explore how connecting with the collective musical joy of their classmates alters how they understand the music their peers, parents, or others like, or how they might express joy through nonmusical endeavors. The continually differing experiences of "joy" and "joyful multiplicity" become more central than divides between joy and other emotions or divergent conceptions of joy. In such instances, music-making does not involve what Susanne Langer would call the "unambiguous" communication of forms of feeling,[79] but rather the intermixing of musical-emotional experiences and humans' changing self-stories.

As detailed in chapter 3, Deleuze and Guattari explain bounded, sedentary locations as "striated spaces" and mobile, heterogeneous locations teeming with variable free action as "smooth spaces." Both smooth spaces and the ongoing integration of smoothing and striation emphasize variable relations in. Rather than connecting to a place striated by stagnant meanings, connecting with involves human multiplicities who alter in and through the evolving meanings they ascribe to their surroundings. Musical connecting with can occur within and between local and global planes of immanence.

The local plane of immanence includes one's immediate teaching and learning environments as well as places in close geographic proximity to teachers and students. In this plane, musical connecting with might involve students whose narratives about the places of—and their places within—music classes or neighborhoods differ through experiences such as sharing compositions, performing with increased expressivity and technical facility, or planning a community-wide musical event. More broadly, students might experience a sense of connection with members of their local community by learning about what forms of music-making unites and divides them, or by collaboratively creating or performing music with them. Such action recalls Christopher Small's assertions about musical endeavors having the capacity to affirm one's community membership—in which groups say, "This is who we are"—as well as to serve as acts of exploration—in which individuals and groups "try on identities to see who we think we are."[80]

Extending Small's ideas, including his attention to the individual and collective construction of meaning, students and educators inspired by Deleuze's work might ask: What musical connecting with incites divergent imaginings of who we might become? In what ways might we ascribe value to that becoming? For instance, students and teachers might question how musical events could illuminate the problems of our current "we," including its omissions and troubling ethical assumptions. Such investigations necessitate treating one's own and others' narratives as variable, incomplete, and open to the unsettlement demanded by connecting with.

Looking beyond one's everyday surroundings, Deleuze and Guattari hint at the relationship between artistic endeavors and a global plane of immanence. They explain that a musical plane of composition "carries a kind of *deframing* following lines of flight that pass through the territory only in order to open it onto the universe, that go from house-territory to town-cosmos."[81] The global plane of immanence forms not when teachers, students, and others capture the foreign and bring it inward, but when they wander nomadically outward, becoming foreign to themselves in the process.[82] Applying such thinking to narratives of connecting with involves embracing the variations in musical meaning-making that individuals bring to cross-cultural meetings as well as the diverse narrative alterations that arise through their interactions.

Educators and students can value these diverging connections in their own right rather than subsuming them under existing systems or norms. For instance, I regret that during my Ghanaian travels I often lacked an awareness of my own meaning-making process. I viewed my drumming teachers as having knowledge and skills that I wanted to learn, and at times I idolized how the entire village gathered around and participated in musical engagements. Yet, I rarely considered that my developing understandings interfaced with and, in turn, altered my own narrative; I was not just learning new musical practices but breaking down preconceptions about what it meant to be and become musical and to live a musical life.

Additionally, I neglected to recognize that my very presence altered the stories of those with whom I interacted. By not attending to my own and others' narratives, I missed both potentially rich reflective experiences and possibilities for deeper, mutually engaging exchanges. I wish that I would have considered how I might have connected with my teachers and other community members in ways that they found meaningful for their own changing narratives. For instance, when a drumming teacher asked me a question about the trumpet and classical music, I gave a curt response and steered the conversation back toward his culture. I regret that I did not inquire further about what meaning he attributed to Western music and what else he wanted to know.

In short, in addition to troubling my desire to adopt new musical practices, I might have reconceived of my drumming education as a multidirectional endeavor that integrated with others' stories as much as it did with my own. Even within this text, my narratives extend largely from my own limited American-centric experiences. My global connecting with, not only musically but in terms of philosophical dialogue, educational practices, and ways of being in the world, demands further development.

Musically Connecting With . . . With . . . With . . .

In considering how these three planes of immanence might intersect, overlap, and even meld, imagine two classes in different locations who share concerns about the social or economic problems in their immediate communities. Subsequently, they might connect with each other by composing or performing music aimed at interrogating the way a specific issue—say various forms of discrimination—affects their individual communities, in the process attending to alterations in their integrated cognition, embodiment, emotions, and sociality. Perhaps they also trade news articles and personal stories, exploring how the local manifestations of their problems interplay with globalized practices. Eventually, the groups might further connect musically by creating a joint composition or performance in response to their inquiries, at various points reflecting on how their personal narratives evolve over the course of the project.

This emphasis on connecting within and across the global, self, and local planes of immanence contrasts the long-standing philosophical centering of different types of musical practices, including divisions between musical genres or styles and between forms of engagement such as creating, performing, and listening.[83] While such distinctions may inform and function in integration with attention to connecting with, highlighting connecting with involves musical and pedagogical deliberations that derive from considerations about the evolving connections such actions enable. In other words, rather than beginning from standards or preset goals, aims and paths develop and alter in integration with imaginings of and reflections on possible meaningful local, global, and self connections.

In addition to attending to how teachers and students might make meaning out of musical events in the moment, connecting with highlights how current musical engagements interface with individuals' past and potential future narratives.[84] For instance, a teacher working with students who seek admission into selective traditional schools of music should take their aspirations into account when debating the formation of various musical connections; in such situations, global and local connecting with might involve—although not rely solely upon—engaging with students, faculty, and graduates of such institutions. Conversely, teachers might take seriously students who envision their potential future narratives as leading toward membership in fiddle groups, rock bands, classical music audiences, or online music composition communities.

This does not mean that music educators should not aim to expand the depth and breadth of musical connecting with that students value. Attention to students' interests and curiosities does not mean neglecting all other possibilities; doing so would form a territorialized yard without an escape. However, while teachers can assist students in reimagining their past experiences and thinking creatively about their futures, such understandings grow from and evolve in integration with students' current narratives and meaning-making. Potentialities necessarily extend from, and at times flee, meaning-laden contexts.

Yet, while some might keep one eye to the past and the other to the future, Deleuzian-inspired educators and students trouble the stagnation of "past" and "future." They instead favor visions that wander among the uncertainty of "now" and "could be." By focusing not on labels and limits but on the productive potential of "with," differing ways out transform musical yards and homes.

Limitations and (Re)considerations

One possible problem of music-making being good for connecting with is that if teachers and students repeat their connections over time, they may territorialize their practices. While the connections themselves may still form a plane of immanence, even changing connections can demarcate a territory. For example, if a music maker primarily connects with their emotions by listening to the same song day after day, even though the connections may form uniquely and evolve moment to moment, the predictable practices territorialize the music maker's self and environments. Likewise, if the aforementioned teachers who engage in music-making centered on countering forms of discrimination undertake the same actions year after year, while the students and specific connective relations may vary, they have territorialized their curricula and pedagogies. Although such actions may be good for other purposes, because they limit imaginative potentialities, they inhibit the deterritorialization essential to Deleuze's artistic philosophizing.

Returning to an understanding of the Deleuzian refrain as necessitating three parts—a home, a yard, and a way out—provides a means of conceptualizing connecting with that acknowledges current practices while resisting complacency. Take the example of a cellist engaging with Bach's *Cello Suite No. 1 in G major*. The musician might territorialize a home and yard by learning the notated rhythms and pitches and by imitating the stylistic interpretations of other performers, perhaps connecting with their emotions and embodiment through the process. While the newness of this connecting with may already serve as a step out of the yard, the cellist might consider further escapes by reimagining the directionality of individual notes or phrases through newly discovered historical or theoretical understandings. They might also experiment with escapes fostered by uniquely responding to the embodied, contextual-specific possibilities of each passing musical moment, or by thinking creatively about how and where they might perform the piece. Similarly, teachers retaining what they may have initially considered innovative pedagogy and curricula might do so with an eye toward possible moments of departure. Even minor openings in one's gated perimeter can serve as a counter to the systemic regulation of educative practices prevalent in contemporary societies.

Deleuze, however, would likely emphasize more substantial forms of deterritorialization. A Deleuzian-inspired cellist may question the proportion of time spent playing Bach versus pieces by or responding to those from marginalized groups. The cellist might ask questions such as: Why ever perform in concert halls? How does the label "cellist" limit my and others' potential musical and educative narratives? This might lead to the formation of groups that include virtual, folk, or non-Western instruments, or events that involve attendees in music creation and performance.

A related problem is that connecting with can devolve into chaotic situations that inhibit further connections. Consider a class of students engaged in electronic composition. If the students spend day after day laughing at random sounds or thoughtlessly adding and deleting preset loops, then they may create a territory too unstable for a way out. Without some eventual guidance and constraints, students may not have enough musical ground from which to wander. In integration with sites of escape, connecting with necessitates developing the skills, knowledge, and experiences needed to form diverse territories. Students who begin by composing within a certain form and then look for possible points of rupture, or those who compose freely and then seek similarities and differences between their practices and existing forms navigate a liminal space, simultaneously territorializing and deterritorializing.[85] Just as music relies on the refrain as content for its deterritorializations, connecting with demands bounded yards of refined musical understandings and techniques as much as it does points of exit.

Another potential problem of music-making being good for connecting with is that aiming for connectivity can hide serious ethical problems; deeming something "good for" is not the same as finding it "good" in the ethical sense. Deborah Bradley reveals how feelings of connection and communal joy during potent musical experiences can hide the "seeds of fascism."[86] Writing about a performance of the Missisauga Festival Youth Choir at a Prison Fellowship Convocation, she describes the energy aroused when the South African delegates, many imprisoned during the apartheid era, spontaneously danced upon finding deep personal meaning in one of the choir's songs.[87] Choir members later recalled those moments as some of their most meaningful musical experiences. Yet, Bradley problematizes the lack of critical thinking surrounding the event, summarizing, "The feelings arising from being included in a collective 'we' are so powerful... feel so good and so unconditional, that we seek to replicate those experiences without thought to their potential outcomes."[88]

While humans' earliest life experiences generally lead them to value connection over disconnection, Bradley's example suggests the possible ethical nature of music-making that fosters disconnection. If the Prison Fellowship Convocation had included a jarring musical composition, perhaps revealing the perspectives of crime victims or prison guards, might participants have experienced a sense of disconnection that encouraged them to question their complicity in an uncritical celebration of freedom? Likewise, take, for example, Ted Hearne's composition *Privilege*, which focuses on the advantages and disadvantages endowed to certain members of twenty-first-century societies. Such musical experiences may cause participants to feel disconnected from their selves and local and global places as they reflect on the inequalities to which they may contribute and from which they may benefit.

Individuals may deem such disconnections important in and of themselves, and they may also facilitate the formation of previously unimagined connecting with. For instance, while participating in *Privilege* may temporarily provoke individuals to experience disconnection, by imagining how they might work against unjust systems, teachers and students may eventually form creative musical connections inspired by initially unsettling endeavors. Conceiving of disconnection not as a permanent state but as a part of ongoing deterritorializing and territorializing processes can enable new connecting with that resists the isolation and hopelessness accompanying sustained disconnection.

Yet, one can still imagine situations in which both connection and disconnection obfuscate and propagate unethical thinking and action. Given that connecting with does not provide a means for evaluating the ethical quality of musical practices, teachers and students might engage in the practice of "considering," detailed in chapters 4 and 5, alongside their deliberations about musically educative connections. Considering musical connections by imagining them from multiple cognitive, embodied, emotional perspectives—including not only those that currently exist but those that might exist—and subsequently judging their ethical implications can assist teachers and students in fostering more ethical musical connections. By integrating ethical considerations with the formation of diverse musical connecting with, teachers and students challenge systems aimed at reducing them to cogs in amoral and often immoral global and local economic practices.

A final limitation of music-making being good for connecting with is that this position makes no claim about the educative nature of such experiences. Are all musical connections educative? If not, what makes certain connective experiences educative? What distinguishes variations in the quality of one's musically educative experiences? These questions prompt our continued journeying.

Notes

1. Wayne Bowman, "Music Education in Nihilistic Times," *Educational Philosophy and Theory* 37, no. 1 (2005): 29–46.
2. Ibid., 41.
3. J. Scott Goble, *What's So Important about Music Education?* (New York: Routledge, 2010), 264.
4. This problem is not unique to Goble's work. For example, Allsup makes a similar critique of Elliott and Silverman's philosophy of music education. Randall Allsup, *Remixing the Classroom: Toward an Open Philosophy of Music Education* (Bloomington: Indiana University Press, 2016), 82.
5. For a balanced perspective on the book, including additional related critiques, see Leonard Tan, "Book Review," *Philosophy of Music Education Review* 19, no. 2 (2011): 201–205. I selected Goble's book as an example because the question "What are musical endeavors good for?" figures centrally into his inquiry. Many other philosophers also assert or at minimum imply responses to this question. See, for example, David J. Elliott and Marissa Silverman, *Music Matters: A Philosophy of Music Education*, 2nd ed. (New York: Oxford University Press, 2015); Bennett Reimer, *A Philosophy of Music Education: Advancing the Vision*, 3rd ed. (Upper Saddle River, NJ: Prentice Hall, 2003); and Paul Woodford, *Democracy and Music Education: Liberalism, Ethics, and the Politics of Practice* (Bloomington: Indiana University Press, 2005).
6. State Education Agency Directors of Arts Education, "National Core Arts Standards: A Conceptual Framework for Arts Learning," last updated July 21, 2016, https://www.nationalartsstandards.org/sites/default/files/Conceptual%20Framework%2007-21-16.pdf#, 10.
7. Gilles Deleuze and Félix Guattari, *A Thousand Plateaus: Capitalism and Schizophrenia*, trans. Brian Massumi (Minneapolis: University of Minnesota Press, 1987), 267.
8. Ibid.
9. James Williams, *Understanding Poststructuralism* (Chesham, UK: Acumen, 2005), 126.
10. Deleuze and Guattari, *A Thousand Plateaus*, 265.
11. See, for example, the National Core Music Standards and Model Cornerstone Assessments. State Education Agency Directors of Arts Education, "National Core Arts Standards," 2014, http://nationalartsstandards.org/; National Association for Music Education, "Student Assessment Using Model Cornerstone Assessments," accessed September 6, 2019, https://nafme.org/my-classroom/standards/mcas/.
12. Gilles Deleuze and Félix Guattari, *What Is Philosophy?* Trans. Hugh Tomlinson and Graham Burchell (New York: Columbia University Press, 1994). While Deleuze and Guattari use both the terms "plane of consistency" and "plane of immanence" to refer to the same idea in their earlier writings, they favor "plane of immanence" in their later work.
13. Deleuze and Guattari, *A Thousand Plateaus*, 268.
14. Ibid., 296.
15. Deleuze and Guattari, *What Is Philosophy*, 18.

16. Deleuze and Guattari, *A Thousand Plateaus*, 323.

17. Elizabeth Gould, "Uprooting Music Education Pedagogies and Curricula: Becoming-Musician and the Deleuzian Refrain," *Discourse: Studies in the Politics of Education* 33, no. 1 (2012): 79.

18. Ibid. While Gould implies that it is not national anthems in and of themselves that constitute a refrain but rather how national anthems function, her statements are somewhat ambiguous. I return to the tension between the integrated issues of ontology and function below.

19. Ibid., 76.

20. Ibid., 76, 79.

21. Deleuze and Guattari, *A Thousand Plateaus*, 299.

22. Ibid., 301.

23. Ibid., 300.

24. Ibid., 317.

25. Ibid., 312.

26. Ibid.

27. Elizabeth Grosz, *Chaos, Territory, Art: Deleuze and the Framing of the Earth* (New York: Columbia University Press, 2008), 52.

28. While Deleuze and Guattari generally write about the simultaneous territorializing and deterritorializing forces within a single refrain, they at one point posit the existence of four types of refrains, explaining: "(1) territorial refrains that seek, mark, assemble a territory (2) territorialized function refrains that assume a special function in the assemblage (the lullaby that territorializes the child's slumber, the lover's refrain that territorializes the sexuality of the loved one. . . .) (3) the same, when they mark new assemblages, pass into new assemblages by means of deterritorialization-reterritorialization. . . . (4) refrains that collect or gather forces, either at the heart of the territory or in order to go outside it." Deleuze and Guattari, *A Thousand Plateaus*, 326–327.

29. Ibid., 300.

30. Ibid.

31. Deleuze and Guattari explain music as both striated and smooth space. Ibid., 447–448.

32. Ibid., 318.

33. Ibid., 348.

34. In posing this example, I am not asserting that a Beethoven tune in a symphonic performance can never territorialize or that commercial music can never deterritorialize. In regard to the former, authors such as Christopher Small have detailed the potential for Western classical music to territorialize participants by affirming their current senses of self. Christopher Small, *Musicking: The Meanings of Performing and Listening* (Hanover, NH: Wesleyan University Press, 1998).

35. At the individual level, they suggest the potentially profound effects of artistic endeavors, writing: "The great refrain arises as we distance ourselves from the house, even if this is in order to return, since no one will recognize us any more when we come back." Deleuze and Guattari, *What Is Philosophy*, 191.

36. John Rajchman, *The Deleuze Connections* (Cambridge, MA: MIT Press, 2000), 138. As explained in the following section, Deleuze's, and hence Rajchman's, emphasis on artworks rather than artistic practices is problematic.

37. Gould, "Uprooting Music Education Pedagogies and Curricula," 80. Gould acknowledges that these ideas originated with Deleuze and Guattari, who had adapted

them from LeRoi Jones. See LeRoi Jones, *Blues People* (New York: William Morrow & Company, 1963).

38. Ibid., 76.

39. Estelle Jorgensen, *In Search of Music Education* (Urbana: University of Illinois Press, 1997), 91–92.

40. Ibid.

41. Reimer, *A Philosophy of Music Education*, 38–59.

42. Ibid., 39.

43. Patrick Schmidt, "What We Hear Is Meaning Too: Deconstruction, Dialogue and Music," *Philosophy of Music Education Review* 20, no. 1 (2012): 9.

44. Deleuze and Guattari, *A Thousand Plateaus*, 320.

45. Ibid., 347.

46. Ibid., 303. Additionally, they elsewhere write, "The child's refrain, which is not music, forms a block with the becoming-child of music" (ibid., 300).

47. Ibid., 271.

48. Gould writes, "Deleuze and Guattari suggest that we have 'only lines and movement'; and, they add, 'Schumann.' I might proffer that educators have only encounters and music—deterritorialized interfaces of teaching and learning. And, I would add, students." Gould, "Uprooting Music Education Pedagogies and Curricula," 84.

49. Deleuze and Guattari, *What Is Philosophy*, 164. They posit percepts and sensations as the other two forces that constitute artworks.

50. Deleuze and Guattari, *A Thousand Plateaus*, 319.

51. For further discussion of Deleuze and Guattari's writings about affects, see Lauren Kapalka Richerme, "A Deleuzian Reimagining of Susanne Langer's Philosophy: Becoming-Feeling in Music Education," *Music Education Research* 20 (2018): 330–341.

52. Grosz, *Chaos, Territory, Art*, 56.

53. Gould, "Uprooting Music Education Pedagogies and Curricula," 83.

54. David Lines, "Deleuze and Music Education: Machines for Change," in *Cartographies of Becoming in Music Education: A Deleuze-Guattari Perspective*, ed. Diana Masny (Rotterdam: Sense, 2013), 23–33.

55. Deleuze and Guattari, *A Thousand Plateaus*, 7.

56. Deleuze and Guattari also equate the rhizome's connective processes with music, stating, "By placing all its components in continuous variation, music itself becomes a superlinear system, a rhizome instead of a tree." Like the rhizome, music can serve a connective, deterritorializing function, overturning structuring "codes." Ibid., 95, 11–12.

57. Brené Brown, *Daring Greatly: How the Courage to Be Vulnerable Transforms the Way We Live, Love, Parent, and Lead* (New York: Gotham, 2012), 145.

58. George Lakoff and Mark Johnson, *Philosophy in the Flesh: The Embodied Mind and Its Challenge to Western Thought* (New York: Basic, 1999), 290.

59. This is my own specific example, not Lakoff and Johnson's; I constructed it with an understanding of and the aim of aligning with the arguments made throughout their text.

60. I would like to thank Sandy Stauffer who, while I was writing my dissertation, asked me to consider the difference between the phrases "connect to" and "connect with." While I did not articulate the distinction in terms of transcendence and immanence at the time, these assertions are an outgrowth of my continued contemplation of that question.

61. State Education Agency Directors of Arts Education, "National Core Arts Standards: A Conceptual Framework for Arts Learning," 10.

62. Ibid.

63. June Boyce-Tillman, "Music and the Dignity of Difference," *Philosophy of Music Education Review* 20, no. 1 (2012): 39.

64. Estelle R. Jorgensen and Iris M. Yob, "Deconstructing Deleuze and Guattari's *A Thousand Plateaus* for Music Education," *Journal of Aesthetic Education* 47, no. 3 (2013): 50.

65. Estelle R. Jorgensen, *Pictures of Music Education* (Bloomington, Indiana University Press, 2013), 240.

66. Ibid., 243.

67. Elizabeth Gould, "Music Education Desire(ing): Language, Literacy, and Lieder," *Philosophy of Music Education Review* 17, no. 1 (2009): 51.

68. Ibid., 49.

69. Ibid., 51.

70. Ibid., 49.

71. Ibid., 43.

72. State Education Agency Directors of Arts Education, "National Core Arts Standards: A Conceptual Framework for Arts Learning," 10.

73. Randall E. Allsup, "Music Teacher Quality and the Problem of Routine Expertise," *Philosophy of Music Education Review* 23, no. 1 (2015): 8.

74. Kevin M. Bradt, *Story as a Way of Knowing* (Kansas City: Sheed and Ward, 1997), 107 (italics in the original).

75. Elizabeth Gould, "Music Education Desire(ing)," 49.

76. David Lines, "Deleuze, Education and the Creative Economy," in *Nomadic Education: Variations on a Theme by Deleuze and Guattari*, ed. Inna Semetsky (Rotterdam: Sense, 2008), 138–139.

77. For further investigation of the tension between naming and not naming, see Lauren Kapalka Richerme, "To Name or Not to Name? Social Justice, Poststructuralism, and Music Teacher Education," *Philosophy of Music Education Review* 24, no. 1 (2016): 84–102.

78. Deleuze and Guattari, *A Thousand Plateaus*, 249.

79. Susanne Langer, *Problems of Art: Ten Philosophical Lectures* (New York: Charles Scribner's Sons, 1957).

80. Small, *Musicking*, 95.

81. Deleuze and Guattari, *What Is Philosophy*, 187 (italics in the original).

82. Benedict posits a similar idea, challenging teachers to see themselves, rather than students, as "other." Cathy Benedict, "Defining Ourselves as Other: Envisioning Transformative Possibilities," in *Teaching Music in the Urban Classroom, Vol 1: A Guide to Survival, Success, and Reform*, ed. Carol Frierson-Campbell (Lanham, MD: Rowman & Littlefield, 2006), 3–13.

83. See, for example, Elliott and Silverman, *Music Matters*; and Reimer, *A Philosophy of Music Education*.

84. This idea was in part inspired by John Dewey, *Experience and Education* (New York: Simon & Schuster, 1997).

85. This could also be understood as a liminal space of "relations to" and "relations in."

86. Deborah Bradley, "Oh, That Magic Feeling! Multicultural Human Subjectivity, Community, and Fascism's Footprints," *Philosophy of Music Education Review* 17, no. 1 (2009): 66.

87. Ibid., 61–62.

88. Ibid., 66.

7 When Is Music Education?

TAKE A MOMENT, and recall the last time that you engaged with music. Perhaps it was in the background of a TV show, singing in the shower, in the place where you grabbed a cup of coffee this morning, or through headphones as you moved to your current location. Now, consider to what extent your musical encounter was educative. In what processes did you engage to determine whether or not you experienced education?

The contextually bound, individual, and ephemeral nature of educative experiences makes distinguishing them from noneducative experiences difficult. Students will not find every moment of their classes educative, and individual students will experience education at different times and in various ways. Furthermore, educative experiences occur during planned teaching and learning encounters as well as beyond them, including through students' solo and collective explorations.[1] While teachers can facilitate conditions that make educative experiences more likely to happen, one can never guarantee that an individual will experience education. Music education is not a stagnant "what" but a temporal "when," or in Michael Szekely's words, a process rather than an entity.[2] While the question "What is music education?" solidifies music education into an immobile identity, asking "When is music education?" emphasizes the differing, individually constructed nature of educative experiences.

Philosophers have described the nature of education in various ways. For example, Jean-Jacques Rousseau equates education with the cultivation of plants, stating, "We are born weak, we need strength; we are born totally unprovided, we need aid; we are born stupid, we need judgment. Everything we do not have at our birth and which we need when we are grown is given us by education."[3] Alternatively, John Dewey defines education as experiences that "have continuity and lead toward more growth," distinguishing them from miseducative experiences that arrest and distort growth.[4] Writing more specifically, Vernon Howard defines music education as "education of an understanding that ranges from physical dexterity, to emotive discovery, to perceptual insight, to pattern recognition, to associative hunches to logical argument—in no particularly order and in every combination."[5] Conversely, David Elliott and Marissa Silverman explain music education as "the wide range of educational and musical values and goods . . . [that] come about in and through the processes, encounters, and relationships involved in learning to make and listen to music of many kinds."[6]

These explanations imply or at minimum do not contradict the common assumption that educative experiences evolve along singular, relatively ordered trajectories. For instance, while Dewey argues for the necessity of considering each child's experiences, he also posits the importance of moving toward organized bodies of knowledge,[7] noting the need for "some comprehension of the development which is aimed at."[8] Despite emphasizing divergent starting points and variable routes, Dewey asserts the need for continuity and partially preset goals, although not necessarily ones common to all students. As explicated in chapter 1, contemporary education policymakers go much further, bounding educative ends through overarching, restrictive standards and corresponding assessments.[9]

Although educative experiences can assist students in progressing toward predetermined objectives, Deleuzian-inspired authors Elizabeth Gould, Inna Semetsky, and Michael Szekely detail how they can also facilitate meaningful unplanned and potentially disjointed wanderings.[10] For example, a student who sets out to learn classical violin technique may soon find themself intrigued by creating mash-ups of fiddle music and contemporary rock music. Although the student may develop only minimal facility on the violin, they might still have deep educative experiences through their music listening and creation, and such practices may lead into forms of personally fulfilling lifelong artistic engagement.

A teacher focused on preplanned aims may miss opportunities to facilitate a student's growth along such discontinuous paths. Applying similar thinking to higher education, Eleni Lapidaki asserts, "To deprive learning experiences of the feeling of unpredictability is to deprive music of its immediacy and us of the occasion for a possible transformation, both personal and social."[11] I wonder: What meaningful musical encounters might an explanation of education highlighting multidirectional journeying enable?

Education and Difference

While on an airplane early one Saturday morning I noticed the sun rising in the distance. As the first rays of light peeped above the ethereal white clouds and the vibrant colors of the surrounding sky intermingled and brightened, I found myself having an artistic experience. I simultaneously felt happiness, smiled, and assessed the image as "beautiful." Yet, while still enjoying the advancing sun, I realized that I did not find the experience educative. I eventually began interpreting the sunrise through my limited understanding of visual art; I contemplated the form of the intersecting shapes, their textures, and their colors. Subsequently, I considered how the sunrise related to music, and I imagined a string section crescendoing on a sustained major chord, complete with an intensifying suspended cymbal roll. Through both my application of visual art theory and my internal music composition process, I became aware that my experience of the sunrise, including its inseparable embodied and emotional qualities, was occurring differently. This awareness of difference contrasted my initial encounter, in which I simply enjoyed and appreciated experiencing the sunrise.

Elaborating on the unique qualities that women bring to music teaching and learning, Gould conceives of "music education as difference," which she explains involves a "becoming-toward, not becoming-as, always moving, never remaining."[12] Through this unceasing variation and motion, Gould argues that musically educative experiences can challenge and change boundaries as well as foster divergent ways of seeing and engaging with the world. In my initial encounter with the sunrise, I endowed it with a solidified identity; I experienced and appreciated its beauty, but I did not have what I would call an educative experience. In contrast, as I creatively engaged with the image and connected it with prior learnings, my developing awareness of both the sky's differing and my own differing invoked what I experienced as moments of education. Drawing on this encounter, Gould's work, and Gilles Deleuze's writings, I posit that education occurs when a person becomes aware of difference. While in partial agreement with Gould, my explanation of education necessitates four points of clarification.

First, while both Gould and I use "difference" in the sense of difference as open variation, I also use it to mean distinctions between identities. As noted in chapter 2, Deleuze and Guattari describe the former as continual, heterogeneous difference and the latter as numeric, discrete, homogenous difference.[13] For instance, statements such as "An individual's music creation practices *differ over time*" imply continual differences, while statements such as "Singing is *different from* composing" exemplify discrete differences. (This distinction also mirrors the contrast between "connecting with" and "connecting to" explained in chapter 6. While "connecting with" involves attending to ongoing changing, "connecting to" denotes perceived differences between entities.) I experienced education as my contemplation of visual art and internal composing caused awareness of the sky differing from itself, and I likely would have experienced education had I considered how the sunrise differed from my prior observations of sunrises.

Educational experiences often include aspects of both types of difference. For instance, one might experience music education when they become aware of a choir *differing* as the members increasingly move out of tune while singing a given passage. The individual, their peers, and their teacher may assign value to such awareness, perhaps terming it a "mistake" that *differs from* standard Western performance practices. Both the initial attentiveness to the choir differing from itself and the awareness of the choir differing from an in-tune choir constitute educative experiences.

Second, one might argue that because existence unceasingly differs, humans continually experience education. As humans, and indeed all existence, move through time, we constantly alter; our integrated minds, bodies, emotions, and sociality change with each passing moment. Yet, few would argue that individuals continually experience education. Since Gould posits "music education as difference" as a means of challenging and reimagining current practices rather than an explanation that subsumes all educative experiences, she avoids the need to distinguish educative experiences from noneducative ones.

In order to contrast humans' ongoing differing with education, I offer that education occurs when an individual *becomes aware* of difference. One can differ without being aware of the process, and one can be aware without *becoming* aware of difference. Consider a previous musical experience that you would not consider educative. Perhaps you passively listened to music in an elevator or thoughtlessly played or sang a musical warm-up or exercise. In such instances, you may assert that your awareness enabled you to hear or make music. However, although you continually differ through time, because you are not *aware* of this differing, you would likely not term the experience "educative." Likewise, my initial engagement with the sunrise necessitated a degree of awareness in order to have an artistic experience, but the absence of awareness of difference caused me not to find those moments educative.

This awareness can foreground human qualities other than cognition. Take, for example, Deleuze's story about a person learning to swim. He states: "When a body combines some of its own distinctive points with those of a wave, it espouses the principle of repetition which is no longer that of the Same, but involves the Other—involves difference, from one wave and one gesture to another and carries that difference through the repetitive space thereby constituted."[14] This description demonstrates how an awareness of difference may involve one's body. Education takes place when the swimmer becomes aware of the changing feel of each passing arm and leg movement or variations in the force of the water against the skin as each wave surges and retreats. Such primarily body-based awareness of difference can occur absent the thought: "I am aware of difference." In contrast, a swimmer can thoughtlessly move through the water, undertaking repeated motions without awareness that they occur uniquely with each passing moment and wave; in such instances, no education occurs. While the body always exists in integration with the mind, as well as with one's emotions and sociality, a person's awareness can favor one or more aspects over the others.

In addition to "awareness," musically educative experiences necessitate the process of "becoming." In this sense, I use the term "becoming" to refer to any general change in one's state of being.[15] Consider a music theory instructor who prepares an exam by thoughtlessly labeling chord sequences; they may draw on past experiences with the differences between sounds without becoming aware of how the experience differs from prior endeavors. In other words, the instructor possesses an awareness of difference, but they are not *becoming* aware of difference and therefore not experiencing education. In contrast, a student taking the theory exam may experience education when they become aware that a given chord sequence differs from a previously experienced chord sequence or when they become aware of how theoretical understandings contribute to their own musical differing. Likewise, a child composing in GarageBand who realizes the possibility of adding a clave loop under their existing composition might become aware of their own differing creativity or become aware that their composition is different from prior compositions.

Third, speaking about educative experiences as occurring or not occurring does not mean that individuals experience all educative moments equally. While Gould does not address this point directly, she implies it through her assertions about the uniqueness of women's contributions to music teaching and learning. Someone identifying as female can never experience educative events exactly like someone identifying as male, let alone someone of a contrasting race, socioeconomic status, national origin, or any other ways of being and becoming. More specifically, by asserting that flows, intensities, events, and multiplicities constitute existence, Deleuze and Guattari posit that existence resists replication both between individuals and over time; the force and quality of life's continual diversification unceasingly alters.[16]

It follows that becoming aware of difference and differing can occur in varying ways, unique to each situation and individual, and its particularity continually changes with each passing moment. A singer focusing on their mouth and throat on two consecutive days may become aware of their differing more intensely on the first day than on the second, or vice versa. The quality and depth of their experience and to which additional aspects of themselves and their surroundings they attend will also likely alter over the course of a single musical engagement.

Fourth, the aforementioned explanation of education leaves open the possibility that students engaging with music may have an educative experience that they do not consider a *musically* educative experience. A student may become aware of difference by focusing on their fingertips, finding that they are able to play a difficult passage more quickly and accurately. Yet, if they focus so much on their body that they essentially ignore the resulting sound, then they may have an educative experience similar to that of a person learning to play a sport. Such an experience may lead to deeper future musical and musically educative experiences, but absent awareness of sound, the person may not deem it a "musical experience" in the moment.

While people can assert that they experience music absent feeling a sense of connection, since humans often engage in musical practices in order to connect with themselves and others, musically educative experiences tend to involve the integration of connectivity and becoming aware of difference. For instance, a student listening to a musical performance might experience music education when they connect with their emotions while simultaneously becoming aware of how those emotions—in integration with their cognition, body, and sociality—differ from moment to moment. Likewise, a teacher leading a songwriting project at a local prison might experience music education when, upon hearing certain lyrics, they become aware of a sense of connection with the creator.

An explanation of education emphasizing difference and differing more easily facilitates diverse, changing trajectories than, for instance, those including phrases such as "pattern recognition" and "learning to make and listen to music of many kinds."[17] Focusing on differing resists delimiting music education to certain skills or conceiving of boundaries between different "kinds" of music as immobile or impermeable. Yet, my explanation of education does not deny the possibilities of motion along preset paths; I could aim to analyze the sunset like a given art critic or to re-create it in the style of a specific artist while still becoming aware of the sky's or my own differing. Given the limitations of teaching and learning that develop solely along preplanned trajectories, my explanation demands further exploration of the roles directionality and continuity do and might play in musically educative endeavors.

Awareness of Differing Rhizomatic and Arboreal Motion

Deleuze and Guattari's concept of the rhizome reveals contrasts that can inform musically educative experiences from moment to moment as well as over various longer time frames. According to Deleuze and Guattari, "The rhizome operates by variation, expansion, conquest, capture, offshoots."[18] Botanical rhizomes, like ginger, meander freely, without a preset path or endpoint. In contrast, arboreal (tree-like) motion involves vertical, hierarchical growth. A tree's roots, trunk, and leaves exist in a given order, serve specific functions, and are limited in the type and directions of their off-shoots.[19]

This contrast between rhizomes and trees mirrors Randall Allsup's distinction between what he terms "open forms" and "closed forms." Allsup writes that open forms include generative, contemporary music practices that are often participatory and may be open-source.[20] On the other hand, in agreement with arboreal motion, Allsup explains closed forms as stable, structured, historically agreed-on music-making norms.[21] While one can imagine tree-like participatory musical engagements or musical hybridization practices that emphasize hierarchies and preset plans, such endeavors generally develop through the ongoing variability and different entryways indicative of rhizomatic growth. Conversely, the predilection for perfection and submission to existing ideals necessary for closed forms tends to align with the predetermined trajectories of a tree's roots, trunk, and branches. The primary difference between rhizomatic and arboreal motion, however, is not the musical practices themselves, but the nature of engagement.

In music education, arboreal motion includes becoming aware of difference in a sequential, preset order; the quarter note comes before the sixteenth note, and one cannot compose without a certain amount of music theory knowledge and technical proficiency. Similarly, immobile curricula and pedagogies favor the tree's association with the verb "to be" over the evolving possibilities of the rhizome's framework of "and . . . and . . . and . . . ."[22] Arboreal teaching and learning roots skills and concepts via stabilizing repetition. For example, one could conceive of learning to improvise as progressing in an arboreal manner, perhaps moving from root notes to a blues scale to a variety of scales. Improvising with facility on a single scale sets the foundation for a second scale, and so on. Those immobile musical "roots" can enable a lifetime of vertical musical growth derived from their solid grounding, but they resist horizontal integration and experimentation that relies on contrasting musical skills and understandings.

Conversely, a rhizomatic image of thought involves relations of sheer difference.[23] Felicity Colman explains, "To think in terms of the rhizome is to reveal the multiple ways that you might approach any thought, activity, or a concept—what you always bring with you are the many and various ways of entering any body, of assembling thought and action through the world."[24] Drawing on such embodied-emotional-social contemplation, teachers acting rhizomatically might encourage students to come to and move within musical endeavors via different routes and to gain various, changing skills and understandings in any order. The beginning ukulele player is not deemed unfit for the concert band, and the student interested in composing with DJ software must not first learn Western notation. Instead of meeting predetermined standards, learning becomes a process of discovery enacted through wandering experimentation.[25]

Similarly, Panagiotis Kanellopoulos offers a rhizomatic vision of improvisation. He explains: "Each musical gesture contains endless possibilities for continuation, and its impact on the continuation of the improvised piece is uncertain."[26] This emphasis on divergent, spontaneous paths forward recalls a botanical rhizome's potential to grow in any direction. In such instances, possibility precedes planned scales or other constraints. Moreover, students may move rhizomatically when they compose absent attention to preset forms, or when they transition seamlessly from engaging with mariachi to Carnatic music to creating music that defies easy categorization. Gregg Lambert summarizes that rhizomatic thinking involves "forgetting what was already known beforehand in order to discover what remains to be thought."[27]

The contrast between trees and rhizomes also highlights potential differences in movement continuity. Educational practices that foreground continuous, uninterrupted growth contrast the rhizome, which "may be broken, shattered at a given spot, but it will start up again on one of its old lines, or on new lines."[28] Gould exemplifies such rhizomatic motion by emphasizing what teachers and students bring to musical engagements "in order to decode music and social relations as they exist and recode them in new and different configurations only to decode them again."[29] This evolving cycle of coding, decoding, and recoding implies a conception of music education as a potentially disjointed process. New configurations may temporarily cease student and teacher growth in order for reimaginings of individual and collective directionality. The class that pauses midway through a composition project in order to determine whether they should change their aims, split into individual endeavors, or engage in listening resists the uninterrupted arboreal growth emphasized by the authors of most contemporary music standards.

The philosophical figuration[30] of the rhizome can also inform understandings about relations between individual educative experiences. Deleuze and Guattari write, "The tree and the root inspire a sad image of thought that is forever imitating the multiple on the basis of a centered or segmented higher unity."[31] In other words, like the transcendent "relations to" detailed in chapter 6, arboreal thought presupposes certain unified totalities that subsume and order difference. Such thinking can encourage teachers and students to consider a Javenese gamelan group as a part of the totality of "world music" and to consider "world music" as only part of the totality of "music education." The gamelan ensemble is a segment in need of other world musics, and music education is not complete without classical music and Western musical terminology. Conversely, rhizomatic practices involve conceiving of individual music-making experiences as positive in their own right rather than as incomplete parts of a standardized or idealized musical or educative whole.

Along the same lines, becoming aware of difference can include the rhizomatic formation of connections between disparate concepts, experiences, and practices. Deleuze and Guattari explain, "Unlike trees or their roots, the rhizome connects any point to any other point, and its traits are not necessarily linked to traits of the same nature."[32] They name "lived events, historical determinations, concepts, individuals, groups, [and] social formations" as well as "semiotic chains, organizations of power, and circumstances relative to the arts, sciences, and social struggles" as examples of evolving rhizomatic connections.[33] For instance, while watching the sunrise from within the plane, I became aware of difference while my thoughts rhizomatically flowed from visual art to music and I began silently composing sounds to accompany the changing image before me. In music education, such wandering might occur as students form free-flowing connections between musical practices or between music classes and their experiences in other subjects as well as environmental, social, and political events outside of school. While the tree's roots restrain practices to their classroom origins, the rhizome opens outward in all possible directions, connecting rather than subsuming differences in the process.

What is most troubling, however, is not arboreal growth and its related thinking in themselves, but that individuals have presupposed such practices as natural and universal. For classical philosophers, the arboreal image of thought corresponds to "common sense."[34] One must begin with and build from a set of accepted premises rather than consider imaginative middles in which seemingly unrelated ideas intersect, meld, and mutate. Likewise, the ubiquity of detailed, systematically ordered music standards can make playing extended improvisations before learning any scale or aiming for expressivity prior to hearing the word "quarter note" seem beyond the realm of possibility.

Although the preceding discussion may imply a strict binary or opposition between rhizomes and trees, Deleuze and Guattari instead view it as a pluralism, in which two ideas or practices coexist.[35] Claire Colebrook explains, "You begin with the distinction between rhizomatic and arborescent only to see that all distinctions and hierarchies are active creations, which are in turn capable of further distinctions and articulation."[36] Deeming action arboreal or rhizomatic necessitates attention to one's differing, multiply situated historical and social contexts, including norms and deviations, habits and experimentations. The teacher who facilitates engagement with hip-hop year after year with little variation may rhizomatically challenge the arboreal territory of the music education profession, but they create their own tree-like structure within their classroom and school.

Furthermore, one can never completely disentangle rhizomatic experiences from arboreal ones. Asserting the permeable boundary between trees and rhizomes, Deleuze and Guattari write, "Trees have rhizome lines, and the rhizome points of arborescence."[37] Music-making may tend toward either rhizomatic or arboreal motion, but it is rarely purely one or the other. Even within solidified, arboreal curricula, changing musically connective experiences can illuminate moments of rhizomatic rupture, and rhizomatic educative practices can never fully escape the structuring weight of tradition.

Although Deleuze and Guattari favor rhizomatic movement over arboreal growth, they neither advocate for the complete elimination of hierarchies and systems of organization nor for a static rhizomatic-arboreal by-product. They explain, "A new rhizome may form in the heart of a tree, the hollow of a root, the crook of a branch,"[38] and elsewhere they note that trees may burgeon into rhizomes.[39] Envision botanical rhizomes intermixing with the roots, trunks, and branches of multiple trees. The rhizomes continually grow horizontally, connecting with diverse parts of the trees and other nearby entities while creating offshoots at various points and in different directions. Simultaneously, the trees grow upward, perhaps intermingling their roots and branches with various rhizomes or even transforming into rhizomes.⁴⁰ Arboreal growth enables new territories for rhizomatic breakaways and vice versa.

Educators might find inspiration in imagining rhizomes interconnecting with trees when considering the nature of students' educative experiences, perhaps attempting to integrate primarily rhizomatic educative experiences with primarily arboreal ones. For example, a teacher might facilitate primarily rhizomatic motion by encouraging students to seek out, combine, reinterpret, and extend different existing styles of music as well as to create their own original musical styles, processes, and products. As students become interested in specific genres or forms of musical engagement, the teacher might facilitate primarily arboreal educative experiences by guiding students' familiarization with accepted practices within a given style. In turn, teachers can open spaces for students' further rhizomatic exploration, perhaps including how their music-making might serve marginalized individuals or bring awareness to global problems.

In short, rhizomatic educative encounters wander outward from uncertain middles along possibly disjoined paths without seeking a clear end or whole. Welcoming educative experiences oscillating between more rhizomatic and more arboreal ways of being and becoming resists perceiving well-worn standards and curricula as "common sense." Attending to varying integrations of rhizomatic and arboreal motion, however, does not distinguish higher-quality educative experiences from lower-quality ones.

Quality and Educative Experiences

Deeming some educative experiences "high quality" and others "low quality" in part contradicts Deleuze's project. A division between high and low is problematic because it creates a strict dichotomy and static hierarchy, minimizing attention to the fluidity within and between such designations. However, since teachers and students inevitably need to make decisions about how to use their limited time together, ideas about the value of certain experiences necessarily affect their actions. Rather than a solidified answer, examining how music educators and students might use Deleuze's work to interrogate variations in the quality of specific educative experiences offers a middle point open to further deliberations.

Deleuze's philosophizing suggests that distinctions about quality might relate to the opening of possibilities. Writers such as David Cole and Semetsky have elaborated on this idea, positing the value of educational "epiphanies" and processes such as "becoming-rhizome," respectively.⁴¹ Likewise, Ronald Bough explains Deleuzian teaching and learning as emphasizing "discovery and creation within the ever-unfolding domain of the new."⁴² These authors suggest that, for Deleuze, the more educative experiences foster creative thinking and action, the higher their quality. In music education, this might mean that a lesson focused on performing a given musical passage as many different ways as possible constitutes a higher-quality educative experience than one aimed at replicating a specific interpretation. More broadly, Deleuze's writings suggest that music education curricula focused on creative cross-cultural connections or innovative participatory music endeavors hold more value than those repeating more commonplace practices such as Kodály, music appreciation, or large ensemble competitions.

Determining the quality of an educative experience solely on the extent to which it opens possibilities is problematic because it neglects attention to individuals' meaning-making. Imagine students who become aware of differing potentialities through electronic composition projects or through performing music in new venues, but who do not place value on such action. While these experiences meet both my definition of education and a Deleuzian focus on creativity, I wonder: What is lost when teachers' and students' values play no role in considerations about quality?

Deleuze in part attends to the individual and evolving nature of educative experiences. Recalling his own university teaching, he explains learning as a process that connects with individuals' pasts, presents, and potential futures. Writing about students participating in his courses, Deleuze states, "Nobody took in everything, but everyone took what they needed or wanted, what they could use."[43] By encouraging engagement uniquely appropriate for each student's divergent interests and becomings, Deleuze suggests the need for attention to individual meaning-making. However, he provides no further insights about how individuals' values and aims might interface with and inform teaching and learning. Similarly, while authors such as Cole and Semetsky imply that student preferences may play a role in their proposed Deleuzian educational processes, they do not directly account for the meaning-laden nature of students' divergent educational experiences.

Since focusing on possibilities alone enables abstract understandings of quality that may contrast the significance with which teachers and students endow certain experiences, I propose that any conception of quality must involve at least some attention to the meaning—or lack there of—that individuals make from the event. Yet, attending primarily to meaning-making in the moment omits the multifaceted effects of educative endeavors, including their life-long implications. Consider a student who imagines creative possibilities for intersections of music and social justice, but whose minimal technical skills cause them to feel uncomfortable making music in public. No matter how innovative or insightful their educative epiphany, if the student lacks the facility to enact it, then few would argue that they experienced a high quality music education.

Changing Narratives

If humans are narrative beings, then like all experiences, teaching and learning integrate with each individual's continually evolving stories. Yet, students may not possess an awareness of how individual educative experiences impact their differing narratives, and indeed, many music teaching and learning endeavors may have only an imperceptible effect on them. Janet Miller makes a similar assertion about the unproblematized identity constructs of "teacher" common in American educational literature, noting that writers often craft such "teacher stories" as unitary, universal, complete, and noncontradictory.[44]

These finished stories resist further development, confining storytellers to their existing ms. Miller explains, "Many of us are grounded in a notion of 'experience' that fails to interrogate how our notions of meaningful experience too are socially and discursively produced."[45] If students and teachers enter classrooms with certain narratives about their musical selves, and those stories do not alter as a result of their experiences, then the transformative possibilities of Deleuze's potentiality-driven education remain unrealized.

I offer that while educative experiences can occur absent considerations of their role in one's narratives, high quality educative experiences often involve individuals becoming aware of how their narratives are changing or might change in the future. In other words, while educative experiences necessitate an awareness of difference, high quality educative experiences occur when such awareness is meaningful enough that it informs one's self-stories. Such action retains Deleuze's emphasis on creative potentialities while honoring both individuals' divergent meaning-making processes and the long-term implications extending beyond the classroom. A narrative from a graduate music education student who teaches a section of music for the Classroom Teacher course for preservice elementary education majors illustrates this position.

She recounted to me the story of an older student, a retired navy serviceman who, in his fifties, decided that he wanted to teach. He entered her class expressing that he had no musical talent and perceived the class as a ridiculous requirement that he only took because the university mandated it. Yet, toward the end of the semester, the man explained that in the course of his fieldwork he saw an elementary teacher use music to teach another subject and recognized how helpful music was in that circumstance; he wanted to learn more. While prior to this transformation the student clearly learned information and skills that enabled him to pass the class assignments, absent this alteration to his narrative, these understandings had little meaning for him and would likely not have impacted his future work. The student finished the semester no longer perceiving himself as unmusical, and he intended to use music frequently in his own classroom.[46] The student's narratives of himself, music, teaching, and learning had changed, indicating a high quality educative experience.

The same holds true for students who come to find meaning in composing music and subsequently become aware that, no longer solely passive music consumers, they now identify as musicians. Likewise, imagine students who come to understand that their music-making can play a role in a local community's identity formation, or who find that through gaining more facility on an instrument they can express aspects of their feelings and inner lives that had long remained hidden. In each case, the students may become aware that their narratives about the nature of and interactions between themselves, music, and society have altered or have the potential to alter. In contrast, in and of themselves, learning proper technique, how to distinguish musical styles, or the meaning of various chord symbols rarely leads to changes in one's narrative.

Time and Voice

It is important to note that just because a teacher does not realize that a student's narrative has changed does not indicate the absence of such an occurrence. Since only individuals can fully understand their own narratives, teachers' comprehension of students' narratives depends on what students willingly divulge. Students will rarely say, "My narrative has changed," but teachers can surmise this information by observing how their communications, actions, and dispositions develop over time. Yet, students may not experience changes to their narratives for weeks or even years after educative experiences. While students within any one music class might not perceive themselves as musical, those who in adulthood sing lullabies to a newborn baby may only then become aware of the impact that their P–12 music education had on their self-stories. Music educators can make curricular and pedagogical decisions attentive to such possibilities, but they will never know the full effects of their work.

Part of becoming aware that one's narrative has altered or has the potential to alter can involve changing how and with whom students share their stories. Jerome Bruner explains that attending to humans' narrative construction of reality involves contemplating the way in which an individual tells the story; one cannot separate the value of a story's content from the act of expression.[47] It follows that recounting the same story to a different audience or via a changed medium, including moving from speech or writing to forms of artistic expression, can indicate high quality educative experiences. Such instances include moments when, no longer feeling the need to keep parts of their narratives hidden, students openly share them—including through music-making—with teachers, parents, and community members.

Miller, however, reminds educators that simply fostering spaces in which marginalized voices can express themselves does not necessarily grant meaning to their worldviews.[48] Autobiography can still serve a normalizing function if, under the guise of inclusiveness, the narratives of often silenced individuals become subsumed under existing understandings of education. Instead, "By encouraging an educator to examine disjunctures, ruptures, break-ups and fractures in the 'normal school' version of the unified life-subject and her own and others' educational practices, autobiography can function to 'queer' or to make theory, practice, curriculum *and* the self unfamiliar."[49] This queering challenges singular conceptions of "acceptable" educators' and students' musical selves as well as the pedagogies that function in and through such standardized understandings.[50]

While individual narratives can serve a primarily arboreal function if told solely in ways that reinforce existing practices, they also have the potential to function rhizomatically by challenging boundaries, including existing hierarchical ways of knowing and doing. Such practices may include the "counterstories" that Gloria Ladson-Billings asserts enable marginalized individuals to name their realities.[51] Tellers of counterstories resist the universality and completeness that enable normative narratives to function as aids to existing forms of oppression.

Imagine musical counterstories through which students express their social-emotional-embodied-cognitive narratives by re-creating and perhaps augmenting music with which they relate or by composing or improvising their own story-songs. Such action recalls Jeananne Nichols' description of a struggling transgendered youth who came to understand songwriting as a "way to make people listen."[52] Through their counterstories, individuals and groups refuse complicity in both silence and "normal" music-making that opposes potential disruptions from subjugated voices.

Facilitating Musically Educative Experiences

If high quality educative experiences involve awareness of alterations to individuals' current and possible future narratives, then music educators can provide students opportunities to share how their musical narratives—both inside and outside of formal education—do and might change. This communication can occur through evolving combinations of dialogue, writing, and artistic practices. Teachers facilitating such exchanges might benefit from recalling Mikhail Bakhtin's distinction between epics and novels discussed in chapter 1.[53]

Rather than encouraging students to author epic stories in which they become flawless, valorized heroes, teachers might foster novel-like narratives that embrace uncertainty and failure. This could occur through questions and prompts that assist students in expressing the unfinished creative potential of their stories. Metaphorically, music educators can encourage students to celebrate their scarred, fallible Harry Potter personas rather than feeling obligated to portray themselves with Promethean courage that, if attainable at all, is inevitably short-lived.

Furthermore, music educators might consider how their own narratives alter through music-making and teaching. In one of his longest passages on education,

Deleuze makes a very subtle distinction about teachers' roles in educative experiences. He writes, "We learn nothing from those who say: 'Do as I do.' Our only true teachers are those who tell us to 'do with me.'"[54] Teachers saying "Do as I do" act as models who focus on arboreal growth and differences between identities. Such pedagogues may, for instance, demonstrate the "correct" or "appropriate" way to phrase a given passage and demand that students follow their example. Any alternate phrasing *differs from* the teacher's superior one, reinforcing the teacher's existing narrative.

Conversely, teachers who say "Do with me" emphasize evolving difference as they, for example, explore together the possibilities of divergent expressive choices. Such educators might use their facial expressions to draw attention to their own changing emotions as they experiment with making music alongside students; the teacher and students *differ* over time through newly forming understandings of their music-making and each other. Phrases including "I do with you" and "Let's do together" can further highlight and foster this collaboration.[55] Learning with their students, teachers saying "Do with me" become not just fellow students but co-wanderers focused on differing musically educative experiences.

Although I have certainly had similar moments teaching in undergraduate and PreK–12 classrooms, I provide the following example of experiencing such differing when facilitating a graduate seminar. As I circulated around the room, I realized that the two small groups had come to contrasting positions regarding the role of language in deepening enjoyment of music. I pointed out their contrasting positions and a debate ensued between the two groups. As I listened to their arguments, I realized that I (a) had not previously fully considered either side of this debate, and (b) was terrified that one of the students was going to look at me and say, "Well, what do you think?" I wasn't anywhere close to articulating perspectives as reasoned as their own, and I dreaded being asked to do so. I was differing with them, and it was terrifying. Luckily, the class ended without anyone asking my opinion, and I felt relieved; my differing was never revealed. Yet, as I reflected on that experience, I realized that I missed an opportunity to acknowledge my own transforming narrative by joining in those confused moments alongside the students; rather than differing *with* me, the students had differed *without* me.

Following the incident, while still devoting the majority of class time to students' construction of their own knowledge, I made it a point to share openly my own differing. I often took a few minutes in the middle of classes to explain how my thinking on a subject had changed based on students' comments, and I sometimes ended classes by noting a question or problem with which I still struggled as a result of our dialogue. While generally happy after the fact to have taken such actions, I could usually best describe my cognitive-embodied-emotional-social state at the time as "vulnerable." I worried that students would judge my underdeveloped thinking, and that I might have to recant or revise my statements as students challenged my evolving deliberations.

Yet, differing *with* students necessitates sharing our experimentations, uncertainty, failures, and growth. High quality educative experiences happen not just when teachers reconsider content, pedagogy, values, traditions, and potentialities, but when they encourage students to become aware of their own changing narratives by allowing students to see the often vulnerable *process* of alteration.[56] Such action recalls Gould's statement: "Dancing together, teachers and students enact a philosophy of doing, experimentation, affirmation, connection, and difference: philosophy as experience."[57]

"Differing with" can occur through engagement with even the most familiar of content; there always exist countless ways to teach any given material, and students' contrasting experiences provide teachers an endless stream of information worthy of further inquisitiveness, investigation, and reflection. Yet, recalling the need to attend to their own survival, teachers might at times ponder what material and pedagogy can best support their personal curiosities. Writing about his own university teaching, Deleuze asserts, "You give courses on what you're investigating, not on what you know."[58] Similarly, Allsup writes, "If I were the president of Julliard, I would insist that my faculty continue to teach what they know, but also facilitate a class about which they are ignorant."[59] In addition to overhauling existing courses and creating new ones with careful attention to students' and communities' interests, music educators can use their own wonderments to inform everything from overarching curricular decisions to everyday content selection to engagement with unexpected student ideas and actions. The practices that educators find meaningful have increased potential to foster changes to their own narratives, making it more likely that they will have high quality educative experiences *with* students.

However, just as educative journeying inevitably involves the integration of tree-like and rhizomatic motion, teachers necessarily say and enact "Do as I do" and "Do with me." An educator intrigued by one student's interpretation of a musical phrase or another's compositional choices may still model more traditional techniques from which students might decide to select. Moreover, students excited to, for example, create a musical event supporting those at a women's shelter likely need a teacher to model certain interpersonal engagements. In such moments, teaching and learning become not about "Do as I do" or "Do with me," but about how focusing on either directive opens new possibilities for subsequent attention to the other. "Do as I do" enables a reimagining of "Do with me" and vice versa.

Largely absent from my preceding explanations is how such action might interface with musical experiences. Lessons focused too much on educative experiences may end up centered on verbal or spatial knowing and doing, including through activities such as historical readings or theory worksheets. In this sense, I concur with Elliott and Silverman that while such understandings can deepen musical experiences, they occur distinct from musical experiences.[60] Since, as detailed in chapter 6, meaningful musical moments often involve a sense of connection, teachers might question how individuals' experiences of becoming aware of difference may precede, follow, or integrate with connective musical encounters.

In order to facilitate educative experiences, musically connective experiences, and intersections of the two, music educators might create lessons with attention to the time spent on each. In addition to reflecting on when students will likely become aware of differing during a given lesson and when they have opportunities to experience musically connecting to and with, music educators might ask: At what points during the class might students experience neither education nor musical connections, and what alternatives might I consider? When and how might these educative and musically connective experiences occur differently for various students, particularly those who often face marginalization? How might my own and students' differing narratives inform and change through these musical and educative processes?

Alongside such planning, students and teachers might welcome deviations that arise as participants differ through unanticipated, creative teacher-student and student-student interactions. Students' inquisitiveness or prior experiences can facilitate meaningful rhizomatic wanderings that alter a teacher's preset plans. The balance between awareness of difference, musical connectivity, and other experiences necessarily alters with the needs of a given time and place. In short, teachers drawing on Deleuze's writings about potentialities might focus less on when education and musical connectivity *are* and more on imagining and experimenting with when they *might be*.

Possible Limitations

Conceiving of music education that emphasizes the integration of connecting and an awareness of difference is still limiting because it enables educative experiences focused on a single human quality. In particular, repeated primarily cognitive educative experiences can reinforce the cognitive-centric standards and assessments permeating contemporary educative practices. Similarly, while rhizomatic motion may lead teachers and students to engage musically with their multiple environments, such action need not necessarily occur. Without added contemplation, teachers and students may form musically educative connections solely with their immediate locations while neglecting or even harming those in their local and global communities.

As explicated in chapter 6, "connecting with" can occur within and between the self, local, and global planes of immanence. Integrating these ideas with the writings above, teachers might consider how "Do as I do" and "Do with me" can involve differing musical connections focused on students' embodiment, emotions, and sociality as well as their local, global, and glocal places. "Do as I do" might involve demonstrating thoughtful engagements with members of a virtual musical community, while teachers might say "Do with me" as they show curiosity about how someone living in another country makes meaning out of engaging with a specific musical practice. Alternatively, a teacher could say "Do as I do" as they compose an emotionally charged song in response to a local medical epidemic, subsequently asking students to "Do with me" as they brainstorm how to share students' music-making with community members and policymakers.

Yet, without continual complicating, these qualities and places can stagnate, limiting further educational journeying. For example, teachers may assume the existence of certain local styles of music-making that occurred in prior years without understanding how intersections with globalized music-making caused them to alter over time. Investigating the question "When is music education?" becomes deeper and potentially more meaningful when engaged in alongside the practices detailed in chapters 2 and 3, including exploring social, emotional, embodied narratives and experimenting with narratives of becoming-nomad.

Another limitation is the possibility that an individual becomes aware of difference, and therefore has an educative experience, while engaging in what many deem unethical thinking and action. My response to such assertions is twofold. First, an awareness of difference may encourage processes needed for ethical engagement. Ethical practices come from active, creative contemplation rather than obedience to stagnant rules.[61] As such, becoming aware of difference may assist individuals in resisting solidified directives and singular worldviews. This awareness can contribute to the dispositions needed for imagining multiple perspectives and judging. Second, despite this potential, I concede that one can imagine scenarios in which an individual becomes aware of difference in an unethical manner. For instance, a white supremacist could continually become aware of their differing hatred of non-Aryan individuals.

Authors such as Elliott and Silverman and those working within the Germanic *Bildung* tradition suggest that the term "education" applies only to ethical experiences.[62] Conceiving of ethics and education as inseparable has the advantage of resisting deliberations about education that do not attend to its ethical qualities. However, such action becomes problematic if how one understands "ethics" remains ambiguous and unquestioned. As noted in chapter 4, given that philosophers have debated the problems and possibilities of specific ethical schools of thought for millennia,[63] each teacher might benefit from acknowledging the ethical assumptions that they work from and perhaps considering alternatives.

Disconnecting the questions "When is music education?" and "In what more ethical music teaching and learning practices might teachers and students engage?" draws independent attention to teachers' and students' ethical processes, enabling them to interrogate and perhaps reimagine them. I propose that music educators and students might use various ethical philosophies, including the practice of "considering" detailed in chapters 4 and 5, to interface with and inform musically educative experiences. Such action ensures that ethical considerations complement inquiries about educative experiences, rather than becoming secondary to or omitted from them.

"Considering" musically educative experiences involves imagining them from as many diverse embodied-cognitive-emotional-social perspectives as possible and then judging with the willingness to justify one's decision to others. In such instances, considering itself can become an educative process as teachers and students become aware of difference, perhaps including their own differing narratives. High quality educative experiences occur not only through engagement with musical content but via deliberations about the ethical possibilities of music teaching and learning.

Ending in the Middle

In summary, I explain educative experiences as occurring when one becomes aware of difference. Educative experiences develop through varying combinations of predetermined arboreal trajectories and uncertain, at times disjointed rhizomatic wanderings. Since rhizomatic educative experiences remain relatively rare, educators aiming to facilitate the ongoing integration of arboreal and rhizomatic growth may need to emphasize the latter.

While Deleuze's work suggests that creative, potentiality-driven educative practices are the most valuable, I argue that questions of quality necessitate attending to students' meaning-making. I propose that high quality educative experiences change students' self narratives, including about who they are and might become. Teachers might facilitate this transformation by journeying *with* students. Musically educative experiences occur when students become aware of differing while connecting to their multiple human qualities and local and global places.

Having explored the possibilities of complicating, considering, and connecting music education, I anticipated that I would arrive at an unobstructed summit with panoramic views. Yet, I find myself fumbling amidst fog and trees, not sure in what direction I am or should be moving. I admittedly still find great joy in arboreal educative moments, at times wondering if welcoming unplanned deviations holds as much value as delivering my cultivated knowledge to students, not to mention receiving such information from my own respected mentors.

Alternatively, I relish sitting back and letting students chart their own courses, fearful that my intervention might both squelch their desire to keep journeying and limit the understandings I personally gain from their collective endeavors.

I reside in a liminal space, unsure of what path to take, when to retreat, and when to bushwhack. Perhaps investigating potential integrations of and interactions between complicating, considering, and connecting will illuminate additional possible paths. I invite you to continue wandering *with* me.

Notes

1. See, for example, Lucy Green, *How Popular Musicians Learn: A Way Ahead for Music Education* (Burlington, VT: Ashgate, 2002).

2. Michael Szekely, "Musical Education: From Identity to Becoming," in *The Oxford Handbook of Philosophy in Music Education,* ed. Wayne Bowman and Ana Lucía Frega (New York: Oxford University Press, 2012), 177.

3. Jean-Jacques Rousseau, *Emile or On Education,* trans. Allan Bloom (New York: Basic, 1979), 38.

4. John Dewey, *Experience and Education* (New York: Macmillan, 1997), 25–26.

5. Vernon Howard, *Learning by All Means: Lessons from the Arts* (New York: Peter Lang, 1992), 21.

6. David J. Elliott and Marissa Silverman, *Music Matters: A Philosophy of Music Education,* 2nd ed. (New York: Oxford University Press, 2015), 151.

7. John Dewey, *The Child and the Curriculum* (Chicago: University of Chicago Press, 1902), 11.

8. Ibid., 19.

9. See, for example, "ESEA Flexibility: Highlights of State Plans," US Department of Education, last modified December 2012, http://www2.ed.gov/policy/elsec/guid/esea-flexibility/resources/esea-flex-brochure.pdf; Stephanie Horsley, "Globally Convergent Accountability Policies and the Cultural Status of State Funded School Music Programs: A State-Level Comparison," in *Proceedings of the 17th Biennial International Seminar of the Commission on Music Policy: Culture, Education, and Media,* ed. Peter Gouzouasis (Vancouver: University of British Columbia, 2014); and "Race to the Top Program Executive Summary," US Department of Education, last modified November 2009, http://www2.ed.gov/programs/racetothetop/executive-summary.pdf.

10. Elizabeth Gould, "Dancing Composition: Pedagogy and Philosophy as Experience," *International Journal of Music Education* 24, no. 3 (2006): 197–207; Inna Semetsky, *Deleuze, Education and Becoming* (Rotterdam, The Netherlands: Sense, 2006); Szekely, "Musical Education: From Identity to Becoming."

11. Eleni Lapidaki, "Uncommon Grounds: Preparing Students in Higher Music Education for the Unpredictable," *Philosophy of Music Education Review* 24, no. 1 (2016): 68.

12. Elizabeth Gould, "Women Working in Music Education: The War Machine," *Philosophy of Music Education Review* 17, no. 2 (2009): 137.

13. Gilles Deleuze and Félix Guattari, *A Thousand Plateaus: Capitalism and Schizophrenia,* trans. Brian Massumi (Minneapolis: University of Minnesota Press, 1987), 484.

14. Gilles Deleuze, *Difference and Repetition*, trans. Paul Patton (New York: Columbia University Press, 1994), 23.

15. In writing about "becoming aware of difference," I am not drawing on Deleuze and Guattari's concept of "becoming." In chapter 2, I explain that Deleuze and Guattari argue that one can become minoritarian but not majoritarian. As detailed further in the "Awareness of Differing Rhizomatic and Arboreal Motion" section of this chapter, I argue that, in addition to rhizomatically becoming aware of difference, one can become aware of difference when moving along arboreal trajectories. Since this arboreal motion would constitute becoming-majoritarian, it is inconsistent with Deleuze and Guattari's concept of becoming. Deleuze and Guattari, *A Thousand Plateaus*, 106.

16. See, for example, Deleuze and Guattari, *A Thousand Plateaus*; and Jean-François Lyotard, *Libidinal Economy*, trans. Iain Hamilton Grant (Bloomington: Indiana University Press, 2004).

17. Howard, *Learning by All Means*, 21; Elliott and Silverman, *Music Matters*, 151.

18. Deleuze and Guattari, *A Thousand Plateaus*, 21.

19. Ibid.

20. Randall Allsup, *Remixing the Classroom: Toward an Open Philosophy of Music Education* (Bloomington: Indiana University Press, 2016), 48.

21. Ibid.

22. Ibid., 25.

23. Ibid., 23.

24. Felicity Colman, "Rhizome," in *The Deleuze Dictionary*, ed. Adrian Parr (Edinburgh: Edinburgh University Press, 2005), 233.

25. Gregg Lambert, *In Search of a New Image of Thought: Gilles Deleuze and Philosophical Expressionism* (Minneapolis: University of Minnesota Press, 2012), 53.

26. Panagiotis A. Kanellopoulos, "Freedom and Responsibility: The Aesthetics of Free Musical Improvisation and its Educational Implications—A View from Bakhtin," *Philosophy of Music Education Review* 19, no. 2 (2011): 127.

27. Lambert, *In Search of a New Image of Thought*, 31.

28. Deleuze and Guattari, *A Thousand Plateaus*, 9.

29. Elizabeth Gould, "Uprooting Music Education Pedagogies and Curricula: Becoming Musician and the Deleuzian Refrain," *Discourse: Studies in the Cultural Politics of Education* 33, no. 1 (2012): 83.

30. As noted in chapter 2, Deleuze uses philosophical figurations to complicate rather than explicate. Elizabeth Adams St. Pierre distinguishes between philosophical figurations and metaphors, asserting, "A figuration is not a graceful metaphor that provides coherency and unity to contradiction and disjunction. . . . A figuration is no protection from disorder, since its aim is to produce a most rigorous confusion as it jettisons clarity in favor of the unintelligible." St. Pierre, "An Introduction to Figurations—A Poststructural Practice of Inquiry," *International Journal of Qualitative Studies in Education* 10, no. 3 (1997): 280–281.

31. Deleuze and Guattari, *A Thousand Plateaus*, 16.

32. Ibid., 9.

33. Ibid., 7, 9.

34. Lambert, *In Search of a New Image of Thought*, 59–60.

35. Claire Colebrook, *Understanding Deleuze* (Sydney, Australia: Allen & Unwin, 2002), xxviii.

36. Ibid.
37. Deleuze and Guattari, *A Thousand Plateaus*, 34.
38. Ibid., 15.
39. Ibid., 17.
40. Deleuze and Guattari explain, "Trees may correspond to the rhizome, or they may burgeon into a rhizome." Ibid., 17.
41. David R. Cole, *Educational Life-Forms: Deleuzian Teaching and Learning Practice* (Rotterdam, The Netherlands: Sense, 2011); Semetsky, *Deleuze, Education and Becoming*.
42. Ronald Bough, "Search, Swim and See: Deleuze's Apprenticeship in Signs and Pedagogy of Images," *Educational Philosophy and Theory* 36, no. 3 (2004): 341.
43. Gilles Deleuze, *Negotiations: 1972–1990*, trans. Martin Joughlin (New York: Columbia University Press, 1995), 139.
44. Janet Miller, *Sounds of Silence Breaking: Women, Autobiography, Curriculum* (New York: Peter Lang, 2005), 51.
45. Ibid., 52.
46. Rose Sciaroni, conversation with author, October 7, 2015.
47. Jerome Bruner, *Acts of Meaning* (Cambridge, MA: Harvard University Press, 1990), 113.
48. Miller, *Sounds of Silence Breaking*, 222.
49. Ibid., 223 (italics in the original).
50. Ibid.
51. Gloria Ladson-Billings, "Just What Is Critical Race Theory and What's It Doing in a Nice Field Like Education?" *International Journal of Qualitative Studies in Education* 11, no. 1 (2010): 13.
52. Jeananne Nichols, "Rie's Story, Ryan's Journey: Music in the Life of a Transgender Student," *Journal of Research in Music Education* 61, no. 3 (2013): 270.
53. Mikhail Bakhtin, *The Dialogic Imagination*, ed. Michael Holquist, trans. Caryl Emerson and Michael Holquist (Austin: University of Texas Press, 1981). See further discussion in the "Limits of Poststructuralism" section in chapter 1.
54. Deleuze, *Difference and Repetition*, 23.
55. I am grateful to Cecilia Ferm-Thorgersen and Hanna M. Nikkanen for suggesting these variations following a presentation of an early draft of this chapter at the 2015 International Society for Philosophy of Music Education Conference in Frankfurt, Germany.
56. For further explanation of the potential benefits and drawbacks of vulnerable experiences in music education, see, for example, Lauren Kapalka Richerme, "Vulnerable Experiences in Music Education: Possibilities and Problems for Growth and Connectivity," *Bulletin of the Council for Research in Music Education*, no. 209 (2017): 27–42.
57. Gould, "Dancing Composition," 205.
58. Deleuze, *Negotiations*, 139.
59. Randall Allsup, "The Eclipse of Higher Education or Problems Preparing Artists in a Mercantile World," *Music Education Research* 17, no. 3 (2015): 258.
60. Elliott and Silverman, *Music Matters*, 218.
61. Elizabeth Gould, "Social Justice in Music Education: The Problematic of Democracy," *Music Education Research* 9, no. 2 (2007): 234.
62. See, for example, Elliott and Silverman, *Music Matters*; Marja Heimonen, "'Bildung' and Music Education: A Finnish Perspective," *Philosophy of Music Education Review* 22, no. 2 (2014): 188–208; and Warner Jank, "Didaktik, Bildung, Content: On the Writings of Frede V. Nielsen," *Philosophy of Music Education Review* 22, no. 2 (2014): 113–131.

63. See, for example, Marcia W. Baron, Philip Pettit, and Michael Slote, *Three Methods of Ethics: A Debate* (Malden, MA: Blackwell, 1997); Tom L. Beauchamp, *Philosophical Ethics: An Introduction to Moral Philosophy,* 3rd ed. (Boston: McGraw Hill, 2001); John Deigh, *An Introduction to Ethics* (Cambridge, UK: Cambridge University Press, 2010); and Noel Stewart, *Ethics: An Introduction to Moral Philosophy* (Cambridge, UK: Polity Press, 2009).

8 Rhizomatic Journeying

SOMETIMES I THINK that my teaching and music-making have changed substantially since I began contemplating the relationship between music education and society. At other moments, I feel as though I have gone nowhere in my thought, feelings, and action. Both notions reveal my predilection for progress—for seeing myself and my work in relation to starting and ending points rather than embracing journeying for its own sake. Yet, my engagement with poststructuralist philosophy has created tension in my yearning for closure that I know (and ultimately desire) to be but an illusion.

It is problematic to conceive of complicating, considering, and connecting as having a destination. While engaging in these processes may lead one's individual work and the music education field more broadly in new directions, relations within and between them remain primary. These wandering interactions move rhizomatically outward from an uncertain middle, interfacing not only with music teaching and learning but with the larger sociocultural milieus in which these practices reside. In turn, like a botanical rhizome that adjusts its pathways when confronted with tree roots, rocks, different soils, and other entities, teachers and students necessarily alter their complicating, considering, and connecting in integration with their changing circumstances.

Complicating, Considering, and Connecting Practices

While this book necessarily reads linearly, moving from complicating to considering to connecting, these practices need not occur in a specific order. For example, if a student raises an ethical question or shows a curiosity that could lead to musical connecting, then educators need not redirect their attention to complicating people and places prior to traversing the paths actualized by their immediate situations. Systematized motion from one process to another limits opportunities for teachers and students to draw on the potentialities of unanticipated moments that permeate each endeavor.

Yet, to connect without considering the ethics of such action may exclude or denigrate certain people and groups. To consider without complicating may reinforce cognitive-centric worldviews or omit how one's actions may affect diverse individuals in one's immediate community and beyond. To complicate without connecting may inhibit understandings of and experiences with the meaning-laden aspects of musical endeavors, and so on. Embracing the unplanned events promoting the immediate favoring of one process does not mean that the other processes do not subsequently demand attention.

In order to understand further the interrelated nature of these three processes, music educators and students might draw inspiration from the physics phenomenon of quantum superposition. Prior to measurement, quantum particles can exist in an infinite number of places. Just as one cannot "locate" a single wave in a rippling pond, quantum particles can defy clear positioning. Scientists use the term "superposition" to describe this indefinite locatedness.[1]

Conceiving of complicating, considering, and connecting as superposed means imagining that, before teachers or students directly engage with one or more of them, they exist simultaneously and in ongoing integration. Such an image enables music educators and students to select the one or more processes most meaningful in a given moment, avoiding a checklist or unidirectional engagement. Additionally, just as particles return to their superposed states following measurement, music educators and students who have undertaken a specific process can imagine it as returning to a state of superposition. Doing so furthers a conception of complicating, considering, and connecting as unceasing processes rather than as tasks accomplished once and forgotten.

Unlike quantum particles, the nature and becomings of complicating, considering, and connecting constantly alter in integration with individuals' narratives. While measuring a particle's position changes its momentum, it does not alter how scientists define momentum. In contrast, the experience of complicating informs how teachers and students conceive of and engage with considering and connecting as well as how they complicate in future moments.

The student or teacher who complicates local musical environments cannot help but bring that information to their ethical considerations and deliberations about potential connections, fundamentally changing what it means for them "to consider" and "to connect." Similarly, a student's stated curiosity may change how a teacher subsequently complicates, even if they remain unaware of this differing. As such, in addition to focusing on how complicating, considering, and connecting relate *to* one another, teachers and students might highlight the immanent relations *in* a complicating-considering-connecting superposition. Each practice holds value not only for how it interacts with the others but for how it fosters previously unimagined conceptions of what these processes are and might become.

Having explored the integrated, evolving nature of complicating, considering, and connecting, how might music educators and students begin welcoming them into their practices? Gilles Deleuze would likely deem this question problematic; to posit a single starting point arborifies experiences, creating a stagnant base and a resulting immobile hierarchy. Instead, music educators and students might experiment with diverse entryways by imagining a superposed middle from which these practices might flow.

One way that music educators and students might embrace this middle is by designating spaces for active engagement with it. Music educators might set aside time to complicate, consider, and connect their practices at the start of each instructional year and term, and they might make time in their opening lessons for students to do the same. Moreover, teachers can attend to complicating, considering, and connecting as part of their everyday lesson planning as well as use them as a means of regularly reflecting on their practices. This includes exploring what complications, considerations, and connections students previously found most meaningful and using that information to imagine creative future actions.

Part of this reflection might also involve pondering when one engages in music education practices absent complicating, considering, and connecting. Teachers and students might ask: What parts of our teaching and learning seem overly simplified? When do we neglect the complexity of our selves and multiple places? At what points do ethical considerations feel most divorced from our practices? Likewise, while acknowledging that disconnection may at times hold value, they might reflect on when their musical practices inhibit connections between their changing selves and their local and global communities. Moving creatively outward from these voids resists the tendency to build on limited aspects of one's current teaching and learning.

As previously hinted, another way in which teachers and students might complicate, consider, and connect their work is by maintaining a receptivity to fleeting spaces of possibility. Regardless of the complicating, considering, and connecting that occurred prior to a given musically educative endeavor, teachers and students might enter their practices with an openness to what Randall Allsup explains as "moments of awareness" that may "flicker before they burn."[2] Since one can never fully anticipate the unplanned wandering that might arise as unique teacher and student narratives intermix, complicating, considering, and connecting can occur when teachers and students foster a willingness to take hold of and experiment with inspired moments.

Because such events invoke contrasting ephemeral experiences informed by individuals' pasts and potential futures, complicating, considering, and connecting involve difference and differing unique to each person. This variation within and between integrating narratives can foster awareness that one's narrative is changing or has the potential to change, or, in other words, high quality educative experiences. Deleuze, however, would likely note the striated nature of delimiting these three processes and of engaging in ordered practices such as lesson or unit planning.

Teachers and students can travel more deeply into Deleuze's project by smoothing the boundaries between complicating, considering, and connecting and by asking who and what these practices exclude. Recalling Deleuze and Guattari's assertions about the ongoing integration of smoothing and striation, this smoothing will alter, although not necessarily undermine, the possibilities for complicating, considering, and connecting. Moreover, even somewhat striated conceptions of these three practices can smooth rigidly structured aspects of contemporary education paradigms. Voicing our own divergent visions of music education while welcoming ongoing variation and critical deliberation offers a counter to an educational climate that seeks to confine teachers and students through standardization and career readiness.

Complicating, Considering, and Connecting Policy

Teachers, teacher educators, and students, however, exist not in isolation but rather work within and are in part constituted by political systems. One cannot simply abandon or ignore the rhetoric and regulations that permeate twenty-first-century education. In addition to heeding calls by authors such as Richard Colwell, Ron Kos, Patrick Schmidt, and Paul Woodford for more attention to policy and politics in music teacher education,[3] music teachers and teacher educators might reimagine how they engage in and with such discourse and action.

Utilizing the practice of complicating, students and teachers could interrogate policy documents by asking: How does this policy account for or affect students' noncognitive qualities, including their diverse bodies and emotional well-being? To what extent does this policy benefit economically and socially privileged students and communities while excluding or even harming those with limited or different resources? How does this policy acknowledge or impact students' and teachers' multiple musical places? Such inquiries can assist music educators and students in resisting treating the inclusions and exclusions of policy discourse as necessary and unquestionable.

As I reflect on how I have tended to engage with policy in undergraduate and graduate classes, I realize that I often explain them as things, describing what "is" as though my account occurred absent any analysis or interpretation. Conversely, Linda Zerilli writes that for Hannah Arendt, it is "the judging activity of the spectators, not the object they judge or its maker, that creates the public space."[4] In other words, public space, which for Arendt is also political space, forms not when one acknowledges or explains a policy document, but when individuals imagine policies from multiple perspectives and then judge them. This can include wondering why policymakers authored a specific mandate, including their possible ulterior motives, and considering how the policy does or might impact diverse students. Through these discussions, participants resist conceiving of policy as an object that they must accept or ignore, striving instead to understand it as a process realized through the acts of imagining and judging.

Although teachers and teacher educators might perceive the term "policy" as only referring to top-down mandates, such as the American Every Student Succeeds Act (ESSA), policy can also denote documents and actions over which they likely have more direct influence. Patrick Jones distinguishes "hard policies" that use carrots and sticks in order to mandate certain results, including evaluations of preservice and practicing teachers and school rankings, from "soft policies" that shape perceptions and values by "co-opting rather than coercing."[5] Soft policies include curricula, course materials, admission requirements, and the work of music associations.[6]

Even absent planned resistances, administrators and educators inevitably deviate from policymakers' aims as they integrate hard policies into existing soft policies and habitual practices. As David Tyack and Larry Cuban's research reveals, reforms do not change schools as much as schools change reforms.[7] While teachers and teacher educators might participate in the creation of hard policies whenever possible, since soft policies, such as curricula, propagate or inhibit hard policies, individuals often possess more control over the broader practice of policy than is readily apparent.

Since the force of schooling and teaching traditions can minimize potentially meaningful innovations, administrators, educators, and students might question to what extent reactions against certain policies result in part from apprehension about embracing the unknown. In Arendt's words, the discomfort often aroused through the loss of familiar habits is not a reason to dismiss alternatives.[8] Working within this awareness, when those complicating and considering specific policies still find them troubling, they might empower themselves to adapt hard policies via rhizomatic soft policies that fit the needs of their changing individual circumstances. Rather than ignoring policies that they deem problematic, administrators, music educators, and students embracing Deleuze's emphasis on possible ways of living might creatively subvert or reimagine these policies.

As noted throughout this text, music educators and students might also consider how they engage with policies outside of education that impact their local and global communities. Given the importance of narrative to my project, I briefly examine intersections between storytelling, politics, and the processes of complicating, considering, and connecting. Grassroots organizer and researcher Marshall Ganz argues that because storytelling remains mindful of the past while simultaneously open to alternative futures, it assists individuals in handling deviations from a "script" by "constructing shared understandings of how to manage the risks of uncertainty, anomaly, and unpredictability."[9] Since narratives rely on embodied understandings, they resist the apathy that abstract, cognitive-centric policy discourses can engender.

Ganz argues that since storytelling constructs agency and enables access to the emotional "resources" that motivate action, it "may be what most distinguishes social movements from interest groups and other forms of collective action."[10] He exemplifies these assertions in telling his personal story about politically mobilizing Mexican agricultural workers alongside Cesar Chavez in California. By transforming thousands of individual stories—including religious, political, and cultural ones—into a shared story, participants created a collective sense of "solidarity, dignity, and power."[11] While stories can assist educators and students in interfacing with existing policies, they can also facilitate awareness about the need for new policies and other forms of political action.

More broadly, educational stakeholders can utilize narratives to incite political engagement by telling what Ganz terms "public stories." According to Ganz, a "public story" includes three elements: a story of self, which explains why one was called to engage in certain actions; a story of us, which tells why a class, community, or organization was called to its shared purposes, visions, and aims; and a story of now, which details current challenges and choices as well as "the hope to which 'we' can aspire."[12] For example, one might tell how their own experiences with discrimination (story of self) led them to join a group with shared understandings about the pervasiveness of such problems and the need for more empathy (story of us). A recent news story indicates the necessity of taking an immediate stand against discriminatory practices, moving beyond vitriol and toward a more inclusive vision of humanity (story of now).

These three stories—of self, us, and now—imply the formation of connections among individuals and between individuals and their multiple places. Yet, while not necessarily antithetical to "connecting with," because Ganz's description does not acknowledge how individuals and groups change through the process of storytelling, he implies "connecting to" stagnant entities. Alternatively, teachers and students focusing on their own and others' differing might connect with themselves by considering the evolving nature of their ethical callings, and they might connect with others by reflecting on how exchanging stories and goals informs their understandings, aims, and narratives. They can also connect with the potentialities of the here and now by exploring how concerns and possibilities form and creatively develop over time. Attending to how individuals and groups transform in and through political storytelling processes provides a more accurate portrayal of such practices and may nurture additional opportunities for critique and innovation.

Artistic endeavors can serve a particularly important function in integrating the practice of connecting with and Ganz's assertions about storytelling. For example, imagine framing a composition project or interactive performance in terms of connecting with stories of selves, us, and now. Perhaps students tell musical stories about their experiences with bullying, or, following Randall Allsup and Eric Shieh's description of students using music to address the aftermath of an oil spill, maybe they focus on social or environmental problems impacting their local communities.[13] Such action affords students opportunities to reflect on their own differing values in integration with the significant issues of their time and places. It can also assist them in developing understandings about the political potential of music-making.

The practices of complicating and considering can also complement Ganz's writings. Given that narratives have the potential to reinforce problematic or limited ideals, teachers and students might complicate their stories of self, us, and now by interrogating the assumptions they make about humans' sociality, embodiment, emotions, glocal places, and nature of music-making. Subsequently, they might imagine alternatives or extensions in light of the revealed omissions or troubling hierarchies. Complicating can also involve experimenting with how artistic endeavors might arouse experiences such as empathy in deeper or different ways than verbal stories alone. Since any sort of unified story risks subjugating and silencing certain voices, ongoing, multifaceted ethical considerations play a crucial role in resisting stagnant grand narratives.

Considering musical stories of selves, us, and now demands viewing those stories from as many diverse perspectives as possible and subsequently judging them. Such action resists the unthoughtful formation of narratives and political goals that may inadvertently harm others. When possible, teachers and students might seek out opportunities for often silenced persons to share their experiences directly. Yet, this does not mean simply fitting new stories into existing storylines. As political philosopher Enrique Dussel writes, "The excluded should not be merely included into the old system—as this would be to introduce the Other into the Same—but rather ought to participate as equals in a new institutional moment (the new political order). This is a struggle not for inclusion but for transformation."[14] As such, those considering divergent stories of individual selves continually reconstitutes musical narratives of "us" and "now" in and through their dialogue and imaginings.

In short, teachers and students might reinterpret Ganz's ideas as involving: a story of one's changing self, complicated and considerate stories of us, and connective stories of now. Rather than conceiving of policy and policymaking as top-down processes separated from one's everyday practices, they might view themselves as policymakers and explore how they can enact policy rhizomatically, affecting change from the middle outward.

Complicating, Considering, and Connecting Research

While this text has primarily focused on music teaching and learning, the processes of complicating, considering, and connecting can also inform research endeavors. Elizabeth Gould explains traditional quantitative, qualitative, and philosophical music education research as "unable to initiate change because it does not and cannot engage radical imagination."[15] Although I do not find change strictly antithetical to contemporary research practices, I agree that such work often remains confined to prescribed procedures and ends, wanting for creativity and separated from life beyond the academy. Janet Miller makes a similar statement about the role of autobiography in research, teaching, and learning, writing: "To 'tell your or my story' as singular, unified, chronological, and coherent, is to maintain the status quo, to reinscribe already known situations and identities as fixed, immutable, locked into normalized conceptions of what and who are possible."[16] It follows that the norms, limits, and values hidden within and propagated by current research methods and products necessitate interrogation.

Music education researchers might complicate their work by considering the assumptions about people and places that underlie their questions and methods. What qualities, including embodiment, emotion, and sociality, do researchers ignore or minimize within a single study or across multiple studies? When are variations within or between teachers' and students' meaning-laden environments, including certain individuals and ways of being and becoming musical, overlooked, or subsumed under overarching norms? To what extent are one's inquiries placeless or grounded in the values and practices of particularly privileged locations? While researchers may not find it meaningful or feasible to address humans' multiple qualities and locations in any one study, contemplating the assumptions that underlie their writing and methods (or nonmethods)[17] may assist them in acknowledging further limitations of individual studies. Additionally, in order to avoid the reinforcement of currently excluded people, places, music-making, and aspects of humanity, scholars might imagine and experiment with how they can diversify their research trajectories and wanderings over time.

It follows that complicating music education research necessitates embracing uncertainty rather than definitive answers. Using Jacques Derrida's practice of deconstruction to explain the limits of language, Petter Dyndahl argues that music education researchers "must endeavor to tolerate a system of meaning and understanding that is characterized by ambiguity, differences, and deferrals."[18] Building on such thinking, researchers might interrogate when simplified research procedures and products become problematic while simultaneously contemplating when and what imaginative sojourns might contribute to their work. I wonder: In addition to and integration with traditional forms of scholarly writing, can we as individuals and as a research community foster research practices and writings that open possibilities rather than aim toward conclusions? What would it look like if researchers, reviewers, and readers welcomed messiness, complexity, and ambiguity as much as any clear "result" or "emergent theme"? Inspired by the concept of the rhizome, might researchers conceive of their work not as permanently filling a gap between existing research, but rather as gaps, knowns, and curiosities that transform in and through their meetings?

Likewise, music education researchers could experiment with how they communicate their work. Drawing on Roberta Lamb's piece "Tone Deaf/Symphonies Singing: Sketches for a Musicale," Gould demonstrates the possibilities of what she calls "academic writing as literary Trojan horse."[19] She explains that rather than simply combining literature and research, such researchers create work that "aspires to leap off the page from visual to sound, singing, murmuring, chanting. . . . Discursive ideas are handled as motives. . . . The story is told and untold. Then retold."[20] Similarly, Gould herself has complicated traditional forms of scholarly communication by using dance to respond to a paper at a philosophy conference and embedding musical recordings within a philosophical text, with the intent that readers play them while reading specific parts of the piece.[21] These examples serve not as models in need of replication but as inspiring points of rupture through and from which others might journey. The question becomes not whether researchers should simplify and organize *or* complicate and confuse but rather how these practices might continually integrate, constituting and altering each other in the process.

Music education researchers might use the practice of considering to examine existing and proposed studies from as many perspectives as possible, including the social-embodied-emotional ones of traditionally omitted or subjugated music makers. They could question: What would those with contrasting viewpoints say about my and others' research, and how might such imaginings inform one's current and future work? Going further, I am curious about how teacher educators might engage students conducting research in ethical imagining and judging during various stages of their inquiries. For example, consider a research class in which students worked together to examine their proposed topics and research questions through multiple divergent viewpoints and subsequently brainstormed how they might make their studies more ethical. How might starting from a place of humility and critical ethical awareness and returning to these evolving positions again and again over the course of the study affect teachers' and students' research experiences as well as their teaching and learning more broadly?

At the conclusion of studies, researchers might ask how their work can inform the creation of more ethical policies as well as contribute to dialogue about the role of ethics in their institutions and everyday encounters. While considering what research and research practices might facilitate to more ethical music teaching and learning need not always serve as the primary guiding force behind research decisions, I wonder what it might look like to imagine one's research as having not only a topical or methodological trajectory, but also an ethical one.

Researchers "connecting with" various individuals might acknowledge and explore how all involved alter in and through their meetings. For instance, policymakers can learn from researchers' findings, while researchers can in turn grow through policymakers' insights about political processes and the current political climate. "Connecting with" can also include challenging divides within institutions, transforming the physical and intellectual boundaries that separate different schools of thought, methodologies, and disciplines. Recalling Gould's statement about explorations that begin with music "rather than what we think music is," I wonder how we might begin with research—with the raw potentiality of inquisitiveness and sustained inquiry—rather than from what we think research is.[22]

Researchers could also experiment with how our practices foster connections with our personal narratives, including how our stories change in the process. Since what constitutes "research" and "researching" evolves in and through culturally situated individual and collective narratives, it is problematic if the stories one tells—both about research and through research—omit the norms and habits that influence and ultimately limit such work. Miller explains, "Changing what it means 'to be' or 'to become' a teacher, or a student, or a researcher cannot happen by 'telling my or your story,' if that story simply repeats or reinscribes the already normalized and descriptive identity categories of 'woman,' 'man,' 'student,' 'researcher,' or 'teacher.'"[23] Connecting with one's self-stories involves an openness to how researching can inform one's becomings and imaginative narrative turns.

In philosophical research, this might include attending to how one's work draws on and changes in integration with their own stories, as I have attempted to do throughout this text. While my own understandings about the potential for such action remain in their infancy, I hope to learn from others who take the risk of communicating their unfinished ventures. Through a willingness to share the vulnerability of embracing scholarly thinking and writing as acts that constitute and reconstitute our evolving selves, we can ask what kind of researchers, educators, and students we might become and how researching can assist us in our journeying.

Continued Journeying

In the middle of writing this book, I was fortunate enough to walk around downtown Longyearbyen, which, located one hundred miles north of the Arctic Circle, is the northernmost settlement on Earth. Weeks earlier, Estelle Jorgensen had challenged me to find my philosophical voice,[24] and I had hoped that my travels would give me a chance to reflect on her provocation. As I hopelessly struggled with the daunting task, the following thought entered my head: I am a person who journeys to the northernmost settlement on Earth, and in this moment, that is my philosophical voice. While I at first tried to dismiss the thought as simplistic, I could not let it go.

My voice is the evolving "I" who travels, both physically and imaginatively, the I who has had great privilege and experienced repeated failure, and the I who expresses herself via music-making and philosophizing. I am as much philosopher as narrative and narrator; I create embodied-emotional arguments that derive in and through experience. My philosophical voice cannot be the same as those who have come before me or as the Deleuzian "people-to-come"; it will never match that of my contemporaries who have traversed markedly different physical, emotional, social, and intellectual journeys. My voice cannot be "lost" or "found," only silenced or embraced—restrained or encouraged to grow. It will always exist in an uncertain middle, differing day after day.

Only later did I realize that the thought had come to me while on an island (Svalbard) with no trees. Upon returning to mainland Norway, I felt jarred when seeing the imposing birch trunks that lined the highway exiting the airport. I welcomed the comfort of their patterned shapes and familiar green hues. Simultaneously, I mourned the loss of the barren landscape, weathered glaciers, and encompassing fog that offered both a previously unimagined way of experiencing the world and a renewed sense of my own precarious, insignificant human life. Despite my return to a place of forests, my journeying has destined me to occupy a liminal space informed by the unceasing integration of tree-like and rhizomatic growth; I still crave the former while being intrigued and challenged by the latter.

And so I wonder: What is your philosophical voice? You are someone reading a philosophical book, someone who will likely soon look into a student's eyes, someone who has made and will make music—whatever that means to you. From where are you coming and what potentialities lie on trails only you can blaze? Are you willing to step beyond the trees, even if only temporarily? What might I and others learn from your evolving narratives?

I end with the words of one of my mentors, Roger Rideout: "Let your passion and curiosity guide you. You will always be on the right path."[25] We can spend our days chasing a "right path" that is of someone else's limited creation, but passion and curiosity will not be our guides. We can thoughtlessly follow passion and curiosity along a path without imagining multiple perspectives and judging "right" and "wrong." Or, we can wander awkwardly and uncertainly, complicating, considering, and connecting multiple paths—paths valued not for their destinations but as meaningful in their own right. My journey—and maybe yours—proceeds from the middle.

Notes

1. Lauren Kapalka Richerme, "To Name or Not to Name? Social Justice, Poststructuralism, and Music Teacher Education," *Philosophy of Music Education Review* 24, no. 1 (2016): 84–102. Superposition can also refer to properties such as spin.

2. Randall Allsup, *Remixing the Classroom: Toward an Open Philosophy of Music Education* (Bloomington: Indiana University Press, 2016), 141.

3. Richard Colwell, "Music Teacher Education in This Century: Part I," *Arts Education Policy Review* 108, no. 1 (2006): 15–27; Ron Kos, "Developing Capacity for Change: A Policy Analysis for the Music Education Profession," *Arts Education Policy Review* 111, no. 3 (2010): 97–104; Patrick Schmidt, "Reinventing from Within: Thinking Spherically as a Policy Imperative in Music Education," *Arts Education Policy Review* 110, no. 4 (2009): 39–47; Paul Woodford, *Democracy and Music Education: Liberalism, Ethics, and the Politics of Practice* (Bloomington: Indiana University Press, 2005).

4. Linda Zerilli, *Feminism and the Abyss of Freedom* (Chicago: University of Chicago Press, 2005), 160. Zerilli clarifies that while Arendt credits this idea to Kant, it is her own idiosyncratic reading of him that enabled it. As noted in chapter 5, Arendt problematically designates schools and families as "pre-political." Writers such as Judith Butler have problematized this distinction, noting the detrimental effects it may have for women, the elderly, and others who have traditionally resided in what Arendt would consider private rather than public life. In agreement with Butler, I argue that a strict demarcation between public and private excludes or minimizes the potential contributions of certain individuals, and that one can never fully separate public from private life. Judith Butler, *Notes Toward a Performative Theory of Assembly* (Cambridge, MA: Harvard University Press, 2015), 44–45.

5. Patrick Jones, "Hard and Soft Policies in Music Education: Building the Capacity of Teachers to Understand, Study and Influence Them," *Arts Education Policy Review* 110, no. 4 (2009): 30.

6. Ibid. While I have elsewhere problematized the terms "hard policies" and "soft policies," I find these distinctions helpful for the purposes of this chapter. Lauren Kapalka Richerme, "Reimagining Policy: Power, Problems, and Public Stories," *Arts Education Policy Review* 120, no. 2 (2019): 94–102.

7. David Tyack and Larry Cuban, *Tinkering toward Utopia* (Cambridge, MA: Harvard University Press, 1995).

8. Hannah Arendt, "Some Questions of Moral Philosophy," in *Responsibility and Judgment*, ed. Jerome Kohn (New York: Schocken, 2003), 107.

9. Marshall Ganz, "The Power of Story in Social Movements," 2001, https://dash.harvard.edu/handle/1/27306251.

10. Ibid.

11. Ibid., 9.

12. Marshall Ganz, "Telling Your Public Story: Self, Us, Now," 2007, https://philstesthomepage.files.wordpress.com/2014/05/public-story-worksheet07ganz.pdf.

13. Randall Allsup and Eric Shieh, "Social Justice and Music Education: The Call for a Public Pedagogy," *Music Educators Journal* 98, no. 4 (2012): 47–51.

14. Enrique Dussel, *Twenty Theses on Politics,* trans. George Ciccariello-Maher (Durham, NC: Duke University Press, 2008), 89.

15. Elizabeth Gould, "Writing Trojan Horses and War Machines: The Creative Political in Music Education Research," *Educational Philosophy and Theory* 43, no. 8 (2011): 877.

16. Janet Miller, "Autobiography and the Necessary Incompleteness of Teachers' Stories," in *A Light in Dark Times: Maxine Greene and the Unfinished Conversation*, ed. William C. Ayers and Janet L. Miller (New York: Teachers College Press, 1998), 152.

17. For a detailed description of Deleuze's nonmethodological rigor, see chapter 1.

18. Petter Dyndahl, "Music Education in the Sign of Deconstruction," *Philosophy of Music Education Review* 16, no. 2 (2008): 140.

19. Gould, "Writing Trojan Horses and War Machines," 884.

20. Ibid.

21. Elizabeth Gould, "A Response to Estelle Jorgensen and Iris M. Yob's 'Deconstructing Deleuze and Guattari's *A Thousand Plateaus* for Music Education'" (presentation, International Society for the Philosophy of Music Education, Helsinki, Finland, June 9–13, 2010); Elizabeth Gould, "Legible Bodies in Music Education: Becoming Matter," *Action, Criticism, and Theory in Music Education* 6, no. 4 (2007): 201–223.

22. Elizabeth Gould, "Women Working in Music Education: The War Machine," *Philosophy of Music Education Review* 17, no. 2 (2009): 128.

23. Miller, *Sounds of Silence Breaking*, 152.

24. Estelle Jorgensen, Skype call with the author, June 24, 2016.

25. Roger Rideout, written message to the author, May, 2005.

Bibliography

Abramo, Joseph. "Mystery, Fire and Intrigue: Representation and Commodification of Race in Band Literature." *Visions of Research in Music Education* 9/10 (2007): 1–23.
Abril, Carlos. "Music That Represents Culture: Selecting Music with Integrity." *Music Educators Journal* 93, no. 1 (2006): 38–45.
Ahmed, Sara. *The Cultural Politics of Emotion*. New York: Routledge, 2004.
Aigen, Kenneth. "Philosophical Inquiry." In *Music Therapy Research: Quantitative and Qualitative Perspectives*, edited by Barbara Wheeler, 447–484. Phoenixville, PA: Barcelona Publishers, 1995.
Alcoff, Linda. "Cultural Feminism versus Post-structuralism: The Identity Crisis in Feminist Theory." *Journal of Women in Culture and Society* 13, no. 3 (1988): 405–436.
Allsup, Randall E. "The Eclipse of Higher Education or Problems Preparing Artists in a Mercantile World." *Music Education Research* 17, no. 3 (2015): 251–261.
———. "Music Teacher Quality and the Problem of Routine Expertise." *Philosophy of Music Education Review* 23, no. 1 (2015): 5–24.
———. *Remixing the Classroom: Toward an Open Philosophy of Music Education*. Bloomington: Indiana University Press, 2016.
Allsup, Randall E., and Eric Shieh. "Social Justice and Music Education: The Call for a Public Pedagogy." *Music Educators Journal* 98, no. 4 (2012): 47–51.
Allsup, Randall E., and Heidi Westerlund, "Methods and Situational Ethics in Music Education." *Action, Criticism, and Theory for Music Education* 11, no. 1 (2012): 124–148.
Ambirajan, S. "Globalisation, Media and Culture." *Economic and Political Weekly* 35, no. 25 (2000): 2141–2147.
Appiah, Kwame Anthony. *Cosmopolitanism: Ethics in a World of Strangers*. New York: W. W. Norton, 2006.
Arendt, Hannah. *Between Past and Future: Exercises in Political Thought*. New York: Viking, 1968.
———. *Essays in Understanding, 1930–1954*. Edited by Jerome Kohn. New York: Harcourt Brace, 1994.
———. "Imagination." In *Lectures on Kant's Political Philosophy*, edited by Ronald Beiner, 79–84. Chicago: University of Chicago Press, 1982.
———. *The Life of the Mind*. San Diego, CA: Harcourt, 1971.
———. "Some Questions of Moral Philosophy." In *Responsibility and Judgment*, edited by Jerome Kohn, 49–145. New York: Schocken, 2003.
Averill, James. "A Constructivist View of Emotion." In *Theories of Emotion*, edited by Robert Plutchik and Henry Kellerman, 306–312. New York: Academic Press, 1980.
Ayers, William. "Doing Philosophy: Maxine Greene and the Pedagogy of Possibility." In *A Light in Dark Times: Maxine Greene and the Unfinished Conversation*, edited by William C. Ayers and Janet L. Miller, 3–10. New York: Teachers College Press, 1998.
Bakhtin, Mikhail. *The Dialogic Imagination*. Edited by Michael Holquist, translated by Caryl Emerson and Michael Holquist. Austin: University of Texas Press, 1981.

Baltzis, Alexandros. "Globalization and Musical Culture." *Acta Musicologica* 77, no.1 (2005): 137–150.
Baron, Marcia W., Philip Pettit, and Michael Slote, eds. *Three Methods of Ethics: A Debate.* Malden, MA: Blackwell, 1997.
Barrett, Margaret S., and Sandra L. Stauffer. "Resonant Work: Toward an Ethic of Narrative Research." In *Narrative Soundings: An Anthology of Narrative Inquiry in Music Education,* edited by Margaret S. Barrett and Sandra L. Stauffer, 1–16. New York: Springer Science+Business Media, 2012.
Beauchamp, Tom L. *Philosophical Ethics: An Introduction to Moral Philosophy,* 3rd ed. Boston: McGraw Hill, 2001.
Belsey, Catherine. *Poststructuralism: A Very Short Introduction.* Oxford: Oxford University Press, 2002.
Benedict, Cathy. "Defining Ourselves as Other: Envisioning Transformative Possibilities." In *Teaching Music in the Urban Classroom,* Vol. 1, *A Guide to Survival, Success, and Reform,* edited by Carol Frierson-Campbell, 3–13. Lanham, MD: Rowman & Littlefield Education, 2006.
———. "Naming Our Reality: Negotiating and Creating Meaning in the Margin." *Philosophy of Music Education Review* 15, no.1 (2007): 23–36.
———. "Processes of Alienation: Marx, Orff and Kodaly." *British Journal of Music Education* 26, no. 2 (2009): 213–224.
Bennett, Andy. *Popular Music and Youth Culture: Music, Identity and Place.* New York: Palgrave, 2000.
Bennett, Peggy D. "Sarah Glover: A Forgotten Pioneer in Music Education." *Journal of Research in Music Education* 32, no. 1 (1984): 49–64.
Biesta, Gert. "How to Exist Politically and Learn from It: Hannah Arendt and the Problem of Democratic Education." *Teachers College Record* 112, no. 2 (2010): 556–575.
Bogue, Ronald. *Deleuze's Way: Essays in Transverse Ethics and Aesthetics.* New York: Routledge, 2007.
Bough, Ronald. "Search, Swim and See: Deleuze's Apprenticeship in Signs and Pedagogy of Images." *Educational Philosophy and Theory* 36, no. 3 (2004): 327–342.
Bourdieu, Pierre. *The Field of Cultural Production: Essays on Art and Literature.* Translated by Randal Johnson. New York: Columbia University Press, 1993.
Bowman, Wayne. "Cognition and the Body: Perspectives from Music Education." In *Knowing Bodies, Moving Minds: Towards Embodied Teaching and Learning,* edited by Liora Bresler, 29–50. Boston: Kluwer Academic Publishers, 2004.
———. "Music as Ethical Encounter." *Bulletin of the Council for Research in Music Education,* no. 151 (2000): 11–20.
———. "Music Education in Nihilistic Times." *Educational Philosophy and Theory* 37, no. 1 (2005): 29–46.
———. *Philosophical Perspectives on Music.* New York: Oxford University Press, 1998.
———. "A Somatic, 'Here and Now' Semantic: Music, Body, and Self." *Bulletin of the Council for Research in Music Education,* no. 144 (2000): 45–60.
———. "Why Narrative? Why Now?" *Research Studies in Music Education* 27, no. 1 (2006): 5–20.
Bowman, Wayne, and Kimberly Powell. "The Body in a State of Music." In *International Handbook of Research in Arts Education:* Part 2, edited by Liora Bresler, 1087–1108. Dordrecht, The Netherlands: Springer, 2007.

Boyce-Tillman, June. "Music and the Dignity of Difference." *Philosophy of Music Education Review* 20, no. 1 (2012): 25–44.
———. "Towards an Ecology of Music Education," *Philosophy of Music Education Review* 12, no. 2 (2004): 102–125.
Bradley, Deborah. "In the Space between the Rock and the Hard Place: State Teacher Certification Guidelines and Music Education for Social Justice." *Journal of Aesthetic Education* 45, no. 4 (2011): 79–96.
———. "Oh, That Magic Feeling! Multicultural Human Subjectivity, Community, and Fascism's Footprints." *Philosophy of Music Education Review* 17, no. 1 (2009): 56–74.
Bradt, Kevin M. *Story as a Way of Knowing*. Kansas City, MO: Sheed and Ward, 1997.
Braidotti, Rosi. *Nomadic Subjects: Embodiment and Sexual Difference in Contemporary Feminist Theory*. 2nd ed. New York: Columbia University Press, 2011.
———. *Transpositions: On Nomadic Ethics*. Cambridge UK: Polity Press, 2006.
Britton, Allen, Arnold Broido, and Charles Gary. "The Tanglewood Declaration." In *Documentary Report of the Tanglewood Symposium*, edited by Robert A. Choate. Washington, DC: Music Educators National Conference, 1968.
Brown, Brené. *Daring Greatly: How the Courage to Be Vulnerable Transforms the Way We Live, Love, Parent, and Lead*. New York: Gotham, 2012.
Bruner, Jerome. *Acts of Meaning*. Cambridge, MA: Harvard University Press, 1990.
———. "Life as Narrative." *Social Research* 71, no. 3 (2004): 691–710.
———. *Making Stories: Law Literature Life*. Cambridge, MA: Harvard University Press, 2002.
———. "The Narrative Construction of Reality." *Critical Inquiry* 18, no. 1 (1991): 1–21.
Butler, Judith. *Notes Toward a Performative Theory of Assembly*. Cambridge, MA: Harvard University Press, 2015.
Carpenter, Nan Cooke. "Music in the Medieval Universities." *Journal of Research in Music Education* 3, no. 2 (1955): 136–144.
Casey, Edward. "How to Get from Space to Place in a Fairly Short Stretch of Time: Phenomenological Prolegomena." In *Senses of Place*, edited by Steven Feld and Keith Basso, 13–52. Santa Fe: School of American Research Press, 1996.
Choksy, Lois. *The Kodály Method: Comprehensive Music Education from Infant to Adult*. Englewood Cliffs, NJ: Prentice Hall, 1988.
Clandinin, D. Jean, and Jerry Rosiek, "Mapping a Landscape of Narrative Inquiry: Borderland Spaces and Tensions." In *Handbook of Narrative Inquiry: Mapping a Methodology*, edited by D. Jean Clandinin, 35–76. Thousand Oaks, CA: Sage, 2007.
Cole, David R. *Educational Life-Forms: Deleuzian Teaching and Learning Practice*. Rotterdam, The Netherlands: Sense, 2011.
Colebrook, Claire. "Creative Evolution and the Creation of Man." *The Southern Journal of Philosophy* 48 (2010): 109–132.
———. *Deleuze: A Guide for the Perplexed*. New York: Continuum, 2006.
———. *Gilles Deleuze*. New York: Routledge, 2002.
———. *Understanding Deleuze*. Sydney, Australia: Allen & Unwin, 2002.
College Board, The. "International Arts Education Standards: A Survey of the Arts Education Standards and Practices of Fifteen Countries and Regions." 2013. https://www.nationalartsstandards.org/sites/default/files/College%20Board%20Research%20-%20International%20Standards_0.pdf.

Colman, Felicity. "Rhizome." In *The Deleuze Dictionary*, edited by Adrian Parr, 11–13. Edinburgh: Edinburgh University Press, 2005.

Colwell, Richard. "Music Teacher Education in This Century: Part I." *Arts Education Policy Review* 108, no. 1 (2006): 15–27.

Coulson, Mark. "Attributing Emotion to Static Body Postures: Recognition Accuracy, Confusions, and Viewpoint Dependence." *Journal of Nonverbal Behavior* 28, no. 2 (2004): 117–139.

Cresswell, Tim. "Introduction: Theorizing Place." In *Mobilizing Place, Placing Mobility: The Politics of Representation in a Globalized World,* edited by Ginette Verstraete and Tim Cresswell, 11–32. New York: Editions Rodopi, B. V., 2002.

———. *Place: A Short Introduction*. Malden, MA: Blackwell, 2004.

Damasio, Antonio R. *The Feeling of What Happens: Body and Emotion in the Making of Consciousness*. Orlando, FL: Harcourt, 1999.

Davies, Stephen. *Musical Meaning and Expression*. Ithaca, NY: Cornell University Press, 1994.

Deigh, John. *An Introduction to Ethics*. Cambridge, UK: Cambridge University Press, 2010.

Deleuze, Gilles. *Difference and Repetition*. Translated by Paul Patton. New York: Columbia University Press, 1994.

———. *Negotiations: 1972–1990*. Translated by Martin Joughin. New York: Columbia University Press, 1995.

Deleuze, Gilles, and Félix Guattari. *Kafka: Toward a Minor Literature*. Translated by Dana Polan. Minneapolis: University of Minnesota Press, 1986.

———. *A Thousand Plateaus: Capitalism and Schizophrenia*. Translated by Brian Massumi. Minneapolis: University of Minnesota Press, 1987.

———. *What Is Philosophy?* Translated by Hugh Tomlinson and Graham Burchell. New York: Columbia University Press, 1994.

de Sousa Santos, Boaventura. "Globalizations." *Theory, Culture & Society* 23, no. 2–3 (2006): 393–399.

Department of Education. "National Curriculum in England: Music Programmes of Study." 2013. https://www.gov.uk/government/publications/national-curriculum-in-england-music-programmes-of-study.

Dewey, John. *The Child and the Curriculum*. Chicago: University of Chicago Press, 1902.

———. *Experience and Education*. New York: Macmillan, 1997.

Dussel, Enrique. *Twenty Theses on Politics*. Translated by George Ciccariello-Maher. Durham, NC: Duke University Press, 2008.

Dyndahl, Petter. "Music Education in the Sign of Deconstruction." *Philosophy of Music Education Review* 16, no. 2 (2008): 140.

Ekman, Paul. "All Emotions Are Basic." In *The Nature of Emotion: Fundamental Questions*, edited by Paul Ekman and Richard J. Davidson, 15–19. New York: Oxford University Press, 1994.

Eliot, T. S. *Four Quartets*. Orlando, FL: Harcourt, 1943.

Elliott, David J. *Music Matters: A New Philosophy of Music Education*. New York: Oxford University Press, 1995.

Elliott, David J., and Marissa Silverman, *Music Matters: A Philosophy of Music Education*, 2nd ed. New York: Oxford University Press, 2015.

———. "Rethinking Philosophy, Re-viewing Musical-Emotional Experiences." In *The Oxford Handbook of Philosophy in Music Education,* edited by Wayne D. Bowman and Ana Lucía Frega, 37–52. New York: Oxford University Press, 2012.

Elpus, Kenneth. "Music Teacher Licensure Candidates in the United States: A Demographic Profile and Analysis of Licensure Examination Scores." *Journal of Research in Music Education* 63, no. 3 (2015): 314–335.

Elpus, Kenneth, and Carlos Abril. "High School Music Ensemble Students in the United States: A Demographic Profile." *Journal of Research in Music Education* 59, no. 2 (2011): 128–145.

Fisher, Walter R. *Human Communication as Narration: Toward a Philosophy of Reason, Value, and Action*. Columbia: University of South Carolina Press, 1987.

Fiske, Harold. "Engaging Student Ownership of Musical Ideas." In *The Oxford Handbook of Philosophy in Music Education*, edited by Wayne D. Bowman and Ana Lucía Frega, 307–327. New York: Oxford University Press, 2012.

Fitzpatrick, Kate R. "Cultural Diversity and the Formation of Identity: Our Role as Music Teachers." *Music Educators Journal* 98, no. 4 (2012): 53–59.

Forman, Murray. *The 'Hood Comes First: Race, Space, and Place in Rap and Hip-Hop*. Middletown, CT: Wesleyan University Press, 2002.

Freire, Paulo. *Pedagogy of the Oppressed*. Translated by Myra Bergman Ramos. 1970, Reprint. New York: Continuum, 2000.

Froehlich, Hildegard, and Carol Frierson-Campbell. *Inquiry in Music Education*. New York: Taylor and Francis, 2012.

Fusar-Poli, Paolo, Francesco Barale, Jorge Perez, Philip McGuire, Pierluigi Politi, Anna Placentino, Francesco Carletti, et al. "Functional Atlas of Emotional Faces Processing: A Voxel-Based Meta-Analysis of 105 Functional Magnetic Resonance Imaging Studies." *Journal of Psychiatry & Neuroscience* 34, no. 6 (2009): 418–432.

Ganz, Marshall. "The Power of Story in Social Movements." 2001. https://dash.harvard.edu/handle/1/27306251.

———. "Telling Your Public Story: Self, Us, Now." 2007. https://philstesthomepage.files.wordpress.com/2014/05/public-story-worksheet07ganz.pdf.

Gaut, Berys. *Art, Emotion and Ethics*. New York: Oxford University Press, 2007.

Gay, Geneva. *Culturally Responsive Teaching: Theory, Research, and Practice*. New York: Teachers College Press, 2010.

Goble, J. Scott. *What's So Important about Music Education?* New York: Routledge, 2010.

Goehr, Lydia. *The Imaginary Museum of Musical Works: An Essay in the Philosophy of Music*. New York: Oxford University Press, 2007.

Goetze, Mary. "Challenges of Performing Diverse Cultural Music." *Music Educators Journal* 87, no. 1 (2008): 23–25, 48.

Goldstein, Rebecca Newberger. *Plato at the Googleplex: Why Philosophy Won't Go Away*. New York: Pantheon, 2014.

Gould, Elizabeth. "Dancing Composition: Pedagogy and Philosophy as Experience." *International Journal of Music Education* 24, no. 3 (2006): 197–207.

———. "Devouring the Other: Democracy in Music Education." *Action, Criticism, and Theory for Music Education* 7, no. 1 (2008): 29–44.

———. "Feminist Imperative(s) in Music and Education: Philosophy, Theory, or What Matters Most." *Educational Philosophy and Theory* 43, no. 2 (2011): 130–147.

———. "Legible Bodies in Music Education: Becoming Matter." *Action, Criticism, and Theory in Music Education* 6, no. 4 (2007): 201–223.

———. "Music Education Desire(ing): Language, Literacy, and Lieder." *Philosophy of Music Education Review* 17, no. 1 (2009): 41–55.

———. "Nomadic Turns: Epistemology, Experience, and Women University Band Directors." *Philosophy of Music Education Review* 13, no. 2 (2005): 147–164.
———. "A Response to Estelle Jorgensen and Iris M. Yob's 'Deconstructing Deleuze and Guattari's *A Thousand Plateaus* for Music Education.'" Presentation, International Society for the Philosophy of Music Education. Helsinki, Finland, June 9–13, 2010.
———. "Social Justice in Music Education: The Problematic of Democracy." *Music Education Research* 9, no. 2 (2007): 229–240.
———. "Thinking (as) Difference: Lesbian Imagination and Music." *Women and Music: A Journal of Gender and Culture* 11, no. 1 (2007): 17–28.
———. "Women Working in Music Education: The War Machine." *Philosophy of Music Education Review* 17, no. 2 (2009): 126–143.
———. "Writing Trojan Horses and War Machines: The Creative Political in Music Education Research." *Educational Philosophy and Theory* 43, no. 8 (2011): 874–887.
———. "Uprooting Music Education Pedagogies and Curricula: Becoming Musician and the Deleuzian Refrain." *Discourse: Studies in the Cultural Politics of Education* 33, no. 1 (2012): 75–86.
Green, Denise. *Metonymy in Contemporary Art: A New Paradigm*. Minneapolis: University of Minnesota Press, 2005.
Green, Lucy. *How Popular Musicians Learn: A Way Ahead for Music Education*. Burlington, VT: Ashgate, 2002.
Greene, Maxine. *Releasing the Imagination: Essays on Education, the Arts, and Social Change*. San Francisco: Jossey-Bass, 1995.
Grosz, Elizabeth. *Chaos, Territory, Art: Deleuze and the Framing of the Earth*. New York: Columbia University Press, 2008.
———. *Volatile Bodies: Toward a Corporeal Feminism*. Bloomington: Indiana University Press, 1994.
Hansen, David T. *The Teacher and the World: A Study of Cosmopolitanism as Education*. New York: Routledge, 2011.
Heimonen, Marja. "'Bildung' and Music Education: A Finnish Perspective." *Philosophy of Music Education Review* 22, no. 2 (2014): 188–208.
———. "Music Education and Global Ethics: Educating Citizens for the World." *Action, Criticism, and Theory for Music Education* 11, no. 2 (2012): 73–74.
Hess, Juliet. "Performing Tolerance and Curriculum: The Politics of Self-Congratulation, Identity Formation, and Pedagogy in World Music Education." *Philosophy of Music Education Review* 21, no. 1 (2013): 66–91.
Higgins, Kathleen. "Refined Emotion in Aesthetic Experience: A Cross-Cultural Comparison." In *Aesthetic Experience*, edited by Richard Shusterman and Adele Tomin, 106–126. New York: Routledge, 2008.
Hochschild, Adam. "Globalisation and Culture." *Economic and Political Weekly* 33, no. 21 (1998): 1235–1238.
Hoek, Antoinette. "South African Unit Standards for a General Music Appraisal Programme at NQF Levels 2–4, with Special Reference to Ensemble Specialisation for Available Instruments." 2001. https://pdfs.semanticscholar.org/3709/f6d49e f6d469457a20e6b9ff936da1ce1895.pdf?_ga=2.162131961.454580314.1567603790-1463185 626.1567603790.
Horsley, Stephanie. "Globally Convergent Accountability Policies and the Cultural Status of State Funded School Music Programs: A State-Level Comparison." In *Proceedings of*

the 17th Biennial International Seminar of the Commission on Music Policy: Culture, Education, and Media, edited by Peter Gouzouasis, 72–78. Vancouver: University of British Columbia, 2014.

Howard, Vernon. *Learning by All Means: Lessons from the Arts.* New York: Peter Lang, 1992.

Hroch, Petra. "Deleuze, Guattari, and Environmental Pedagogy and Politics: *Ritournelles* for a Planet-Yet-to-Come." In *Deleuze and Guattari, Politics and Education: For a People-Yet-to-Come,* edited by Matthew Carlin and Jason Wallin, 49–76. New York: Bloomsbury Academic, 2014.

Jank, Warner. "Didaktik, Bildung, Content: On the Writings of Frede V. Nielsen." *Philosophy of Music Education Review* 22, no. 2 (2014): 113–131.

Jones, LeRoi. *Blues People.* New York: William Morrow & Company, 1963.

Jones, Patrick M. "Hard and Soft Policies in Music Education: Building the Capacity of Teachers to Understand, Study, and Influence Them." *Arts Education Policy Review* 110, no. 4 (2009): 27–32.

Jorgensen, Estelle R. *In Search of Music Education.* Urbana: University of Illinois Press, 1997.

———. *Pictures of Music Education.* Bloomington: Indiana University Press, 2013.

———. *Transforming Music Education.* Bloomington: Indiana University Press, 2003.

Jorgensen Estelle R., and Iris M. Yob, "Deconstructing Deleuze and Guattari's *A Thousand Plateaus* for Music Education." *Journal of Aesthetic Education* 47, no. 3 (2013): 36–55.

Kanellopoulos, Panagiotis A. "Freedom and Responsibility: The Aesthetics of Free Musical Improvisation and its Educational Implications—A View from Bakhtin." *Philosophy of Music Education Review* 19, no. 2 (2011): 113–135.

Kertz-Welzel, Alexandra. "Lessons from Elsewhere? Comparative Music Education in Times of Globalization." *Philosophy of Music Education Review* 23, no. 1 (2015): 48–66.

Kivy, Peter. *Music Alone: Philosophical Reflections on the Purely Musical Experience.* Ithaca, NY: Cornell University Press, 1990.

Klein, Alyson. "ESEA Reauthorization: The Every Student Succeeds Act Explained." EdWeek, November 30, 2015. http://blogs.edweek.org/edweek/campaign-k-12/2015/11/esea_reauthorization_the_every.html?r=501001509.

Kos, Ronald P. "Developing Capacity for Change: A Policy Analysis for the Music Education Profession." *Arts Education Policy Review* 111, no. 3 (2010): 97–104.

Koza, Julia. "Listening for Whiteness: Hearing Racial Politics in Undergraduate School Music." *Philosophy of Music Education Review* 16, no. 2 (2008): 145–155.

———. "My Body Had a Mind of Its Own: On Teaching, the Illusion of Control, and the Terrifying Limits of Governmentality (Part I)." *Philosophy of Music Education Review* 17, no. 2 (2009): 98–125.

Kratus, John. "Music Education at the Tipping Point." *Music Educators Journal* 94, no. 2 (2007): 42–48.

———. "The Role of Subversion in Changing Music Education." In *Music Education: Navigating the Future.* Edited by Clint Randles. New York: Routledge, 2015.

Krulwich, Robert. "Socrates (In the Form of a 9-Year-Old) Shows Up in a Suburban Backyard in Washington." *National Public Radio,* March 27, 2013. http://www.npr.org/sections/krulwich/2013/03/27/175455214/socrates-in-the-form-of-a-9-year-old-shows-up-in-a-suburban-backyard-in-washingt.

Kruse, Adam. "Panel: Diversity & Inclusion in Music Education." Presentation, Big Ten Academic Alliance Music Education Conference. College Park, MD, October 5–7, 2016.

Ladson-Billings, Gloria. "Just What Is Critical Race Theory and What's It Doing in a Nice Field Like Education?" *International Journal of Qualitative Studies in Education* 11, no. 1 (2010): 7–24.

———. "Toward a Theory of Culturally Relevant Pedagogy." *American Educational Research Journal* 32, no. 3 (1995): 465–491.

Lakoff, George, and Mark Johnson. *Philosophy in the Flesh: The Embodied Mind and Its Challenge to Western Thought.* New York: Basic, 1999.

Lambert, Gregg. *In Search of a New Image of Thought: Gilles Deleuze and Philosophical Expressionism.* Minneapolis: University of Minnesota Press, 2012.

Langer, Susanne. *Problems of Art: Ten Philosophical Lectures.* New York: Charles Scribner's Sons, 1957.

Lapidaki, Eleni. "Uncommon Grounds: Preparing Students in Higher Music Education for the Unpredictable." *Philosophy of Music Education Review* 24, no. 1 (2016): 65–83.

Lena, Jennifer. *Banding Together: How Communities Create Genres in Popular Music.* Princeton, NJ: Princeton University Press, 2012.

Lieblich, Amia, Rivka Tuval-Mashiach, and Tamar Zilber. *Narrative Research: Reading, Analysis, and Interpretation.* Thousand Oaks, CA: Sage, 1998.

Lines, David. "Deleuze, Education and the Creative Economy." In *Nomadic Education: Variations on a Theme by Deleuze and Guattari*, edited by Inna Semetsky, 129–142. Rotterdam, The Netherlands: Sense, 2008.

———. "Deleuze and Music Education: Machines for Change." In *Cartographies of Becoming in Music Education: A Deleuze-Guattari Perspective*, edited by Diana Masny, 23–33. Rotterdam, The Netherlands: Sense, 2013.

Locke, David. "The African Ensemble in America: Contradictions and Possibilities." In *Performing Ethnomusicology: Teaching and Representation in World Music Ensembles*, edited by Ted Solis, 168–188. Berkeley: University of California Press, 2004.

Lundqvist, Lars-Olov, Fredrik Carlsson, Per Hilmersson, and Patrik N. Juslin. "Emotional Responses to Music: Experience, Expression, and Physiology." *Psychology of Music* 37, no. 1 (2009): 61–90.

Lyotard, Jean-Francois. *The Inhuman.* Translated by Geoffry Bennington and Rachel Bowlby. Stanford, CT: Stanford University Press, 1991.

———. *Libidinal Economy.* Translated by Iain Hamilton Grant. Bloomington: Indiana University Press, 2004.

Magid, Brandon. "Music & Meditation—Devising an Empathy Concert at Your School." Presentation, Big Ten Academic Alliance Music Education Conference. Ann Arbor, MI, October 10–12, 2018.

Manabe, Noriko. "Globalization and Japanese Creativity: Adaptations of Japanese Language to Rap." *Ethnomusicology* 50, no. 1 (2006): 1–36.

Mantie, Roger. "Bands and/as Music Education Antinomies and the Struggle for Legitimacy." *Philosophy of Music Education Review* 20, no. 1 (2012): 63–81.

Marks, John. "Ethics." In *The Deleuze Dictionary*, edited by Adrian Parr, 85–87. Edinburgh: Edinburgh University Press, 2005.

Massumi, Brian. "Translators Forward: Pleasures of Philosophy." In *A Thousand Plateaus: Capitalism and Schizophrenia*, translated by Brian Massumi, ix–xv. Minneapolis: University of Minnesota Press, 1987.

May, Todd. *Gilles Deleuze: An Introduction.* Cambridge, UK: Cambridge University Press, 2005.

———. "When Is Deleuzian Becoming?" *Continental Philosophy Review* 36 (2003): 139–153.
May, Todd, and Inna Semetsky, "Deleuze, Ethical Education, and the Unconscious." In *Nomadic Education: Variations on a Theme by Deleuze and Guattari*, edited by Inna Semetsky, 143–158. Rotterdam, The Netherlands: Sense, 2008.
Mead, Virginia Hoge. "More Than Mere Movement: Dalcroze Eurhythmics." *Music Educators Journal* 82, no.4 (1996): 38–41.
Mehta, Jal. *The Allure of Order: High Hopes, Dashed Expectations, and the Troubled Quest to Remake American Schooling*. New York: Oxford University Press, 2013.
Memmie, Albert. *The Colonizer and the Colonized*. Boston: Beacon Press, 1965.
Miller, Janet. "Autobiography and the Necessary Incompleteness of Teachers' Stories." In *A Light in Dark Times: Maxine Greene and the Unfinished Conversation*, edited by William C. Ayers and Janet L. Miller, 145–154. New York: Teachers College Press, 1998.
———. *Sounds of Silence Breaking: Women, Autobiography, Curriculum*. New York: Peter Lang, 2005.
Molnar-Szakacs, Istvan, and Katie Overy. "Music and Mirror Neurons: From Motion to 'e'Motion." *Social Cognitive and Affective Neuroscience* 1, no. 3 (2006): 235–241.
National Association for Music Education. "Broader Minded: Think beyond the Bubbles." 2014. Accessed January 5, 2016. http://www.nafme.org/wp-content/files/2014/05/Broader-Minded-Brochure.pdf.
———. "Music Model Cornerstone Assessment: Artistic Process: Creating 8th Grade General Music." 2017. https://nafme.org/wp-content/files/2014/11/Grade_8_GenMus_Creating_MCA.pdf.
———. "National Standards for Music Education." 2014. Accessed September 4, 2019. https://nafme.org/wp-content/files/2014/06/Archived-1994-Music-Standards.pdf.
———. "Student Assessment Using Model Cornerstone Assessments." Accessed September 6, 2019. https://nafme.org/my-classroom/standards/mcas/.
National Coalition for Core Arts Standards. "National Core Arts Standards." 2014. http://www.nationalartsstandards.org/.
Nichols, Jeananne. "Rie's Story, Ryan's Journey: Music in the Life of a Transgender Student." *Journal of Research in Music Education* 61, no. 3 (2013): 262–279.
Noddings, Nel. *Happiness and Education*. New York: Cambridge University Press, 2004.
O'Toole, Patricia. "I Sing in a Choir but I Have 'No Voice!'" *The Quarterly Journal of Music Teaching and Learning* 4, no. 5 (1994): 65–76.
———. "Threatening Behaviors: Transgressive Acts in Music Education." *Philosophy of Music Education Review* 10, no. 1 (2002): 3–17.
Pabich, Randall. "Learning to Live Music: Musical Education as the Cultivation of a Relationship Between Self and Sound." In *The Oxford Handbook of Philosophy in Music Education*, edited by Wayne D. Bowman and Ana Lucía Grega, 131–146. New York: Oxford University Press, 2012.
Parr, Adrian. *Deleuze and Memorial Culture*. Edinburgh: Edinburgh University Press, 2008.
Partti, Heidi, and Heidi Westerlund, "Envisioning Collaborative Composing in Music Education: Learning and Negotiation of Meaning by Operabyyou.com." *British Journal of Music Education* 30, no. 2 (2013): 207–222.
Peters, Michael. "Education and Philosophy of the Body: Bodies of Knowledge and Knowledges of the Body." In *Knowing Bodies, Moving Minds: Towards Embodied Teaching and Learning*, edited by Liora Bresler, 13–28. Boston: Kluwer Academic, 2004.

Phelps, Roger, Lawrence Ferrara, and Thomas Goolsby, *A Guide to Research in Music Education*. 4th ed. Metuchen, NJ: Scarecrow Press, 1993.
Poster, Mark. *Critical Theory and Poststructuralism: In Search of a Context*. Ithaca, NY: Cornell University Press, 1988.
Rajchman, John. *The Deleuze Connections*. Cambridge, MA: The MIT Press, 2000.
Regelski, Thomas A. "The Good Life of Teaching or the Life of Good Teaching?" *Action, Criticism, and Theory in Music Education* 11, no. 2 (2012): 42–48.
———. "Music and Music Education: Theory and Praxis for 'Making a Difference.'" *Educational Philosophy and Theory* 37, no. 1 (2005): 7–27.
Reichling, Mary. "On the Question of Method in Philosophical Research." *Philosophy of Music Education Review* 4, no. 2 (1996): 117–127.
Reimer, Bennett. *A Philosophy of Music Education: Advancing the Vision*, 3rd ed. Upper Saddle River, NJ: Prentice Hall, 2003.
Richerme, Lauren Kapalka. "A Deleuzian Reimagining of Susanne Langer's Philosophy: Becoming-Feeling in Music Education." *Music Education Research* 20 (2018): 330–341.
———. "Difference and Music Education." In *Music Education: Navigating the Future*, edited by Clint Randles, 16–28. New York: Routledge, 2014.
———. "A Feminine and Poststructural Extension of Cosmopolitan Ethics in Music Education." *International Journal of Music Education* 35, no. 3 (2017): 414–424.
———. "Measuring Music Education: A Philosophical Investigation of the Model Cornerstone Assessments." *Journal of Research in Music Education* 63, no. 3 (2016): 274–293.
———. "Nomads with Maps: Musical Connections in a Glocalized World." *Action, Criticism, and Theory for Music Education* 12, no. 2 (2013): 41–59.
———. "Reimagining Policy: Power, Problems, and Public Stories." *Arts Education Policy Review* 120, no. 2 (2019): 94–102.
———. "To Name or Not to Name? Social Justice, Poststructuralism, and Music Teacher Education." *Philosophy of Music Education Review* 24, no. 1 (2016): 84–102.
———. "Uncommon Commonalities: Cosmopolitan Ethics as a Framework for Music Education Policy Analysis." *Arts Education Policy Review* 117, no. 2 (2016): 87–95.
———. "Vulnerable Experiences in Music Education: Possibilities and Problems for Growth and Connectivity." *Bulletin of the Council for Research in Music Education*, no. 209 (2017): 27–42.
Robertson, Roland. "Glocalization: Time-Space and Homogeneity-Heterogeneity." In *Global Modernities*, edited by Mike Featherstone, Scott Lash, and Roland Robertson, 25–44. London: Sage, 1995.
Robinson, Jenefer. *Deeper Than Reason: Emotion and Its Role in Literature, Music, and Art*. New York: Oxford University Press, 2005.
Rorty, Richard. "Analytic Philosophy and Narrative Philosophy." Draft of lecture, University of California, Irvine, 2003. Richard Rorty Papers.
Rousseau, Jean-Jacques. *Emile or On Education*. Translated by Allan Bloom. New York: Basic, 1979.
Rudolph, John. *Scientists in the Classroom*. New York: Palgrave, 2002.
Schmidt, Charles P., and Stephen F. Zdzinski. "Cited Quantitative Research Articles in Music Education Research Journals, 1975–1990: A Content Analysis of Selected Studies." *Journal of Research in Music Education* 41, no. 1 (1993): 5–18.

Schmidt, Patrick. "Ethics or Choosing Complexity in Music Relations." *Action, Criticism, and Theory for Music Education* 11, no. 1 (2012): 149–168.
———. "Reinventing from Within: Thinking Spherically as a Policy Imperative in Music Education." *Arts Education Policy Review* 110, no. 4 (2009): 39–47.
———. "What We Hear Is Meaning Too: Deconstruction, Dialogue and Music." *Philosophy of Music Education Review* 20, no. 1 (2012): 3–24.
Scott-Kassner, Carol, and Mary Goetze. "The Struggle for Authenticity and Ownership: A Brief Overview of the Past and Future in Multicultural Approaches to Music Education." *The Mountain Lake Reader* (2006): 8–15.
Semetsky, Inna. *Deleuze, Education and Becoming*. Rotterdam, The Netherlands: Sense, 2006.
Shaw, Julia. "The Skin That We Sing: Culturally Responsive Choral Music Education." *Music Educators Journal* 98, no. 4 (2012): 75–81.
Small, Christopher. *Musicking: The Meanings of Performing and Listening*. Hanover, NH: University Press of New England, 1998.
Sogon, Shunya, and Makoto Masutani. "Identification of Emotion from Body Movements: A Cross-Cultural Study of Americans and Japanese." *Psychological Reports* 65, no. 1 (1989): 35–46.
St. Pierre, Elizabeth Adams. "An Introduction to Figurations—A Poststructural Practice of Inquiry." *International Journal of Qualitative Studies in Education* 10, no. 3 (1997): 280–281.
Stagoll, Cliff. "Event." In *The Deleuze Dictionary*, edited by Adrian Parr, 87–89. Edinburgh: Edinburgh University Press, 2005.
State Education Agency Directors of Arts Education. "National Core Arts Standards." 2014. http://nationalartsstandards.org/.
———. "National Core Arts Standards: A Conceptual Framework for Arts Learning." Last updated July 21, 2016. https://www.nationalartsstandards.org/sites/default/files/Conceptual%20Framework%2007-21-16.pdf#.
Stauffer, Sandra L. "Place, Music, Education, and the Practice and Pedagogy of Philosophy." In *The Oxford Handbook of Philosophy in Music Education*, edited by Wayne D. Bowman and Ana Lucía Frega, 435–452. New York: Oxford University Press, 2012.
———. "Placing Curriculum in Music." In *Music Education for Changing Times: Guiding Visions for Practice*, edited by Thomas A. Regelski and J. Terry Gates, 175–186. New York: Springer, 2009.
Stauffer, Sandra L., and Margaret S. Barrett. "Narrative Inquiry in Music Education: Toward Resonant Work." In *Narrative Inquiry in Music Education: Troubling Certainty*, edited by Margaret S. Barrett and Sandra L. Stauffer, 19–29. New York: Springer Science+Business Media, 2009.
Stewart, Noel. *Ethics: An Introduction to Moral Philosophy*. Cambridge, UK: Polity Press, 2009.
Szekely, Michael. "Musical Education: From Identity to Becoming." In *The Oxford Handbook of Philosophy in Music Education*, edited by Wayne Bowman and Ana Lucía Frega, 163–179. New York: Oxford University Press, 2012.
Talbot, Brent, and Hakim Mohandas Amani Williams, "Critically Assessing Forms of Resistance in Music Education." In *Oxford Handbook of Philosophical and Qualitative Perspectives on Assessment in Music Education*, edited by David J. Elliott, Marissa Silverman, and Gary McPherson, 83–100. New York: Oxford University Press, 2019.

Tan, Leonard. "Book Review." *Philosophy of Music Education Review* 19, no. 2 (2011): 201–205.
Tobias, Evan S. "Toward Convergence: Adapting Music Education to Contemporary Society and Participatory Culture." *Music Educators Journal* 99, no. 4 (2013): 29–36.
Toscano, Alberto. "Axiomatic." In *The Deleuze Dictionary*, edited by Adrian Parr, 17–18. Edinburgh: Edinburgh University Press, 2005.
Tyack, David, and Larry Cuban. *Tinkering toward Utopia*. Cambridge, MA: Harvard University Press, 1995.
US Department of Education. "ESEA Flexibility: Highlights of State Plans." Last modified December 2012. http://www2.ed.gov/policy/elsec/guid/esea-flexibility/resources/esea-flex-brochure.pdf.
———. "ESEA Flexibility Policy Document." December. 18, 2015. http://www2.ed.gov/policy/elsec/guid/esea-flexibility/index.html.
———. "Race to the Top Program Executive Summary." Last modified November 2009. http://www2.ed.gov/programs/racetothetop/executive-summary.pdf.
Väkevä, Lauri. "Garage Band or GarageBand®? Remixing Musical Futures." *British Journal of Music Education* 27, no. 1 (2010): 59–70.
Waldron, Janice. "User-Generated Content, YouTube and Participatory Culture on the Web: Music Learning and Teaching in Two Contrasting Online Communities." *Music Education Research* 15, no. 3 (2013): 257–274.
———. "YouTube, Fanvids, Forums, Vlogs and Blogs: Informal Music Learning in a Convergent On- and Offline Music Community." *International Journal of Music Education* 31, no. 1 (2013): 95–105.
Warner, Brigitte. *Orff-Schulwerk: Applications for the Classroom*. Englewood Cliffs, NJ: Prentice Hall, 1991.
Williams, James. *Understanding Poststructuralism*. Chesham, UK: Acumen, 2005.
Woodford, Paul. *Democracy and Music Education: Liberalism, Ethics, and the Politics of Practice*. Bloomington: Indiana University Press, 2005.
Yob, Iris. "Cognitive Emotions and Emotional Cognitions." *Journal of Aesthetic Education* 32, no. 2 (1998): 27–40.
Zerilli, Linda. *Feminism and the Abyss of Freedom*. Chicago: University of Chicago Press, 2005.
———. "Toward a Feminist Theory of Judgment." *Signs* 34, no. 2 (2009), 295–317.
———. "We Feel Our Freedom: Imagination and Judgment in the Thought of Hannah Arendt." *Political Theory* 33, no. 2 (2005): 158–188.
Ziarek, Ewe. *An Ethics of Dissensus: Postmodernity, Feminism, and the Politics of Radical Democracy*. Stanford: Stanford University Press, 2001.

Index

Abramo, Joseph, 47
accountability, 2
Ahmed, Sara, 88–89, 95
Alcoff, Linda, 74
Allsup, Randall, 4–5, 68–70, 115, 132, 142, 142, 155
Anderson, Leroy, 77–81, 84–88, 93
Appiah, Kwame Anthony, 97
arboreal, xii, 132–136, 140–141, 145,
Arendt, Hannah, xi, 75–81, 93–95, 98, 153–154
artwork, 28, 60, 107, 109–110
assessment, 2–3, 7, 22, 43, 54–55, 73, 89, 103, 107, 128, 143
audience, 27, 29, 34, 36, 46, 49, 51, 53–54, 80–81, 106–108, 120, 139
Averill, James, 27
Ayers, William, vii

Bach, Johann Sebastian, 120–121
Bakhtin, Mikhail, 15, 140
band, viii, 12, 32, 133; and embodiment, 24–25; and ethics, 77, 79, 81, 84, 86–87; and place, 46, 55–56, 59–61; and sociality, 29–30
Barrett, Margaret, 12–13, 60
Barthes, Roland, 14
becoming, xi, 8, 15, 23, 44, 49, 53; 109–110, 118, a-body-without-organs, 32–37, 112; and Deleuzian ethics, 70, 72–74, 79–81, 151, 157, 159; and education, 129–134, 136–137; nomad, 57–62, 112, 144
Beethoven, Ludwig van, viii, 106, 109
Belsey, Catherine, 14
Benedict, Cathy, 2, 5, 71, 126n82
Bennett, Andy, 54
Beyoncé, viii, 104
Biesta, Gert, 94
Bildung, 144
Bloomington, Indiana, 53
body. *See* embodiment

body-without-organs (BwO), 32–38, 57, 102
Bogue, Ronald, 70, 88
Boston, 43
Boulez, Pierre, 104, 109
Bourdieu, Pierre, 26
Bowman, Wayne, xi, 23, 25, 35, 61, 71, 101
Boyce-Tillman, June, 7, 23, 113
Bradley, Deborah, 7, 121–122
Bradt, Kevin, 60, 115
Braidotti, Rosi, 34, 58–59, 74–75
Brexit, 73
Brown, Brené, 91–92, 110
Bruner, Jerome, 59, 61, 139
Butler, Judith, 95, 164n4

capitalism, 48–49, 56, 74–75
Casey, Edward, 54
Chavez, Cesar, 154
choir, 7, 29, 45, 71, 121, 129
Chopin, Frédéric, 109
Clandinin, D. Jean, 13
classical music, ix, 3, 24, 27–29, 45, 47–48, 67, 74, 101, 103, 104, 106, 109, 118, 120, 128, 134
cognition, xii, 12–14; connecting musically with, 116, 119, 122, 132; and education, 140–141, 145; and embodiment; 22–32, 34–38, moving beyond, 84, 87–88, 90, 92–94, 130, 150, 154
Cole, David, 136–137
Colebrook, Claire, 10, 32–33, 36, 57, 99n13, 135
Colman, Felicity, 133
college, viii, 8, 15, 29, 56, 67, 137–138, 142,
colonialism, 49, 56, 58, 67
Colwell, Richard, 153
common world, 76–80, 87, 89–90, 94–95, 98
community, vii–viii, x, 1, 4, 7, 11, 155, 157; and education, 139, 144; and ethics, 71, 77, 79–81, 84, 93–94, 96–97; and music, 28–29, 102, 114, 117–118, 122; and place, 43, 45–45, 48, 52–53, 60, 150

175

composition, xi, 3–4, 6, 28, 37, 43, 45, 48, 54–56, 67, 73–74, 81, 89, 105, 115, 117–122, 129, 131, 134, 137, 142
complicating, x, xii, 23, 53, 57, 62, 71–74, 78, 90, 107, 117, 144–146, 150–158
connecting, xi–xii, 3, 110–123, 129, 135, 143–145, 150–159
considering, x–xii, 79–81, 84, 86–87, 89–90, 92–98, 122, 145–146, 150–158
cosmopolitan, 49, 97
country music, 104
creativity, vii, ix, 3, 8, 67, 70, 73, 103, 108, 117, 119, 128, 131, 133, 135, 137, 157
Cresswell, Tim, 43, 53–54, 56
Cuban, Larry, 154
culture, 6, 23, 28–29, 45, 47–49, 61, 101–102, 111–112, 116, 118

Dalcroze pedagogy, 25
Damasio, Antonio, 26, 29
Davis, Miles, 104
de Sousa Santos, Boaventura, 50
Deleuze, Gilles, xi–xii, 8, 13, 16, 41n59, 45, 68, 84, 69, 129–130, 137, 141, 142, 151; and Félix Guattari, vii, 5–6, 8–12, 15–16, 30–34, 48–49, 53–62, 69, 74, 88, 91, 102–111, 116–118, 129, 131–132, 134–135. *See also* becoming; body-without-organs; deterritorialize; ethics; event; Guattari, Félix; immanence; multiplicity; nomad; refrain; rhizome; smooth spaces
Dello Joio, Norman, 24–27, 29, 31
Derrida, Jacques, 6–7, 108, 157
deterritorialize, 57, 106–111, 114–115, 121–122
Dewey, John, 12, 68–69, 71, 127–128
dialectics, 5, 30, 108
dialogue, ix, xi, 14, 36, 53, 58, 68–70, 73, 76, 85–86, 94, 96, 119, 140–141, 156, 158
difference, xii, 5–8, 13–14, 23, 48, 108, 116, 152, 157; Deleuzian, 30–31, 33–34, 36–37, 103, 112; and education, 128–135, 138, 141–145, 152, 157; and ethics, 70–71, 73–74, 76, 86, 88–89, 91, 94, 96; and place, 49, 52–53, 59
disconnection, xii, 14, 89, 111, 122, 152
dissensus, 76
DJs, 2, 109, 133

Dussel, Enrique, 156
Dyndahl, Petter, 157

economy and education, 2, 4, 8, 68, 106, 122, 153
education, xii, 1–2, 4–5, 9, 11–12, 22–23, 35, 150, 152–153; definition of, 127–132, 136–145; and ethics, 67, 70–72, 75, 92, 94; and music, 114, 119. *See also* economy and education
Ekman, Paul, 26
Eliot, T. S., 1, 60
Elliott, David, 23, 26, 68, 71, 127, 143–144
embodiment, x–xii, 12, 14, 59, 109, 160; and cognition, 22–38; and education, 129, 132–133, 140–141, 144–145; and ethics, 84, 88–94, 96, 98; and music, 109–111, 114, 116, 119, 121–122; and policy, 155–155; and research, 157–158
emotion, x–xii, 11, 16, 59, 160; and education, 140–141, 144–145; and embodiment, 22–24, 26–32, 34–38; and ethics, 84, 87–94, 96, 98; and music, 110, 112, 114–117, 119–120, 122, 129–130, 132–133; and policy, 154, 155–155; and research, 157–158
empathy, 14, 28, 36–37, 47, 67, 88–90, 155–156
Enlightenment, viii
ethics, ix, xi, 5, 9, 50, 62, 67–68, 90–98, 113, 144, 150, 158; Arendt's, 75–81, 84–91, 93–95, 98; Deleuzian, 68–75, 78–81; situational, 69–70
event, xi, 8, 13, 16, 34, 37, 45, 53, 57, 62, 69–70, 104, 131
Every Student Succeeds Act (ESSA), 154
Eurocentric, 102, 114
Ewe music, 25, 31, 101, 103, 112
exclusions, ix, xi, 5–6, 23, 44, 46, 50, 52, 56–57, 60–61, 79–80, 153, 156–157

feminism, 8, 58, 116
Fiske, Harold, 23
folk music, 53, 109, 121
Fossom, Hanne, 12
Foucault, Michel, 6–8, 12, 69
Freire, Paulo, 85

gamelan music, 3, 27, 47, 134
Ganz, Marshall, 154–156
GarageBand, 74, 131
Gay, Geneva, 62n7
gender, 23, 32, 34–35, 61, 67, 74, 94, 131.
 See also transgender
general music, 8
Ghana, 25, 101, 103, 111, 118
global, xii, 2, 4–5, 22, 44, 136, 154; connecting with, 102, 116–119, 122, 143–145, 152; definition of, 46–53, 56–57, 59–60; and ethics, 67, 69, 73, 90, 95–97
globalization, 4, 43, 48–50, 119, 144
glocal, 44, 50–53, 56–57, 59–60, 144, 156,
Goble, J. Scott, 23, 101–102
Goethe, Johann Wolfgang von, 104
Goetze, Mary, 48
Gould, Elizabeth, 5, 8, 12, 29, 45, 50, 59, 68, 71, 75–76, 95, 105, 107, 109–110, 113–116, 128–131, 134, 142, 156, 158–159
Green, Denise, 8
Greene, Maxine, 13, 76
Grosz, Elizabeth, 105, 110
Guattari, Félix, 8. See also Deleuze, Gilles
guitar, viii, 27–28, 55, 74

habit, vii, 1, 11, 34, 56–57, 70, 72, 85, 90, 96, 107, 111, 113, 135, 154, 159
Hansen, David, 49–50
Harry Potter, 15–16, 140
Hearne, Ted, 122
Hegel, Goerg Friedrich, 104
Heimonen, Marja, 48
Hess, Juliet, 47–48
hierarchy, xii, 13, 151, 156; and education, 103, 112, 132, 135–136, 140, 151, 156; and ethics, 68, 72; and location, 47, 52, 56; and mind-body, 23–24, 30, 33, 35; versus rhizome, 9–12
Higdon, Jennifer, 104
Higgins, Kathleen, 29
Hindustani music, 2
hip-hop, viii, 47, 50, 91, 135
Horsley, Stephanie, 2, 4
Howard, Vernon, 127
Hroch, Petra, 72

imagining multiple perspectives, xi, 76–80, 84–86, 88–90, 93–97, 160. See also Arendt
immanence, xii, 102–104, 109–113, 116–120, 141
immigration, 23, 58, 68, 73, 94, 97
improvise, 3, 29, 38, 74, 104, 106, 107, 133, 135
inclusion, ix, 46, 56, 108, 139, 153, 155–156
inequality, 7, 67, 119, 122
informal music making, 48, 56, 91
international education, viii, 2–3, 12, 50,

jazz, 29, 50, 71, 106–107
Johnson, Mark, 24, 26, 111, 114
Jones, Patrick, 154
Jorgensen, Estelle, xv, 3, 5, 8–9, 35, 55–56, 108, 113, 159
judging, 75–81, 84–87, 94, 96, 98, 122, 144–145, 153, 156, 158

Kanellopoulos, Panagiotis, 133
Kant, 8, 68, 75, 90
Kertz-Welzel, Alexandra, 49
Kivy, Peter, 26–27, 29
Kleist, Heinrich von, 104
Kodály pedagogy, viii, 25, 91, 137
Kos, Ronald, 153
Koza, Julia, 8
Kratus, John, 16
Kristeva, Julia, 6

Ladson-Billings, Gloria, 62n7, 140
Lakoff, George, 24, 26, 111, 114
Lamb, Roberta, 158
Lambert, Gregg, 173
Langer, Susanne, 117
Lapidaki, Eleni, 128
LGBTQ+. See sexual orientation
Lines, David, 8, 68, 116
listening, vii, 26, 28, 31, 50–51, 84, 86, 103, 115, 117, 119–120, 128, 132, 134
Liszt, Franz, 106
local, x–xii, 1, 28, 43–47, 49–53, 56–57, 60; and education, 132, 139, 143–145; and ethics, 67, 69, 73, 80, 94–97; and music, 102, 105, 115–117, 119, 122, 151–152; and policy, 154, 156
Locke, David, 25
Lyotard, Jean-Francois, 6–7, 73

majority, 32, 35, 51, 57, 59, 71, 76, 94
Mantie, Roger, 46
marginalization, 13, 34–35, 46, 58, 74, 107, 121, 136, 139–140, 143
mariachi, 45–46, 115, 133
May 1968 protests, 8
May, Todd, 7, 41n57, 48, 72
meaning, vii–viii, xi, 3, 5, 36, 101, 154, 157, 160; and connecting, 114–115, 117–122; and Deleuze, 110–112; and education, 128, 137–139, 142–145; and ethics, 68, 72, 77, 80–81, 89, 98; and music, 22, 24, 43–46, 49, 151–152; and place-making, 54–55, 58–62; and poststructuralism, 7, 14–16
Mexican-American border, 73
Miller, Janet, 138–139, 159
mind. *See* cognition
minoritarian, 32–33, 57, 60, 68, 74–76
mirror neurons, 27–28
Model Cornerstone Assessments, 3
Molnar-Szakacs, Istvan, 27
multicultural music, 2, 47–48, 52–53
multiplicity, 24, 30–32, 116–117, 131
music, 23–32, 55, 101–102, 107–123, 131–132. *See also* band; choir; classical music; country music; Ewe music; folk music; gamelan music; hip-hop jazz; multicultural music; orchestra; popular music; rap; rock music
music technology, vii–viii, 2–4, 10, 45, 48, 51, 55, 74, 81, 103, 109, 120, 128, 131, 133
music theory, 25, 130, 133

National Core Music Standards. *See* standards
narrative, 151–152, 156; of becoming-nomad, 50–62; emotional, social, embodied, 35–38; changing, 138–143, 145; of connecting with, 115–121; and ethics, 93–98; personal, vii, 22–24, 26, 37, 50, 77, 101, 106, 160; philosophy of, xi, xii, 12–16; political, 154–155; and research, 159
New Orleans, 106–107
Nichols, Jeananne, 140
No Child Left Behind, 2
Noddings, Nel, 5
nomad, 24, 57–62, 112, 118, 144

norms, xi, 1, 3, 8, 57, 109, 132, 135, 157; of body, 35, 59; break from, 114, 118; and ethics, 70–74, 78, 92–93; and narrative, 61–62, 139–140, 159; socialized, 7, 29, 32
Norway, 160

O'Toole, Patricia, 14, 29
oppression, 48, 50, 74, 85, 107, 140
orchestra, viii, 29, 52, 72, 128
Orff pedagogy, viii, 25, 78
Overy, Katie, 27

Pabich, Randall, 23
Parr, Adrian, 16
participatory music making, viii, 27–28, 55–56, 74, 101, 132–133, 137
Partti, Heidi, 48
perform, vii, x–xi, 3–4, 8, 103–105, 107–109, 129, 132, 137; and connecting, 112, 115, 117–121, 155; and emotion, 27–28, 32, 34, 36; and ethics, 67, 71, 73, 75–77, 80–81; and mind-body, 22–23, 25, 31; and place, 43, 45–48, 51–54, 56
performative literacy, 45, 113–114
Peters, Michael, 33
philosophical figuration, 33, 35, 57–58, 61, 134
philosophy, xii, 1, 5, 8–17, 101, 110, 135, 142, 158–160
Phoenix, 44–45
place, x, xii, 1–3, 16, 43, 101, 150–153; connecting with, 110–112, 116–119, 122; and ethics, 67, 69, 71, 78, 81, 95; and music, 60–62; and music education, 144–145, Local and global, 44–52, 56–57; and policy, 155–156; and research, 157; smooth and striated, 53–57
plane of immanence. *See* immanence
Poe, Edgar Allen, 14
policy, viii, xi, 2, 4–5, 7, 9, 22, 46, 57, 97, 114, 128, 144, 153–156, 158
politics, 4, 7–8, 45, 48–49, 52, 57–58, 72–75, 78–80, 94, 95, 98, 102, 114, 153–154
popular music, vii, 26, 43, 48, 51, 54, 67, 71, 78, 106, 109
poststructuralism, vii, xi, 5–9, 12–16, 24, 73–74, 150
potentialities, 46, 50, 57, 109, 120, 150, 155, 160; and Deleuzian ethics, 69–70, 73, 78–81, 96, 98; and education, 137–138, 142–143

Powell, Kimberly, 25
power, 23, 28, 32, 73, 91, 96, 116, 122, 134, 155
pragmatism, 101–102
privilege, 34–35, 58, 87, 92, 122, 153, 157, 159
Prometheus, 15–16, 140

quantum particles, 151
Queen, 54

race, viii, 23, 34, 51, 58, 61, 73, 94, 104, 131
Rajchman, John, 9–10, 69, 107
rap, vii–viii, 51, 71, 104
reflection, xii, 1, 14, 25, 32, 34, 36, 106, 115–119, 141–143, 152–153, 155–156, 159; and ethics, 67, 73, 78, 81, 84, 93, 96, 122
refrain (Deleuzian), 102, 104–107, 109–110, 120–121
refugees, 23, 60, 94
Regelski, 71
Reichling, Mary, 10
Reimer, Bennett, 68, 108
relativism, xi, 73–76, 80, 96
research, 156–159
Rideout, Roger, 160
rhizome, 16–17, 49, 61–62, 69, 110, 150, 157, 160; definition of, 9–12; and education, 132–136, 140, 142–143, 145; and ethics, 80, 98; and policy, 154, 156
Robertson, Roland, 51
Robinson, Jenefer, 26–27
rock music, 3, 27–29, 47, 50, 52, 54, 74, 120, 128
Rorty, Richard, 60
Rosiek, Jerry, 13
Rousseau, Jean-Jacques, 127

Schmidt, Patrick, 5, 108, 153
Scruton, Roger, 101
Semetsky, Inna, 72, 128, 136–137
sexual orientation, 34–35, 59, 67, 73–74, 94. *See also* gender; transgender
Shaw, Caroline, 115
Shaw, Julia, 45, 48
Shieh, Eric, 155
Silverman, Marissa, 23, 26, 68, 71, 127, 143–144
Small, Christopher, 28, 117–118
smooth spaces, 52–58, 60–62, 102, 106, 117, 152–153

social justice, 8, 23, 52, 71, 74, 92, 107, 122, 137, 154. *See also* politics
sociality, xii, 22–24, 28–32, 34–38, 59, 110, 114, 141, 156–158; connecting with, 116, 119; and education, 132–133, 140, 144–145; and ethics, 84, 88, 90–94, 96, 98
socioeconomic status (SES), 51, 94, 96, 131
songwriting, 28, 48, 132, 140
Sputnik, 4
St. Pierre, Elizabeth Adams, 33
standards, viii, 2–3, 9, 22–23, 43, 54, 77, 102–103, 112, 114, 119, 128, 133–136, 143
standardization, 2–5, 11, 49, 68, 72, 153
Stauffer, Sandra, x, xv, 12–13, 43, 46, 54, 60
stories. *See* narrative
striated spaces. *See* smooth spaces
superposition, 151
Svalbard, 160
Szekely, Michael, 8, 127–128

Talbot, Brent, 89
Tanglewood Declaration, 47
technology. *See* music technology
tolerance, 47
transcendence, 103–104, 111, 113
transgender, 59, 97, 140
tree, 150, 160. *See also* arboreal
Tyack, David, 154

university. *See* college
ukulele, viii, 133

Väkevä, Lauri, 48
vulnerability, vii, 11–12, 15, 35, 67, 84, 91–92, 97–98, 142, 159

Westerlund, Heidi, 48, 69–70
Williams, Hakim, 89
Williams, James, 6, 103
Woodford, Paul, 68, 71, 153
world music. *See* multicultural music

xenophobia, 47, 58, 67

Yob, Iris, 8–9, 23, 35, 55–56, 113

Zerilli, Linda, 77–79, 153

LAUREN KAPALKA RICHERME is Associate Professor of Music Education at the Indiana University Jacobs School of Music.

www.ingramcontent.com/pod-product-compliance
Lightning Source LLC
Chambersburg PA
CBHW021810220426
43662CB00006B/253